NEW FACULTY

A PRACTICAL GUIDE
FOR ACADEMIC BEGINNERS

Christopher J. Lucas and John W. Murry, Jr.

palgrave

NEW FACULTY

First published 2002 by PALGRAVE™
175 Fifth Avenue, New York, N.Y.10010 and
Houndmills, Basingstoke, Hampshire RG21 6XS.
Companies and representatives throughout the world.

PALGRAVE is the new global publishing imprint of St. Martin's Press LLC Scholarly and Reference Division and Palgrave Publishers Ltd (formerly Macmillan Press Ltd).

ISBN 0-312-29506-5 hardback
ISBN 0-312-29537-5 paperback

Library of Congress Cataloging-in-Publication Data
Lucas, Christopher J.
New faculty : a practical guide for academic beginners / Christopher J. Lucas, John W. Murry, Jr.
     p. cm.
Includes bibliographical references and index.
     ISBN 0-312-29506-5—ISBN 0-312-29537-5 (pbk.)
     1. College teachers—United States. 2. First year teachers—United States. 3. Teacher orientation—United States. I. Murry, John W. II. Title.

LB1778.2.L83 2002
378.1'2'0973—dc21

2001052301

A catalogue record for this book is available from the British Library.

Design by Letra Libre, Inc.

First edition: April 2002
10 9 8 7 6 5 4

Printed in the United States of America.

NEW FACULTY

TABLE OF CONTENTS

ACKNOWLEDGMENTS

Thanks are owed to Shontarius Aiken, Barbara Goodman, Carol Warner, Michelle Schleibaum, and Chris Arnold for assistance with source materials; to the staff of the Faculty Support and Teaching Center at the University of Arkansas-Fayetteville for their cooperation; and to Peggy Catron-Ping for her invaluable editorial scrutiny of successive manuscript drafts. We are indebted to colleagues and peers elsewhere across the country who provided illustrative commentary and anecdotal material used throughout. A special debt of gratitude is owed Sonja Bennett for her assistance in the preparation of the manuscript. Support from Michael Flamini, Meg Weaver, Karin Bolender, Amanda Johnson, and others at Palgrave in carrying this project forward is also greatly appreciated.

ABOUT THE AUTHORS

CHRISTOPHER J. LUCAS is currently Professor of Higher Education and former Head of the Department of Educational Leadership, Counseling, and Foundations in the College of Education and Health Professions, University of Arkansas-Fayetteville. He holds degrees from Syracuse University (B.A.), Northwestern University (M.A.T.), and Ohio State University (Ph.D.). He previously served as Interim Director of the Center for International Programs and Studies and Professor of Education Policy Studies at the University of Missouri-Columbia, and subsequently as Chair of the Department of Educational Psychology and Leadership at Kent State University. He is the author or editor of 14 previous books. Lucas is former president of the American Educational Studies Association, the Society of Professors of Education, and the Council of Learned Societies in Education.

JOHN W. MURRY, JR., is currently Associate Professor of Higher Education and Associate Dean for Graduate Studies, Research, and Faculty Development at the University of Arkansas-Fayetteville. He holds B.S.B.A., M.B.A., J.D., and Ed.D. degrees from the University of Arkansas. He formerly taught at Mesa State College in Colorado and Henderson State University in Arkansas.

PREFACE

A curious feature of modern academic life is the presumption that new faculty members arrive on campus having previously acquired virtually all the habits, knowledge, and skills required for on-the-job success. By some mysterious alchemy, it is assumed, yesterday's graduate students have mastered the skills and tricks of the trade needed as full-fledged faculty in today's challenging academic environment.

Given some minimal orientation to the institution and a congratulatory welcome, accordingly, newcomers are thought to be fully capable of jump-starting their own careers. The tacit assumption is they will neither need nor want to look to others for assistance. On the contrary, as savvy professionals in their own right, so it is held, they can hardly be expected to welcome didactic "hand-holding." Still less will they brook even well-intended "interference" from others.

Whereas many professions require on-the-job training and some type of structured initiation into the workplace, academics are somehow different—or so it is commonly assumed. Ostensibly, they are autonomous, self-reliant, self-directing. Opinion holds therefore they will do well and adapt to what essentially is a competitive "sink-or-swim" institutional environment—a milieu dominated, one might add, in typical situations by strong individualists. As former graduate students who have lived and worked previously in academe, they already enjoy the advantage of an insider's perspective on professorial life. In short, supposedly, faculty newcomers are fully prepared to "hit the ground running."

In fact there is abundant evidence to suggest otherwise, much of it informal and anecdotal, yet compelling all the same. As Sarah M. Dinham of the University of Arizona observes, "When we are faculty newcomers, our accomplishments and successes . . . fade into the background while we cope with the vexations of being new. We must learn our way around; we do not yet know the subtleties of the new organization; we must deal with endless trivial details; we struggle to match our experiences in the new environment with our earlier perceptions of it; we inadvertently break unspoken rules; and we need information when clear answers seem elusive."[1]

Hence, the belief that previous graduate training supplies the essential background information new faculty need for getting off to a good start may be mistaken. As Dinham, continuing, notes, "Graduate school provides teaching opportunities and research experience, but useful as they may be for preparing us for faculty life, these are foremost the experiences of graduate education, not the experiences of faculty status. . . ." The environment may seem superficially familiar, but the role new faculty play within it is quite different. "Altogether then, graduate school can provide some direction for the junior faculty member . . . but the faculty experience will inevitably be filled with surprises."[2]

Some of those "surprises" are apt to be quite unwelcome. Robert Boice of the State University of New York at Stony Brook, shares a poignant self-disclosure from a faculty respondent who at midcareer acknowledged he had been dogged by failure from the outset. Reflecting on a lackluster career, he traced his professional troubles back almost to the beginning: "Once I discovered that I was getting hopelessly behind in all the things I had to do, especially in getting published, I began to give up," he confessed. "I never really did feel that I fit in or that I got the resources I needed. I sometimes tried to tell myself that I got my satisfaction from teaching, but that was never true. Somehow, I think that if I had gotten off to a better start, I could have had a much better career."[3]

While Boice's case study affords a somewhat extreme example, the reality is that some professorial novices *do* flounder at first—for weeks or months on end, some possibly for years. Fortunately, most eventually find their bearings, one way or another. Many go on to pursue successful careers (albeit not without a few false starts and detours). But some do not. It is disquieting to wonder to what extent trial and error spells the difference between those hapless individuals who find the transition to academic life unnecessarily difficult or even impossible to manage and those who adjust easily.

Expertise is not the critical factor. A fledgling scholar may enjoy an exhaustive command of an academic specialization or field of knowledge, yet still experience difficulties settling into campus routines. Again, an individual may have a natural gift for teaching or writing or research, though its possession alone does not necessarily afford a sufficient condition for job success. The real imperative is one of adequate, timely socialization.

With growing recognition that new faculty hires can indeed benefit from guidance and direction, some colleges and universities have begun to offer formal orientation and development programs. These initiatives tend to vary widely in terms of structure, duration, and directiveness. Some are first-rate. Many others are perfunctory at best, consisting perhaps of no more than a single day's workshop conducted at the opening of the new academic term. Others are quite elaborate, extending over a period of weeks or months. Most, however, tend to focus primarily on *institution-specific information:* the humdrum particulars of where offices are located, who to contact for answers to questions about benefits and payroll, how to process paperwork, who to see when particular types of problems arise, basic policies and procedures, and so forth.

Less often is attention paid to more fundamental aspects of fulfilling one's professional role, or to specific strategies faculty members might employ to get off to a good start. It goes without saying, in an institutional environment or climate that tacitly discourages any unseemly display of inexperience or naiveté from new faculty arrivals, that the more basic issues are not likely to get raised at all.

Essentially, there are any number of reasons why orientation activities planned for new faculty rarely touch on the fundamentals of professorial work. Most academic institutions bend over backward, as it were, to avoid conveying the impression of condescending to their new hires or appearing to insult their intelligence by offering overly prescriptive advice and counsel. Little attention is given, for example, to how to organize one's work-related tasks, or to techniques for handling difficult students, personal-time management, consideration of what constitutes good teaching, getting started with a research agenda, the fundamentals of academic publishing, and so on. Once again, the presumption lingers that new faculty members are full-fledged professionals who already understand what their job will demand.

It remains an open question, however, how useful and helpful are formal induction programs for new faculty. Quite possibly, job socialization can be accomplished just as well, if not better, through informal, unplanned information sharing among junior and senior colleagues. Either way, the critical consideration is an institutional climate in which novices' questions are welcomed and treated with the attention they deserve.

Teaching affords a case in point. Most faculty are expected to teach. Yet it is astounding how little attention is paid in any deliberative and explicit way to questions about collegiate teaching as a craft, to the challenge of achieving proficiency and real effectiveness in the classroom. It may not be much of an exaggeration to claim, as have two recent writers, that "newcomers to the professoriate arrive unprepared and uncertain as teachers. Earlier still in their career paths, as graduate teaching assistants, novice teachers exemplify the basic difficulties that continue into first professorial appointments. They worry about not knowing enough, about gaining student respect, and about balancing teaching with other time-consuming demands. They sometimes feel they get too little guidance. And, whether they know it or not, beginning teachers quickly form lasting styles and attitudes."[4]

If new faculty have questions about teaching and feel they may not know nearly enough to proceed with complete confidence, the same applies to initiating a research agenda, writing for publication, balancing out conflicting demands for institutional service, applying for research and service grants, or any other aspect of faculty responsibilities.

Accordingly, this primer is inspired by a conviction, first, that the transition from graduate student to professor can and should be facilitated and guided; and, second, that there are specific initiatives a new faculty member should take at the outset to increase his or her prospects for long-term success in an academic career. Whereas some of the suggestions offered may appear mundane or intuitively transparent, their real utility and power become apparent only after the fact. Strategies for organizing one's work and keeping it organized afford a familiar and homely example.

Other considerations are perhaps a bit less obvious—for example, the importance of clarifying institutional work-performance expectations in ways such that one budgets one's time and sets priorities correspondingly. In either case, ways of developing effective work habits in academe have much to recommend themselves, deriving as they do from the collective wisdom and experience of more seasoned hands with proven track records.

It must be said that elaborate cookbook-like recipes or formulae that profess to guarantee professional success—like most self-help literature—are the stuff of fiction. In most instances, they overpromise and underdeliver. This much conceded, within certain limits there do seem to be at least some ideas and rules of thumb still worth considering on their merits, no matter how trite or self-evident they may appear at first glance. If observed and applied appropriately, depending on individual circumstances, they are capable of serving in tangible ways to sharpen or enhance the focus of the newcomer's academic career, particularly in its earliest formative stages.

Some do's and don'ts have to do with specific behaviors, with ways of taking action. Others involve asking the right questions and deliberately searching out the information needed to guide on-the-job conduct. No matter what, the challenge for the novice is to become aware of what he or she does not know—and then to set out to remedy matters as promptly as possible.

MORNING COFFEE AT THE DOUGHNUT HOLE

It was our custom that first semester back in the late sixties to assemble each weekday morning at a little coffee shop on the edge of campus. There were usually five or six of us gathered around the table. We were all recent graduates of leading doctoral universities, each of us representing a different discipline. What we shared in common in that first year as faculty members at a medium-sized, Midwestern state university was a quite peculiar problem— namely, finding enough to do.

All things considered, we had not been provided much in the way of orientation to our new positions. A distracted, overworked dean had bid us welcome. He did seem friendly enough, though he conveyed the distinct impression his time for us was limited. His remarks were followed by a short address from the chancellor of the university, a less-friendly dignitary who, among other things, ventured the claim that in his opinion productive academic researchers were inevitably good teachers, and vice versa. He expressed his hope that we would eventually turn out to be both, wished us luck—and without further ado, abruptly made his departure. That was it. Total time reserved for orientation? Less than half an hour at most.

Our senior colleagues were friendly enough, in an abstract sort of way, those first few weeks of the term, though they all seemed terribly busy. The contrast was disconcerting to say the least, because we newcomers most decidedly were not. To put it bluntly, we didn't have enough to do to keep busy. Or more accurately, our shared naiveté prevented us from understanding how and why we should have been exceedingly busy.

We had long since settled into our offices, our newly-minted Ph.D. diplomas placed proudly on display for anyone who cared to notice (and no one seemed to do so). Our class handouts and lecture outlines were all typed up and ready for use. Nobody had yet assigned us any student advisees. We had no committee responsibilities. We were not yet on anyone's mailing list, so office correspondence was rare. Our phones almost never rang. Nor did hardly anyone ever drop by for idle chitchat, much less for business. And so, simply to fill time if nothing else, our little band gathered daily at the coffee shop for doughnuts and friendly conversation.

One morning a member of our group proudly announced he had just had a short article accepted for publication in an academic journal. The rest of us offered hearty congratulations. A long silence ensued. Then someone else spoke up hesitatingly, wondering aloud, "Say, is publishing something we all ought to be doing sometime?"

continues

We were naive, indeed. And, of course, conditions were different then; it was another era. A great deal has changed in the decades since. Those entering the professorate nowadays tend to be a lot more savvy, more sophisticated, better informed than we were. Colleges and universities seem to be doing a better job of assimilating new faculty members than they once did. So our situation then may have been somewhat unique. We were an extreme case. But the point is, part of our problem at the time was, *we simply did not know how to be professors.* We had at best a dim comprehension of what was involved, of how we should behave, of what constituted appropriate performance in a milieu or setting we did not yet fully understand.

—a personal reminiscence by a former faculty
member at a Midwestern public university

Literature on the theory and practice of faculty development has grown enormously in recent years. Books devoted exclusively to college teaching or curriculum development number in the dozens. They treat their subject matter at far greater length and in more detail than an omnibus guide can hope to match. The effort here, needless to say, has not been to encompass some of the more arcane, recondite aspects of faculty career theory. Rather, the aim has been to strive for brevity and to focus on a very few practical essentials one can absorb and apply in short order.

Some readers may take exception to, or feel vaguely uncomfortable with, the seeming attention paid to considerations of personal advantage, and to an almost Machiavellian tone of "calculated" self-advancement. But like any "game," the professorial life nowadays (to a greater extent than some are willing to acknowledge) is dominated by undertakings whose successful execution is not always self-evident at first.

The game may be played poorly or it may be played skillfully. Striving to do well as an individual faculty member should not entail any compromise with the highest and best interests of the academic community as a whole. In fact, one could argue, the vitality of the academic enterprise that binds a community of scholars together is helped—not threatened—by people who know and understand the rules that promise to enhance their own effectiveness as individual faculty members.

Our intent as authors of this brief guide has been to supply, in a nutshell, a work that new faculty members will find useful and can read through quickly. We have tried to be as succinct, practical, and genuinely informative as possible. The work we offer is in no way intended to compete directly with the handful or so similar books already in print, several of which we would be the first to concede are quite helpful. On the contrary, we are convinced that newcomers to academe can benefit significantly from perusing many such books, mining them for whatever help they may afford.

Notwithstanding, drawing on our experience in conducting in-service faculty workshops and seminars for new faculty at several different institutions, as we began our planning, we felt there was room for at least one more such primer, particularly if it were responsive *to the actual questions and issues most frequently posed by faculty beginners themselves*. Further, we judged that the most useful approach would be to organize as much of the discussion as possible under the actual categories of work in which faculty typically engage.

What follows opens with a brief treatment of an often-neglected topic: the "culture" of an academic institution and how faculty newcomers become acculturated or socialized to its norms. This discussion leads, naturally enough, to a consideration of the dilemmas of new faculty members engaged in the process of trying to "fit in" and become effective within an unfamiliar organizational environment. The benefits of mentoring relationships are taken up, together with several specific suggestions about what the professorial neophyte most needs to know in order to be successful and what to do in order to secure hard answers to the questions that seem to matter most throughout the initial year or so on the job.

The first major category of faculty work treated is instruction. The discussion emphasizes the steps an inexperienced teacher can take to enhance his or her prospects for effectiveness in the college classroom. We consider, first, both the opportunities and the inherent limitations or constraints of the traditional lecture approach. The discussion is then expanded to explore nontraditional teaching formats; in particular those that seek to transform passive learners into active, participatory learners. Additionally, we thought it would be helpful to review at least some of the major issues surrounding the assessment and evaluation of both teaching and learning.

Faculty at an ever-increasing number of colleges and universities nowadays feel under pressure to publish or otherwise give public demonstration of original research and scholarship. Issues surrounding the much-decried "publish or perish" syndrome are revisited briefly. Here the discussion aims to supply a fresh context for considering how new faculty can best help themselves become productive scholars: preparing scholarly papers for presentation, developing a research agenda, writing an article for submission to an academic or professional journal, drafting a book prospectus, and so on. Also taken up are suggestions for developing that most-valued of professorial skills in research-focused institutions: grantsmanship.

Strangely enough, little attention seems to be paid to another aspect of faculty work, namely, the advising and mentoring of students. In one way or another, in almost all colleges and universities, senior and junior faculty alike are expected to devote time and energy to student advisement. Why advising is important, how it affects faculty careers, and how best to manage the responsibilities entailed are all issues worthy of careful review and are considered in their essentials.

Faculty service comprises the third element of a venerable workload triad in academe, alongside teaching and scholarship. Here attention is given to the various types and levels of professorial service, the advantages and drawbacks of extensive service involvement on a new faculty member's part, and some of the considerations that should come into play when the academic newcomer must decide whether to accept or decline service opportunities proffered.

The discussion of faculty service is followed by a necessarily abbreviated overview of some important legal considerations governing contemporary academic life—the "traps" and "pitfalls" that await the unwary and how best to avoid them. In an increasingly litigious society where recourse to the court system is a first rather than a last resort for resolving conflicts or redressing grievances, ignorance is not bliss; and faculty members are well advised to refrain from engaging in those behaviors most likely to invite legal confrontation. Several specific examples are identified and discussed.

The work concludes with a summary of general suggestions worth heeding by all new faculty members.

A few disclaimers seem in order, the first having to do with terminology. To minimize repetitive phrasing, we have resorted to such near-synonyms as "neophyte" or "novice" to refer to a faculty "beginner" or "newcomer"—someone new to the circumstances of a situation or position. This aptly describes, we would argue, the challenge most faculty members confront starting out. The intended designation in all cases is a college teacher recently graduated with an advanced degree and now employed for the first time in a regular academic position, either at a four-year college or university or perhaps at a two-year community college. Basically, the person to whom this volume is addressed is the inexperienced junior faculty member.

Our use of the terms "novice" or "neophyte" is in no way intended to be condescending or pejorative. As noted previously, most new faculty members in fact are bright, competent, well-educated professionals. To speak of someone as a "novice," after all, is not necessarily to imply he or she is a "rank novice," someone bereft of any relevant job experience altogether. This being said, newness to the collegiate environment usually conduces to a certain naiveté and, for quite understandable reasons, less than full appreciation for what long-term-employment success demands in today's academic world. But once again, inexperience alone implies nothing about a person's intelligence or basal ability. It means simply that a novice still has more to learn.

Terminology aside, the broader challenge of being didactic with new faculty is to avoid a tone of discourse that ends up sounding arrogant or patronizing. The intended beneficiaries, after all, are not "clueless" dullards; and junior colleagues certainly deserve to be treated with the utmost respect. Moreover, some new faculty have been well prepared for taking up their new responsibilities and are capable of effecting a seamless transition from graduate student to professor—in which case, however, the discussions to follow presumably have little relevance.

The more common pattern among doctoral-degree-granting universities, however, as mentioned above, is the tendency to train future graduates as academic specialists, as researchers fitted for jobs in the same type of institution from which they matriculate. Despite the growing popularity of programs such as Preparing Future Faculty (PFF) and others, most doctoral-degree recipients, we judge, still enter the academic marketplace somewhat ill-prepared to assume their new roles as teachers and advisers, especially if they have accepted a position in an institutional setting quite dissimilar from the one they left behind. They may have taught classes as graduate assistants while pursuing their studies, for example. But whether they received much systematic supervision or were given in-depth opportunities to work through instructional problems with both peers and mentors prior to graduating, in our minds at least, remains problematic.

The same holds true of academic service obligations, student advising, and other duties commonly expected of a full-fledged faculty member. Our point is that universities usually do a good job of ensuring subject-matter competency for the graduates they release into the job market. But whether they give adequate attention to other aspects of academic job preparation is less certain. In any event, this guide to professorial life seeks to help new faculty members build on whatever previous training they might have received, above and beyond discipline-related tutelage.

We are sensitive to the point that advice-giving needs to be handled with discretion. It must always be borne in mind that so far as matters of faculty development are concerned, no precepts are absolute or infallible. Nothing is beyond challenge; and practically every rule admits of exceptions and qualifications, depending on the situation at hand. To put it bluntly, few if any ideas work for everyone; and what benefits one person may not prove particularly helpful for someone else. All told, therefore, it is important to remember that the successful pursuit of an academic career is an art, not an exact science. Readers of this work are urged to give every suggestion a fair hearing and a trial run if possible, but ultimately one must pick and choose what works best for oneself.

Finally, readers will note a significant omission—the absence of discussion about adjunct or "non-regular" faculty, those not moving toward a decision on tenure or promotion. The literature on this population is voluminous; and its treatment might require an entire separate volume dealing with issues surrounding the use of part-time, visiting, and adjunct faculty in the academy. On one side, the widespread, ever-increasing reliance of academic institutions on non-tenure-track faculty to carry their curricula affords many people opportunities that would otherwise be nonexistent. Some adjunct faculty do welcome the flexibility and reduced demands of part-time employment. Teaching provides supplemental income without the responsibility and demands of a full-time academic career.

On the other side, the potential for exploitation remains high. For those who wish to teach but are geographically place-bound by reason of spouses' careers or other family responsibilities, for instance, adjunct faculty status is often the only viable option. Not only are they necessarily limited in where they can teach, generally they must accept terms of employment set exclusively by the local institution where part-time work is to be had.

Characteristically, an adjunct is compensated on a "piece-work" basis—that is to say, he or she is paid by the course taught. Alternatively, the salary of an adjunct instructor or professor is likely to be disproportionately low relative to whatever duties are assigned. A part-timer's official status as a faculty member (voting rights and so forth) may be nonexistent or ambiguous at best. Nor are part-time adjunct or visiting faculty always extended the same fringe benefits enjoyed by their full-time colleagues. Most importantly, adjuncts usually hold temporary or term-limited contracts. In effect, they lack much chance of assuming a regular position that could lead to tenure and the economic security it affords.

Hope springs eternal. Under some circumstances, an adjunct faculty member might expend years building up his or her record of professional accomplishments in the expectation of being considered eventually for a regular, full-time position. Undeniably, there are situations in which a productive adjunct faculty member can become the "inside" candidate for a regular tenure-track position, if and when one opens up. Colleagues' familiarity with the adjunct's abilities and achievements might very well confer a distinct advantage over the candidacies of competing applicants. More often though, adjuncts on term appointments are considered ineligible for tenure-track positions. Marginalized and rendered somewhat "invisible" professionally, they serve out on the periphery of the academy's main enterprises.

Although the respective circumstances of regular tenure-track faculty members and nonregular faculty differ substantially, the chapters following may still offer useful suggestions for adjunct faculty, no less than for those with tenure-track appointments. They too need to apprise themselves of the local institutional culture and better understand their working environment if they are to be successful. They sometimes need mentoring. Visiting or adjunct faculty do seek to improve their instruction, to become the best teachers they can. They are often called on to assume advising duties. And, finally, many elect to engage in research and publishing, if only for whatever intrinsic rewards are involved.

It remains to observe, for all of the challenges and difficulties besetting higher education today, that it must be said that academic life can afford exhilarating, satisfying careers for those suited to it by ability, interest, and temperament. However, evidence abounds that even for the most talented, getting off to a good start is critical to long-term success. If in some small way this work assists faculty newcomers to launch their careers effectively, our efforts to assemble tips and hints to facilitate the process will have been imminently worthwhile.

Christopher J. Lucas
John W. Murry, Jr.
Fayetteville, Arkansas

PART I

PRELIMINARY CONSIDERATIONS

CHAPTER 1

INSTITUTIONAL ENVIRONMENT AND THE ACADEMIC COMMUNITY

The Multiple Cultures of the Academy

Every college and university (not to mention each academic unit or department within the institution) exhibits its own distinctive organizational culture. As Ann Austin observes, faculty values and behaviors are shaped in part by three distinct cultures or subcultures: that of the academic profession in general, that of a given academic discipline, and that of the institution itself.[1] For many new faculty members, the process of becoming acculturated at these multiple levels becomes a quest to find out "what is important" and "how things are done around here." Unfortunately, this task often develops into a frustrating search for answers that are neither clear nor readily apparent.

As they join the ranks of the professorate, new faculty members enter a unique work environment, a milieu wholly unlike that of most other occupational settings. Whereas most academics would prefer not to think of it quite this way, for example, the fact of the matter is professors *do* work as salaried employees of a legal corporation. All the same, given the nature of their work, they necessarily enjoy a considerable degree of autonomy and, correspondingly, a great deal of freedom in deciding how to conduct themselves. That degree of independence is both virtually unknown in most other professions and from some quarters remains an object of considerable envy as well as misunderstanding (*"You only teach 9 to 12 hours per week? What do you do the rest of the time?"*).

The defining ideals of academic culture in its broadest sense include, as George Kuh and Elizabeth Whitt expansively phrase it (*The Invisible Tapestry:*

Culture in American Colleges and Universities), "the concepts and symbols of academic freedom, the community of scholars, scrutiny of accepted wisdom, truth telling, collegial governance, individual autonomy, and service to society through the production of knowledge, the transmission of culture, and education of the young."[2]

How these broad themes are embodied and applied in the daily work of a professor depends in large measure on the individual's academic department and his or her disciplinary specialty. As Douglas Toma points out, "Disciplines determine the substantive knowledge with which scholars work, how they organize that knowledge, how they may draw on other disciplines, what types of work their colleagues value, and the language and symbols they use."[3]

Hence, it is a truism to observe that the experience of one faculty newcomer striving to become acculturated and integrated within a community of peers is apt to differ significantly from that of another in a different department or discipline—even within the same institution. It follows that attempts to generalize too freely or broadly about the experiences of faculty neophytes are apt to flounder on the specific circumstances that differentiate them. Once again, each person's initial experience within the academy is to some extent unique.

The work environment or culture of each institution differs as well, both in obvious ways and others less so. Colleges and universities are dissimilar from one another in terms of basic mission and goals. The constituency of a two-year community college, to cite an important example, is substantially unlike that served by a major research-focused university. A private liberal-arts college is inspired by a different system of values and priorities than those of a multipurpose institution with a strong sectarian affiliation. An urban university attracts students with backgrounds dissimilar from those attending a small rural college. Institutions vary greatly as well in terms of resources, operational goals, strategic plans, and their respective visions and aspirations for the future.[4]

Colleges and universities are shaped by powerful external factors—demographic, political, and economic—as well as by received customs, traditions, and habits of operation that emanate largely from within.[5] William Tierney of the University of Southern California observes that "an organization's culture is reflected in what is done, how it is done, and who is involved in doing it." He adds, "It concerns decisions, actions, and communication both on an instrumental and a symbolic level."[6] Overall, drawing from an extensive literature that has grown up around the idea of academic culture, the basic concept serves as a rubric encompassing all of the major artifacts, underlying values, defining beliefs, conventional assumptions, expectations, attitudes, and enduring ways of thinking shared by faculty as these are passed on to new members entering the institution.[7]

Dimensions of Institutional Culture

One of your challenges as a new faculty member is to identify those characteristics of your institution's culture that may or may not be readily detectable at the outset. The admittedly hackneyed metaphor of an iceberg floating in the ocean is as apt as any in that the visible tip comprises only a small fraction of what lies unseen beneath. The same may be said of academic culture. Visible dimensions of institutional culture include the following:

- Explicit rules, regulations, procedures, and organizational structures. The "official" representation of how the institution operates—or is supposed to function—is preserved in faculty, staff, and student handbooks; board of trustee policies; organizational charts; and in similar documents. Handbooks outline rules concerning teaching workloads and other faculty responsibilities, position descriptions, criteria governing promotion and tenure, office hours, governance structures, and so forth.
- Mission and goal statements. Virtually every college and university has an officially sanctioned statement of purpose, goals, and priorities. Mission statements purport to convey a sense for what is considered important and desirable, for what the institution is about. Particularly in their dealing with various public bodies and organizations, academic institutions as corporate entities find it advantageous to invoke explicit declarations of their basic aims and purposes. Mission statements tend to be couched in lofty, inspirational terms and are generally framed in the broadest, most inclusive terms possible, e.g., "to serve the needs of students" or "to foster the production and dissemination of knowledge for the common good of society."
- Rites and ceremonies. "Rites" are formal practices, customs, and observances comprising an institution's normal routines, such as the faculty meeting that opens the school year or the lighting of the university's tower after a football victory. "Ceremonies," on the other hand, are comprised by a series of rites that culminate in some public event, such as homecoming, commencement exercises, or the inauguration of a new president or some other high-ranking official.
- Symbols, emblems, artifacts. Institutional logos, slogans, seals, and other artifacts are tangible, physical expressions of an institution's

identity. Such artifacts are invested with symbolic significance by those who share and participate in the common culture.

* Language and dress. Another key to the culture is the language and jargon used by the organization's members. Seemingly insignificant yet symbolically important are norms governing individual behavior, not the least of which is the approved mode of dress. (In some academic institutions, casual attire worn by faculty is normal and even expected; in others, it is customary for faculty and staff to dress more formally.)

* Mythic narratives, sagas, and legends. Myths, stories, and legends are accounts of past events in the history of the institution that still hold special meaning to members of the organization. Some have a factual basis; some do not, or may have benefited from extensive embellishment. Similar in nature are "sagas," or well-preserved narratives celebrating the accomplishments and noteworthy deeds of particular individuals who have played important roles within the college or university at some point in the past.[8] Legends are instructive when they embody or underscore basic values considered important within the academic community.

While the "visible" components of institutional culture are useful for deciphering and understanding the institution, more important still are the "hidden" dimensions of organizational culture that can only be grasped over time. A. Clay Schoenfeld and Robert Magnan (*Mentor in a Manual, Climbing the Academic Ladder to Tenure*), advise new faculty to give scant attention to the institution's own promotional literature, to distrust preconceptions and prior assumptions, to give credence to first impressions, and to record mentally only what one sees and hears.[9] When it comes to uncovering the culture of a college or university, they advise, it is important to remember that "people learn from what they live rather than from what they are taught."[10]

Prudence dictates that as a faculty newcomer you make a considered effort to invert the culture iceberg and examine what lies beneath. So-called hidden dimensions of organizational culture include participants' beliefs about how the institution operates; specific values that appear to command broad acceptance from a majority of the people in the institution; assumptions that may or may not necessarily be rooted in fact but are widely accepted as true and therefore are rarely questioned; and norms that serve to govern acceptable behavior within the institution.[11]

Of the four, norms are generally the most important formative attributes or characteristics of an organizational culture. As defined by John Kotter and James Heskett, norms are "common or pervasive ways of acting that are found in a group and that persist because group members tend to behave in ways that teach these practices . . . to new members, rewarding those that fit in and sanctioning those that do not."[12] Adherence to prevailing behavioral norms, it has been argued, is more important to the success of new faculty than virtually anything else.[13]

Research conducted by Robert Allen and Saul Pilnick, for instance, indicates that every college or university has its own distinctive normative profile, a profile so characteristic of the institution that it serves as the equivalent of a fingerprint. "No two," they allege, "are exactly alike."[14] If your behavior conforms to the specific pattern of expectations prevailing in your institution, it is likely you will gain acceptance and support from your peers. Contrariwise, if your comportment violates or flouts the norms of the group, even within an otherwise permissive and forgiving environment, you will likely find yourself distanced by your new colleagues.

Allen and Pilnick identify ten distinct norm clusters that help account for why and how faculty members behave as they do. Some normative perceptions, they point out, are "positive" in that they are congruent with, and serve to support, the stated mission and purpose of the institution. Others are "negative" in that they work against, or undermine, institutional intentions, and, further, are in conflict with organizational policies and goals. Both shape behavior. Clusters specified are as follows:

- Pride, loyalty, sense of affiliation. This category defines the degree of pride that faculty and staff member have in their jobs. An example of a positive norm might be expressed as, "Around here we stand up for the college when others unfairly criticize it." A pervasive negative norm might be revealed by widespread assent to the declaration, "In our college, we tend to view major problems as the fault of the administration, not ours."
- Performance and excellence. This normative cluster defines the accepted level of performance expected of faculty. When queried, faculty members might agree, "Administrators do not really care about quality teaching—so why should I?" In contrast, a positive expression might be exemplified by the comment, "In our department we acknowledge faculty who strive for excellence in teaching as in all else."
- Teamwork and communication. A positive illustration of this norm category might be, "In our department we enjoy good rapport and work well together as a team." A negative indicator would be, "Around here, we have hypocrites who are out to advance themselves and tear everyone else down."

- Leadership and supervision. Norms associated with this cluster address faculty perceptions of the quality of leadership prevailing. Indicative of a positive expectation is the remark, "Administrators generally offer a clear vision and help us define our goals for the future." Conversely, negative perceptions might be illustrated by the comment, "Administrators around here are far more interested in looking good than in solving real problems."
- Accountability. The extent to which people in an institution are perceived to be held accountable for their performance affords a valuable clue to the character of the organization's culture. A negative norm would be revealed in widespread assent to the comment, "In my department I am unsure what is really expected of me for promotion or tenure." If positive norms prevail, one would be more likely to find agreement with the declaration, "We have clear guidelines to help us perform our assignments, and then we are rewarded accordingly."
- Collegial relationships. A felt absence of connection with others is disclosed by the comment, "Most of us have no outside interests in common—we do our job and then leave." A positive set of norms might be indicated by, "In our department, if one of our colleagues is getting a 'bum rap,' everyone is concerned. Faculty are truly friends in my unit."
- Student relations. Some norms help define what is considered an appropriate level of interaction between faculty and students. The observation, "At our school faculty work closely to monitor students' academic progress," suggests an environment quite different from one in which the norm is expressed as, "In my department it is customary for faculty to interact mainly through e-mail and to minimize personal contact with students."
- Honesty and responsibility. Notions about stewardship of funds and property help define institutional culture. There is a world of difference, for example, between "Around here we respect the things we use (computers, copiers, and so on)" and the admission, "We tend to be careless with our equipment."
- Faculty training and development. The importance attached to faculty and staff training and development helps shape academic culture. Reflecting a positive norm is the statement, "In our department faculty development is both encouraged and supported financially." A negative perception gives rise to, "A lot of lip service is paid to faculty development, but there is no money to support it."
- Innovation and change. Yet another norm category highlights perceptions of the extent to which creativity, innovation, and change are encouraged and embraced. A positive indicator might be expressed as,

"We keep our sights on the future and constantly look for opportunities to better serve our students." The opposite attitude is found in the comment, "Whenever we propose a change, we are always told 'but we have always done it this way.'"[15]

Peter Seldin, who writes extensively about faculty evaluation and academic culture, suggests there are ten major characteristics that collectively define the academic culture of an institution or department.[16] His list of salient features includes the following:

- Individual autonomy: the degree of freedom, autonomy, and independence that a new faculty member enjoys in teaching, scholarship, and service.
- Structure: the extent to which institutional rules and regulations impact upon what faculty members do, and the nature of their influence—whether they are perceived to thwart or facilitate faculty endeavors.
- Support: the type and amount of resources, financial and otherwise, available to faculty to sustain their teaching and research efforts.
- Identity: the degree to which faculty, staff, and students identify with, and have a sense of loyalty toward, the institution.
- Quality of personnel: the perceived level of trust and confidence among administrators, faculty, staff, and students.
- Cooperation: how closely members of the institution and department work together in achieving shared goals.
- Decision-making: how decisions are made and the extent and quality of faculty involvement in decision-making processes.
- Risk tolerance: the degree to which faculty are encouraged to be innovative and take risks.
- Communication: how communication (formal and informal) flows and how information is shared among members of the institution.
- Community: the extent to which faculty members feel connected to one another and the level of trust and collegiality enjoyed among them.

The Importance of Understanding the Effects of Culture

Schoenfeld and Magnan, among others, emphasize the point that any new faculty member must be comfortable within a particular cultural milieu before he or she can hope to function successfully.[17] And in order to achieve that necessary level of comfort and "fit," some sleuthing is needed

OBSERVING INSTITUTIONAL CULTURE

Each institution has its own particular culture, although it is shaped by the broader academic culture.

Institutional culture determines what is important, what is acceptable, and how business gets done at a particular campus. Culture is shaped by commonly held beliefs, values, and underlying assumptions. . . . Culture is the "invisible glue" that holds [a college or university] together by providing a common foundation and a shared interpretation and understanding of events and actions. Institution-wide patterns of perceiving, thinking and feeling; shared understandings; collective assumptions; and common interpretive frameworks are the ingredients of institutional culture. . . .

Understanding institutional culture is analogous to peeling away the many layers of an onion. The outer skins of the onion are the organization's *artifacts*, the middle layers the *espoused values*, and the inner core the *underlying assumptions*.

Artifacts are those visible products, activities, and processes that form the landscape of the institutional culture. Examples of artifacts include insiders' language and terminology, myths and stories, published mission statements, observable rituals and ceremonies, reward structures, and communication channels.

Espoused values are the articulated beliefs about what is "good," what "works," and what is "right." For example, an institution might value promoting lifelong learning or developing future global citizens, faculty-student contact outside of class, or active learning over formal classroom activities.

At the inner core of organizational culture are the underlying assumptions. These are the deepest ingrained assumptions that have become rarely questioned, taken-for-granted beliefs. They are the most difficult to identify because only cultural insiders can truly understand them, even if they cannot readily articulate them.

Examples include such statements as: acquiring knowledge is more important than transmitting it; community welfare is more important than individual welfare; if it's not invented here, it will not work in our culture; or some disciplines are more influential than others.

. . . When inconsistencies exist between espoused values and underlying assumptions, the assumptions come to light and understanding these assumptions becomes more critical. . . .

Two of the junior faculty who were recognized with outstanding teaching awards (artifact) did not receive tenure even though teaching is said to be important (espoused value). The explanation lies in the underlying assumption—that teaching is not as significant as other factors in the tenure process.

continues

A faculty senate produces a report (artifact) calling for "enhanced academic excellence" (espoused value) and echoing the goals in the strategic plan (artifact).When "weak" departments and programs are slated for elimination, faculty across campus protest because closing academic departments conflicts with their shared view that the campus is a "family" and the family must stay together (underlying assumption).

—Peter Eckel et al., *On Change III, Taking Charge of Change: A Primer for Colleges and Universities* (Washington, D.C.: American Council on Education, 1999), 21–24.

to understand the organizational culture in which you find yourself. The task, fundamentally, is to find out how the prevailing culture creates a sense of shared identity for the organizational unit, what specific behavioral expectations it reinforces or sanctions, and what shared beliefs and assumptions are endorsed.[18] Accordingly, you need to ask yourself questions such as the following:

- Formal organizational charts aside, where does real power and authority reside within the department or division as well as within the college or university? Who are the power brokers and how do they influence decision-making?
- What expectations of you are held by your newly acquired colleagues? What are the actual norms (both formal and informal) with which you will be expected to comply?
- Which academic policies and procedures are held to be most important or authoritative?
- What does the immediate academic unit most value with regard to teaching, scholarship, and service?[19]

New Faculty Socialization

Learning the ropes and becoming acculturated to the norms, values, and behaviors of the group is oftentimes a haphazard affair.[20] It occurs—or fails to take place—with little or no formal planning on the institution's part. As William Tierney points out, socialization tends to proceed not through direct didactic instruction so much as through the "ordinary daily occurrences" that transpire as the newcomer sets about the task of taking on the professorial role.[21]

BEFORE YOU ACCEPT THE POSITION . . .

The best time to ask probing questions about an institution is during the on-campus interview, well *before* you have been offered or accepted a position:

1. Request that time be set aside in the interview schedule for you to talk with students. Ask them about their opinions of the institution. Do they like their teachers? Are faculty members accessible to students? Do professors maintain regular office hours and otherwise make themselves available to those seeking help and mentoring?

2. Take time, if possible, to wander around the campus. Observe carefully. Strike up conversations with people you encounter. Encourage them to share with you their pet peeves and gripes as well as talk about the things they most enjoy about the school. (Brief conversations may not yield an in-depth analysis of the institution, but even cursory impressions are informative.)

3. Visit the campus bookstore. Look through the lists of textbooks required for courses in your field. Do the offerings seem appropriate and up-to-date? How is space within the bookstore utilized? How much room is given over, for example, to displays of trade and scholarly books, compared with sports memorabilia, casual wear, jewelry, souvenirs, stuffed animals, wall posters, and so on?

4. Interview first-year or second-year faculty members. Ask them about the state of campus morale. Find out what they like and dislike about their jobs. Ask about the quality of students in their classes. Try to draw them out about faculty-administration relations and the general "climate" of the institution. (It may be unrealistic to expect much candor, but you can learn from what is withheld as well as what information is disclosed.)

5. Identify the faculty members with whom you would be most likely to work closely, assuming you were offered the position for which you are interviewing. Spend as much time as possible garnering their perceptions and opinions about the institution—their likes and dislikes, their assessments of strengths and weaknesses, their professional hopes and plans for the future.

6. Pay attention to announcements posted on bulletin boards. Flyers reveal a great deal about what is going on around campus, the types of activities in which students are engaged or to which they are attracted, the events to which people give their time, and, generally, the state of the cultural life of the institution.

continues

7. Ask for demographic information on the school's students. How many students are campus residents, how many commuters? Do most students work full-time and attend school part-time? Or are most students attending classes on a full-time basis? How much diversity is there within the student population? What special provision, if any, does the college make for nontraditional students? Are there developmental and support facilities to assist students with academic remediation?

8. Look through the school's catalogue. Note the faculty's credentials and other demographic particulars. Where did they earn their degrees? From nearby graduate institutions or from leading universities across the country? Did they graduate from schools comparable with your own alma mater?

Terry Rosch and Jill Reich posit a four-stage process that junior faculty members typically undergo as they move toward becoming full-fledged members of the group: (1) pre-arrival; (2) encounter; (3) adaptation; and (4) commitment or metamorphosis.[22] The first of these, "pre-arrival," acknowledges the influence of preexisting values, attitudes, and expectations. The faculty neophyte does not arrive as a blank slate, so to speak; he or she has previously acquired an entire set of expectations as a graduate student as well as perceptions deriving perhaps from previous professional work experience.

As advanced-degree candidates, prospective faculty members are exposed to the values, norms, customs, and attributes of the institution they have attended as graduate students. This learning amounts to a kind of "anticipatory" acculturation or socialization to academic life. Unhappily, few institutions do an especially good job of preparing their graduates for the actual challenges they will face once they enter the teaching profession as faculty members in their own right.[23]

Dissonance occurs when new faculty arrive on the campus of a college or university expecting that the place that just hired them will exemplify much the same characteristics as the institutions from which they have recently graduated—and of course that is rarely the case. The most common example is the former graduate student from a major research-oriented university who accepts a position at a small school where the institution's mission emphasizes teaching almost exclusively. All told, academic life is likely to look quite different from the vantage point of the newly credentialed "insider" as compared with the "semi-outsider" perspective afforded by graduate-student status. Needless to add, frustration sets in when the academic neophyte discovers what was considered appropriate and fitting at one institution does not necessarily work at another.

Meanwhile, the "encounter" stage of socialization, according to Rosch and Reich, begins at that point in time when a candidate first begins to form an impression of an institution seeking to recruit him or her for a faculty position.[24] The prospective job-holder's initial perceptions of the school in question ultimately may or may not prove accurate in the long run. Once hired, the new appointee begins checking early perceptions of the work environment against subsequent impressions gained on the job. In some situations, the two coincide. In other cases, earlier images necessarily give way to a somewhat different, perhaps more realistic and less-idyllic picture of the college or department.[25]

At this point, the new faculty member is engaged in the task of discerning what is expected in the way of job performance and possibly in setting professional goals perceived to be congruent with those institutional expectations.[26] The newcomer seeks to identify more clearly his or her basic responsibilities. He or she seeks answers to questions about how other faculty manage their time, about where to go for support and resources, and perhaps about the standards or criteria by which faculty members in the unit are evaluated.

The third stage in the faculty socialization process, according to a number of writers on the topic, is that of "adaptation." At this point, the newcomer works to reconcile whatever contradictions may exist between early expectations and subsequent on-the-job experiences, those involving the work itself, relations with colleagues, and the environmental climate of the institution as a whole.[27]

Much time and energy are consumed learning specifically where offices are located, finding out who to see when problems arise, and, generally, identifying what rules and regulations govern how things are done. For many new faculty members, a degree of disillusionment begins to set in. Colleagues are not quite as collegial or helpful as one might have been led to believe previously. Isolation breeds loneliness. The process of trying to "fit in" as a member of the group, in many cases, generates anxiety and stress.

The fourth phase of the socialization process refers to commitment or metamorphosis. In this stage the newcomer truly begins to settle into the institution's routines. The focus shifts to finding one's niche or place within the unit.[28] The neophyte now starts to internalize the values, beliefs, and norms of the institution. Metamorphosis, as Stephen Robbins judges it, is complete when the new member has achieved a sense of comfort within the organization and feels himself or herself to be an integral part of it.[29]

Rosch and Reich conclude that the socialization process is "a cumulative learning period" when "individuals build upon and draw from their graduate training experiences in assuming the role of assistant professor."[30] But they further suggest that new faculty oftentimes are reluctant to make their needs known, fearing they will be judged negatively by peers and other associates.[31] Female and minority faculty members in particular, or so it is reported, often confront acute socialization problems stemming from fewer networking opportunities than those enjoyed by male or majority-culture colleagues and from a lack of directive mentoring. Newcomers, men and women alike, may prove unable to articulate their needs and problems unless they are prompted to be more forthcoming about their initial adjustment experiences.[32]

In the final analysis, effecting a successful transition from the role of graduate student to that of faculty member in a college or university demands an institutional support system. By the same token, it also requires that you as an involved individual exercise the initiative in ferreting out answers to certain fundamental questions:[33]

- What specifically is expected in the way of teaching, advising, research, and scholarship, and service? What constitutes an appropriate level of performance? How much room exists for negotiating a work assignment and with whom does such negotiation take place?
- What resources are available from the department, college, and institution as a whole to support your professional endeavors? How are these secured?
- Where should you go for feedback on professional progress? Who evaluates performance? By what standards or criteria are various faculty undertakings evaluated?
- What resources or facilities exist to assist you in improving your teaching or research skills? What information can be tapped to improve your ability to advise students or to engage more effectively in professional service activities?
- No one works in total seclusion and isolation from others. How is "good citizenship" defined within the program, department, or division? What is required in order for you to be perceived as a "team player" and a collegial member of the faculty?

Good Academic Citizenship

Of all the aforementioned questions, those dealing with professorial "collegiality" rank among the most problematic. They deserve further

A POSITIVE INSTITUTIONAL ENVIRONMENT: SOME INDICATORS

- Faculty members within each academic unit are focused, share many common priorities, and have a well-developed, clearly-articulated sense of mission within the unit.
- Faculty are committed to shared responsibility for establishing, reviewing, and modifying institutional policies and procedures, as circumstances dictate. Faculty policy contributions are both meaningful and substantive. Administrators listen to the faculty and heed advice; faculty in turn are sensitive to the constraints and imperatives to which administrators must remain responsive.
- Relations between administrative personnel and faculty members are collaborative, collegial, and generally amicable. Good two-way communication prevails. Interaction between faculty and the administration is rarely if ever adversarial in character. Mutual trust facilitates cooperation between both parties and advances the common welfare of the institution.
- The vital role played by support staff in conducting institutional operations is acknowledged, respected, and appropriately rewarded. All useful work is acknowledged and valued.
- The welfare of students is a top institutional priority. Policies and procedures reinforce the importance of meeting students' needs. Students are treated with consideration and respect.
- Faculty members work closely with one another in the pursuit of shared goals and objectives. Schisms, petty factionalism, and interpersonal conflict are strongly discouraged. Collegiality is highly valued. Opportunities are provided for airing disagreements and resolving conflicts as they arise, and problems are addressed promptly and effectively.
- Personnel policies are clear and explicitly stated, but are neither excessively rigid nor inflexible. Institutional routines reflect a shared conviction that everyone is seeking to make positive contributions to the welfare of the institution and its constituents, both internal and external. The basic posture is one of trust and belief in people's good intentions. Faculty, staff, and students alike evidence pride, loyalty, and a strong sense of affiliation with the institution.
- People are rewarded and reinforced for whatever they do well that makes for a positive contribution in advancing the institution's well-being. Considerations of fairness and equity are held uppermost.
- Wise stewardship of resources and accountability for their use are leading operational values.

continues

- The faculty reward system coincides closely with the institution's avowed priorities.
- Continuous improvement is an institutional mandate.
- Faculty, staff, and student morale is high.

consideration. While there is general agreement among faculty that being a "good citizen" and interacting with peers in a collegial manner is important, considerable disagreement attends what academic citizenship really means. As James L. Bess remarks, "Despite some tacit appreciation for collegiality, most working faculty don't even know what it is."[34] When polled about collegiality on their campus, many senior faculty report it barely exists; and first-year faculty report being disappointed by what they perceive to be a lack of collegial relations in their new department.

A standard dictionary definition claims collegiality is characterized by "equal sharing: marked by power or authority vested in each of a number of colleagues."[35] Some suggest that collegiality is "an attitude about professional relationships that leads to genuine collaboration, potentiated individual endeavors, and mutual respect."[36] Others hold that collegiality rests on a "belief in the propriety of order and rationality in the structure and process of deliberations concerning organizational decisions; and belief in and commitment to the value of goodwill among colleagues." In essence, according to Rita Bode, "collegiality assumes order and sustenance, and balance of reason and emotion."[37]

If no single definition marks out clearly what is meant by professorial collegiality, it remains true to say that its presence or perceived absence weighs heavily on how first-year faculty are accepted by their colleagues. The theme is one of "getting along" and being cooperative; of showing a willingness to place the common welfare ahead of the demands of one's own agenda; of readiness to pitch in and do one's share of the work; of courtesy and respect shown toward one's peers.[38]

In spite of an increasing trend in recent years to include collegiality as a criterion in the promotion and tenure process, more than a few critics now oppose its inclusion. Carlin Romano, for example, writing in the *Chronicle of Higher Education,* argues that "collegiality is a judgment we largely base on spoken, personal interaction, where the best-laid euphemism can come undone thanks to an inadvertently curled lip, raised eyebrow, or spontaneous spasm of honesty."[39]

Assessing a colleague's collegiality, it is sometimes argued, is a hazardous business because the judgments required are so subjective in character. Should peer or administrative perceptions of a given individual's "enthusiasm" or "dedication" count as distinct elements in determining a candidate's progress toward tenure? Might one imagine circumstances in which collegiality gets confused with someone's excessive deference to others? Is the person who "goes along to get along" thereby somehow more collegial than someone willing to take a principled stand on a particular issue, even at the risk of alienating colleagues or administrative superordinates who strongly disagree with the position taken?

On the other side of the issue, if "collegiality" is construed as implying no more than decorum and appropriate restraint in dealing with colleagues, of courtesy, respect, and solicitude shown toward others; if it refers primarily to genuine cooperativeness and collaboration rather than attempts to be ingratiating or to win favor; if collegiality has nothing to do directly with seeking approbation and approval from others; if it in no way entails some sort of academic "popularity contest"—then, it is difficult to see how collegiality ought *not* to figure in decisions about promotion and tenure.

Within very broad limits—and in academe they are broader than in almost any other sort of organization—due regard *should* be paid, it is sometimes argued, for whether someone exhibits collegial behavior. On balance, you are well-advised to attend to how you are perceived as a contributing member of the larger academic community. At the very least, if you are seen to be excessively combative, disruptive, and uncooperative, or looked on as someone unwilling to contribute to the common good, you may have a harder time securing tenure than someone who is considered genuinely collegial.

For the uninitiated, the "good citizen" issue can be frustrating and seemingly fraught with great danger. Whether to speak up in a faculty meeting, how much to say, whether to criticize, whether it is acceptable as a nontenured neophyte to offer one's opinion or suggestions in a public forum—all such situations can easily give rise to grossly exaggerated fears of adverse reactions from colleagues. If the working milieu is dysfunctional, it must be said, then whatever anxieties provoke a newcomer to keep his views to himself or herself are probably well founded. Nevertheless, in a healthy organizational environment, where diversity of opinion and free expression are accepted norms, circumspection has little, if anything, to do with authentic faculty collegiality and good citizenship.

COLLEGIALITY:
TWO CANDIDATES FOR TENURE

Two assistant professors were hired at the same time. Sufficient time has elapsed so that both are now under consideration for tenure.

Professor X is unquestionably brilliant and seemingly destined to make major contributions to her field of academic specialization. She has already secured two major research grants and is working on a third. She is acknowledged as an original and innovative scholar. She publishes often, in all the right places, and has delivered numerous papers at national conferences. Unfortunately, she is utterly lacking in interpersonal skills and sensitivity. She intimidates her students, even though they concede her thorough command of her subject-matter. She is regarded by her colleagues as abrasive and unnecessarily combative in her dealings with staff, students, and faculty alike. She appears to go out of her way to alienate others and to pick fights. She is needlessly insulting and seems ready to attack or criticize others at the slightest provocation. She is constantly at the center of a tempest.

Efforts to counsel her have proven uniformly unsuccessful. Attempts to persuade her to modulate her outspoken criticism of others fall on deaf ears. She is openly contemptuous of her department chair, her dean, and other superordinates who have sought to intervene. The faculty is convinced she will never change. They question whether her disruptive behavior will only worsen once she is granted tenure.

Professor Y is affable, collegial, and well liked within his department. He gets along with everyone. He can be counted on unfailingly to accept the assignments or committee chores no one else wants. He works long and hard. Although not considered a great teacher, students report he is "a nice guy," and they are not unduly critical of his instruction. He has written two brief articles in five years, neither of them in well-regarded journals. Overall, his department chair has given him a "minimally satisfactory" rating each year since his initial appointment. His colleagues characterize him as "solid" but "unexceptional."

What considerations ought to be taken into account in determining which, if either, of the two candidates should be recommended for tenure?

Points in Review

- Deciphering and understanding the organizational "climate" or "culture" of an institution is crucial for a new faculty member.
- Good indicators of a healthy work environment include a common, shared sense of mission; a strong tradition of faculty governance; good

faculty-administrator relations; high priority placed on meeting student needs; faculty collegiality; explicit policies and procedures; high morale.

- New faculty members need to identify what norms govern performance expectations. It is critical to ascertain what the institution (administrators, faculty colleagues) require in order for one to be successful.
- Professorial collegiality is important.

CHAPTER 2

FACULTY MENTORING

The Mentoring Relationship

The pairing of a master with an apprentice, or a mentor with a protégé, frames a very ancient tradition in job training and career advancement. Characteristically, the mentor is a senior person who oversees and promotes the career and development of another person, usually a junior, through teaching, coaching, and counseling.[1]

The mentor serves as an exemplar or role model, acting also on occasion as a sponsor or advocate of a subordinate's interests. The mentor is an adviser, a guide, a supportive critic if need be, sometimes a special friend or confidant.[2] Whatever the specific combination of roles, the dynamic of the relationship between mentor and mentee involves an experienced person offering guidance and advice for the benefit of someone less experienced.[3] Basically, the mentor undertakes responsibility for actively fostering or promoting the protégé's success in some type of occupational setting.

Because mentoring involves highly variable interactions, conducted under differing circumstances in a wide range of contexts or settings, mentoring roles cannot always be clearly differentiated.[4] A mentor might serve simultaneously as a sort of guru or teacher, depending on the circumstances, as well as a teammate, helper, rescuer, collaborator, motivator, nurturer, caretaker, door-opener, champion, or professional consultant, and possibly much else besides.[5]

In the absence of any clear or universal definition of mentoring, a commonsensical description emphasizes "a nurturing process in which a more skilled or more experienced person, serving as a role model, teaches, sponsors, encourages, counsels, and befriends a less-skilled or less-experienced person for the purpose of promoting the latter's professional and/or personal development . . . within the context of an ongoing, caring relationship between the mentor and protégé."[6] What the seasoned mentor offers the novice, basically, is "a foundation of effective strategies, useful knowledge, and proven applications that would otherwise be learned through trial and error."[7]

It has often been noted that academic life, though outwardly crowded with people (especially students) is very much a solitary pursuit. For you as a new faculty member, the challenge is to take advantage of every collegial opportunity to counterbalance that solitude.[8] The fact is, newcomers seldom chose to work in isolation from others.[9] Identifying a kindred spirit can ease the sense of isolation you are likely to experience; and finding someone with whom to share and collaborate becomes an equally important source of support. Above all, the encouragement and direction supplied by a mentor may help overcome feelings of estrangement and isolation, hastening the time when one comes to feel a stronger sense of affiliation within the peer community.

What is often noted about teachers working in lower schools applies with even greater force to professors in academe: that much of the work performed, by its very nature, tends to separate and isolate individuals from one another. The teacher locked off in a classroom or library affords the typical case in point. As most newcomers soon discover, if you are to acquire a sense of connectedness with some larger social whole and work in concert with it, forging bonds with peers and establishing collegial relationships will assume great importance.[10]

Consider this panegyric offered by a Purdue University professor reminiscing about the contributions of his senior mentor: "He welcomed me to the faculty by providing me with continuing support and communication He provided me with the necessary background, information, and course materials to make my transition to the college classroom a smooth one. . . . He included me in his publications and research program. He encouraged me to co-author publications with him . . . included me in his grant programs, and included me in graduate committees. . . . He made sure that I did the 'right' things and did not stray off track spending time on projects that had little payback for an assistant professor."

The mentor took pains to see that his protégé established specific goals and worked toward them throughout the year. This senior colleague functioned as a coach, helping his mentee build on his strengths and working with him to overcome weaknesses. "He made sure that my performance was monitored and that feedback was always provided in a positive and reassuring manner." As a result, the former mentee reports, "I have attempted to carry on the tradition that [he] initiated. I regularly meet with new faculty members to discuss their goals and objectives. I discuss the expectations for a new faculty member in a university environment; I monitor

MENTORING:
TWO DIFFERENT EXPERIENCES . . .

No sooner had I arrived on campus, when a senior colleague took me under his wing. As it turned out, he had attended graduate school with my former dissertation supervisor; they had been close friends years before. . . . My new mentor showed me the ropes. He counseled me on the hidden protocols and etiquette appropriate for "the new kid on the block." He was always there to answer my questions—with tact and endless patience.

He fostered in me a growing conviction that I could succeed. His faith in my abilities helped me feel confident and hopeful. He freely shared whatever advice he could about teaching, advising problems, committee assignments, who to watch out for, how to get along with our department chair. He interceded on my behalf with the dean when a problem arose. . . . I owe him a great deal.

Whatever successes I achieved in those first few years are due partly to the man who served as my mentor. I will always feel appreciation and gratitude for the support I received. . . .

—from an interview with a senior
professor in a large Midwestern university

In my first [academic] job, the faculty colleague with whom I shared an office volunteered to be my mentor. He told me he would "keep me out of trouble." He gave me a great deal of advice; and I listened to him, figuring he knew more than I did about the place. He looked on me as his protégé. But as time went on, I realized he expected me to go along with everything he said and never disagree. If I didn't follow up and do what he advised, he became visibly agitated. Once he didn't speak to me for an entire week. Our relations became strained; and I felt I had to ask to be reassigned to an- other office. . . .

The day I moved, another faculty member came up to me and offered congratulations. "We've all been wondering when you'd catch on," he confided. "You've been joined at the hip with [Professor X] since you got here—we all assumed you were 'his boy.' Most of us consider him to be the biggest jerk on the whole faculty. I wouldn't trust a word he says!"

—from an interview with a newly tenured
associate professor in a private liberal arts college

new faculty members with respect to their progress in the promotion and
tenure process; and, most importantly, I try to provide the necessary encouragement to help them succeed in their chosen areas of scholarship,
teaching, and service."[11]

Benefits of Mentoring

Although there exists substantial anecdotal evidence to support the idea
that mentoring new faculty can be extremely helpful, empirical studies
documenting specific benefits have been suggestive only and "far from
conclusive."[12] Some research appears to confirm the notion that a men-
torship in a faculty novice's first year is "critical" in launching the person's
productive career.[13] Another analysis of recent vintage indicates that having a faculty mentor may very well remain important throughout at least
the first three years of a newcomer's first appointment.[14]

Mentoring, it has been alleged, "promotes faculty productivity, advocates collegiality, and [advances] a broader goal of attracting, retaining, and
advancing faculty members. Mentoring supports professional growth and
renewal, which in turn empowers faculty as individuals and colleagues."[15]
At the very least, it has been alleged, the influence of a mentor serves to
reduce a newcomer's isolation during the first few months or so on the job
and thereby makes it likelier that the novice will benefit from the advice
and counsel of others.[16]

Demonstrating longer-lasting advantages, however, has been somewhat
more problematic.[17] "A dearth of information exists regarding evaluative
outcomes for mentoring faculty," two authors note, "and the mentoring
research in postsecondary and higher education has revolved primarily
around whether mentoring relationships have existed for protégés, either
as students or as professionals. . . ."[18]

Nevertheless, mentored protégés compared with unmentored faculty
newcomers, it is claimed by some researchers, do tend to feel more self-
assured about professional risk taking, exhibit greater political savvy, profess to feel more confident about their teaching, and, generally, in the long
run tend to be more prolific researchers. Faculty with mentors have been
found to be more productive, to receive more competitive grants, to publish more, and they indicate higher career and job satisfaction, while
achieving greater long-term success than those not mentored.[19] For these
and other reasons, the considered judgment of many is that "sensitive guidance from established professionals" may indeed represent "the most effective way to ease the initial career transition for new faculty." More
specifically, "a supportive department chair or senior colleague willing to

give advice and respond to questions can remove many hurdles confronting a new professor."[20]

Why Faculty Mentoring
Programs Remain Uncommon

As a general rule, according to Robert Boice of SUNY Stony Brook, who has written extensively on the topic, whereas informal advice giving may be a commonplace in the academic arena, formal mentoring programs for new faculty are neither well developed nor widely utilized across the country.[21] Relatively few colleges and universities, he judges, arrange for the mentoring of their new hires in any systematic or demonstrably effective way. Notwithstanding, in his estimation the number of institutions that are trying to do so has increased at least moderately in recent decades.

The relative paucity of mentoring programs is accounted for by several factors. "The literature on mentoring new teachers is scattered, little-known, and largely conjectural," Boice and his colleagues observe. "Its glib enthusiasm and lack of verification disposes some to dismiss programmatic efforts as a fad."[22] More important still, the taint of faddishness aside, is the tradition holding that effective mentoring, when it occurs at all, is most likely to develop spontaneously, of its own accord, without third-party intervention. Mentors and protégés, or so it is commonly assumed, cannot simply be assigned to one another under the auspices of some formal institutionalized program. Mentoring relationships that are truly functional must evolve "naturally" or spontaneously out of mutual professional attraction. Ultimately their success comes to depend, runs the argument, on some shared perception of common academic interests.

Furthermore, many experienced and new faculty alike tend to view formal mentoring programs with suspicion and distrust because they associate them with "remediation." For some, program participation serves as a possible indicator of professional deficiency, as something that will hinder, not help, one's future career.[23]

Again, new faculty members, already overwhelmed by the pressures of their new assignments, sometimes judge that working with a mentor would prove too time consuming, and that the benefits of having a mentor assigned in some explicit capacity would not be commensurate with the effort invested. Some novices fear the possibility of dependency or even of actual exploitation at the hands of a senior colleague empowered to serve as an "official" guide and role model. Finally, more than a few simply remain unconvinced they need any mentoring in the first place, and are content to strike out on their own as much as possible.

Critics of formal mentoring programs go so far as to claim they actually do a disservice to new faculty and may be indicative of a basic systemic weakness. Typical is the argument recently advanced by two academic psychologists, James Selby and Lawrence Calhoun, who assail such programs as both unnecessary and harmful. A department, they observe, is a community of scholars whose members, ideally, are devoted to teaching and other scholarly pursuits. Years of training and development prepare people for membership in such a community. Presumably then, each new faculty hired should arrive on campus with a clear notion of what will be required for effective participation in the life of that academic community. "Is a person who has successfully completed [extended graduate] training and received the acknowledgment of the graduate faculty," they ask rhetorically, "not ready to take his or her place in a community of scholars?"[24]

"New faculty should have the necessary skills to elicit support from helpful and approachable senior colleagues," they argue. "If new faculty lack the intellectual ability and the personal strengths to assume the responsibility for developing professionally within academic institutions, then attention should be focused instead on strengthening graduate training."[25] A mentoring program, by the very fact of its existence, allegedly conveys a negative message that new members of the academy cannot be expected to succeed on their own, that they are incapable of seizing the initiative in seeking out senior colleagues for advice and guidance as needed.

"If colleges and universities are now systematically producing [faculty] who are not ready to take their place as fully functioning colleagues," they observe, "then perhaps what is needed is not the formalized paternalism of mentoring programs, but an improvement in the quality of doctoral training. . . ."[26] Faculty mentoring may be both necessary and helpful, they conclude, but it hardly justifies the bureaucratic trappings, report writing, time spent attending meetings, and all the rest of the cumbersome baggage that inevitably comes with the institutionalization of something that should be left to work informally on its own.[27]

Lessons Learned from Formal Mentoring

On the other side of the argument, advocates for organized mentoring programs argue that so-called natural mentoring occurs relatively infrequently, and oftentimes fails to help those who might benefit the most from structured collaboration, some women and minority faculty members in particular. What happens in the absence of an institutionally sanctioned program, it is alleged, is that senior colleagues hesitate to volunteer

IT SHOULD BE OKAY TO ASK QUESTIONS . . .

New faculty members should be encouraged to ask questions and solicit information when they need it. Especially if there is no formal faculty development program in place to assist newcomers, and you need answers, no good purpose is served by pretending otherwise.

Secretaries and administrative assistants of various sorts are an invaluable source of information. They can handle routine queries, ranging from where to obtain parking permits or how to submit a purchase requisition to how to replace a missing office key, with a minimum of fuss and bother. Most competent support staff members have a uniquely privileged perspective on the institution's daily operations and its personnel. As the saying goes, they know "where all the bodies are hidden." Seasoned veterans who have been around a long time are usually very keen observers and—to extend the metaphor—they know which closets hold skeletons.

Never miss a chance to learn from custodians, technicians, clerical administrators, and secretaries.

Some questions can be responded to by students. Administrators usually try to be helpful as well. Faculty colleagues are usually flattered when you solicit their advice, and are pleased to offer their opinions.

Most newcomers in their first faculty position—to phrase it bluntly—"don't know what they don't know but need to know."

One intelligent response is *the judicious posing of open-ended questions:* How is success measured around here and what does it take to succeed? Who, in your judgment, is the best person to seek out if I need help with my teaching? Who is a good writer? I am considering applying for a grant; who should I talk to for advice on how to begin? Can you offer any tips or suggestions on how to improve my time management?

Create opportunities for informal discussion and exchanges. Offer to take a more experienced colleague to lunch. Share coffee with a fellow faculty member. Exercise the initiative by introducing yourself to people you do not know yet. Drop in on a colleague for a chat during his or her office hours if no one else is present. By your actions and words, publicize your openness and willingness to learn from others.

advice for fear of being considered presumptive or unduly intrusive. Likewise, in a culture where mentoring is not customary, newcomers may be hesitant to ask questions or seek help for fear of being considered naive or inadequate. People are usually more willing to offer and to receive assistance when such behaviors are accepted norms in the situation.[28] A mentoring program, in effect, helps to legitimate and encourage truly beneficial collaborative liaisons between senior and junior faculty.

Systematic mentoring, defenders claim, not only works better than spontaneous, so-called natural peer counseling, but it is apt to involve a higher percentage of new and junior faculty than would otherwise be true in cases where a laissez-faire approach prevails. Mentoring capable of making a positive difference begins with institution-wide programs aimed at making newcomers feel welcome and connected. Support programs succeed when they make novices feel valued, when they convey the message that initiation rituals are fair and explicit, and that beginners, with an honest effort, can succeed.[29]

Certain features of the most successful programs are fairly obvious. Others, surprisingly, seem somewhat counterintuitive.[30] Either way, the institutional experience of scores of colleges and universities as reported in recent literature on faculty mentoring may be said to suggest the following generalizations:

- The scale of operation of a mentoring program is important. Programs with the best prospects for success reportedly are conducted on a campus-wide basis rather than within smaller academic units such as a department or a particular academic program area.
- New faculty orientation and assigned mentoring ought to be mandatory, or at least strongly encouraged. Program participation needs to be presented to newcomers as an established institutional expectation, not as an entirely voluntary option. Faculty mentors, on the other hand, should be recruited from the ranks of those willing and able to volunteer their time and talents for the task.
- The earlier provision is made for mentoring to begin, the more beneficial and enduring are the outcomes. Successful faculty development programs (including mentoring) start as soon as the intended beneficiaries arrive on campus, well before participants become fully engaged in their work routines.
- Effective mentoring allegedly depends far less on a personality match between a mentor and a protégé and more on the nature of their collaboration—that is, what they do together. Mentoring for new teachers works as well—if not better—between strangers and between faculty in different disciplines than with pairings assembled along more traditional lines, so long as the pair is engaged in a series of structured discussions and activities having a clear, unambiguous focus.
- Gender, ethnicity, program affiliation, or disciplinary specialization (or so it is claimed by some) are likewise relatively unimportant variables

in pairing faculty members. What counts are the quality and regularity of interaction between the experienced and the less-experienced faculty member in the pursuit of specified program objectives.

• Habituation is a key element for success. A paired mentor and mentee must meet regularly, weekly or biweekly, for a period of time extending over several months perhaps, or even longer. Care must be taken to prevent attrition. Intervention typically is needed to prevent program participants from concluding their series of meetings prematurely, before the full benefits of the relationship can be realized.

• It is helpful—some would say essential—that the mentoring program have a coordinator who is responsible for ensuring that mentoring pairs continue to meet on a regular and continuing basis, that progress is monitored, and that participants are provided with feedback as needed.

• Good mentoring programs make provision for interaction, exchange, and discussion among or between paired mentors and protégés in some type of group setting. Some exemplary programs encourage two to four meetings between mentors and protégés each month, to which is added one collective monthly meeting of all new faculty members and their respective mentors.

• Protégés first and foremost seek expressions of interest and support from mentors. What the former tend to appreciate most from the latter is empathy, humor, reinforcement, the presumed benefits of experience, and reliable information about the prevailing organizational culture.

• The most effective mentors are those imbued with an altruistic desire to pass on their knowledge and skills and to facilitate the work of others. The most important attributes of a good mentor include an ability to listen actively, to be present, and to communicate an attitude of acceptance and positive regard. An effective mentor is accessible, empathic, and supportive.[31] Good mentors do not view themselves, nor do they pose, as infallible authorities with a mandate to instruct novices how to do their work in some particular way.

• New faculty members tend initially to seek help or guidance with teaching. Their first priority has to do with the nuts and bolts of classroom performance. Close behind is the felt need to familiarize themselves with their own programs or departments, then with their schools or colleges, and finally with the institution's campus as a whole. Only as they begin to feel more comfortable with their own teaching do they feel able and willing to focus their attention on broader concerns or longer-range career issues.[32]

• The most common topics for discussion between a mentor and a novice typically include any or all of the following: institutional work expectations, how to develop a research and scholarship agenda, grantsmanship, the mechanics of getting published, academic politics, relations with colleagues, preparing for performance evaluations, tenure and promotion criteria, career planning, networking, time management, stress reduction, balancing out personal and professional commitments, professional service, techniques for dealing productively with difficult or antagonistic students, and professional values and ethics—though not necessarily in any particular sequence or order of perceived importance.

The Dilemmas of New Faculty Members

In the vast majority of cases, a newly appointed faculty member will discover upon arrival that very little provision has been made for some kind of structured work socialization or extended institutional acculturation. In some instances, there will be a new-faculty orientation session or workshop of limited scope and duration that newcomers are urged to attend. Pro forma reassurances will be extended to the effect that questions are welcomed, and that help will always be available upon request. Otherwise, there will be little else offered, apart from the welcoming rituals customary on most campuses.

Thereafter the new faculty member will be left by and large to his or her own devices. No one in particular is likely to be appointed—or is apt to volunteer—to act in any special mentoring capacity. Nobody will be expressly identified as a resource person to whom you may come for consultation or assistance.

Meanwhile, at the risk of noting the obvious, what you are most likely to experience at the outset is stress. "Moving from one job to another is rarely easy," observes Robert Menges of Northwestern University's Center for the Teaching Professions. "The difficulties of settling in are compounded when the new position requires geographical relocation, calls for new skills, and entails new responsibilities. All this is true for academics no less than for other professionals, particularly when junior academics assume new positions. . . ." He adds, "Even those who have previous experience as full-time academics feel challenged when they move into a faculty position at a new college or university."[33]

Faculty development specialists concur that tension continues as a prominent feature in the lives of junior faculty—a reality quite at odds with the popular impression of academics absorbed in leisured contemplation and scholarly reflection. As Menges observes, "Anxiety is high for junior faculty. This is no longer anxiety about finding a job; it has been transformed into anxiety about surviving in the job."[34]

Second, "junior faculty feel tremendous pressure from obligations that compete for their time and energy. Often they find themselves taking time from important professional activities and from meaningful personal pursuits in order to meet demands that seem more urgent, and usually those are the demands of teaching."[35]

Third, new faculty are likely to experience a strong sense of isolation or separation from others. As Menges phrases it, "They find fewer connections with colleagues than they expected and than they desire."[36] Finally, new and junior faculty "experience dissonance about the rewards they receive for their work. They spend the great majority of their time in teaching-related activities, yet most of them (at least those at four-year institutions) soon learn that compensation and advancement are strongly dependent on achievements in research and scholarship."[37]

Work-related sources of stress are multiple: committee participation and faculty meetings, the teaching of new classes, expectations of research and publishing productivity, the prospect of future performance reviews, latent uncertainty about what may be involved in seeking tenure and academic promotion, and so on. The challenge always is calculating how to apportion your time so that priorities are observed and work is accomplished. Decisions about allocating time are made all the more difficult, of course, in the face of possible uncertainty or confusion over what job success will demand over the long haul.[38]

What Novices Need to Know

It remains a truism to observe that each individual's situation may be unique when it comes to seeking information deemed important for long-term career success in academe. Junior faculty members differ tremendously in terms of experience, sophistication, background, interests, and needs. Yet common experience does suggest recurrent patterns of questions most likely to demand answers that only fellow faculty members can supply. The following list of topics is intended to be illustrative only:

- Performance Expectations. What is required for professional success? What does the institution value most and reward? How do institutional needs and priorities affect the work of individual faculty members? Which types of activities and accomplishments are most consistent with the faculty reward system? What are the criteria or standards that govern contract renewals, the awarding of tenure, annual salary increments, merit pay, and academic promotions?

• Institutional Culture. What adjectives would faculty of long-standing tenure be most likely to employ to describe or characterize the "climate" or work "environment" of the institution (school, college, department, program)? Is the job culture marked by collaboration and cooperation, or is competition stressed? Is collegiality valued or not? Do faculty members feel nurtured and respected as professionals? What is the state of faculty morale? Is there a rift or tension between academics and administrators? Who exercises authority, and in what specific ways? Are decision-making processes authoritarian or nonauthoritarian? Does the faculty feel disenfranchised or empowered? Are operating policies and procedures clear and explicit or ambiguous and widely misunderstood?

• Institutional Politics. Who wields power? How is it distributed? Who is in charge? How do decisions get made? Is change facilitated or hindered by those who exercise authority? Who are the major players and power-brokers?

• Faculty Evaluation. How is faculty performance assessed? Who is responsible for implementing relevant policies? Is there general satisfaction or dissatisfaction with the procedures employed? Is the system fair and equitable? Why or why not? What documentation must individual faculty members supply? What purposes are served through faculty assessments? What steps need to be taken to make receiving a favorable evaluation more likely?

• Time Management. Are there any proven techniques colleagues find helpful in reconciling the many disparate demands placed on a faculty member's time and energy? If so, which techniques or procedures seem most effective?

• Institutional and Professional Service. Is it possible to avoid feeling overcome by multiple, often time-consuming service responsibilities? Under what conditions is it advisable to take on even burdensome assignments? When is it acceptable to decline opportunities for professional service? How important is service as a component element in an individual's total work profile?

• Teaching and Curriculum Development. Is teaching valued? How much is it esteemed relative to other activities in which faculty typically engage? Do faculty peers and/or administrators review teaching performance in any substantive, meaningful way? How important are student evaluations of a faculty member's classroom instruction? By what standards is my teaching going to be evaluated, if at all? What resources are available to assist me to improve my performance? Are efforts at innovation and experimentation encouraged or discouraged? How does a relatively inexperienced faculty member such as myself develop new courses or redraft existing ones—that is, how free will I be to revamp or restructure a course? Within the context of teaching a specific discipline, what are the best ways of fostering student learning?

- Research and Scholarship. Is published scholarship considered important by the institution? To what extent is it valued, compared with other faculty activities? What forms or expressions of faculty scholarship are prized most? What are the best ways of initiating a research agenda? How do I first get published? What level of research activity or involvement is considered reasonable or necessary?
- Grantsmanship. Does the institution value efforts aimed at securing external grants and contracts? What types of support are available to assist faculty in responding to grant opportunities? What are the attributes or characteristics of successful proposals? How are grants administered? What policies and procedures govern grant applications? What pitfalls should be avoided?

Seizing the Initiative

In the absence of an assigned senior mentor (or an established campus facility devoted to faculty support), it inevitably falls to you as the new faculty member to exercise the initiative in securing assistance or the information you need. Sometimes the act of seeking help may involve soliciting cooperation from a single individual. Other times, the recruitment of a colleague as mentor will depend upon the type of help sought. You might very well turn to several different people for support or direction, depending on the issues at hand.

If the challenge is teaching, it is usually not difficult to identify someone who enjoys a reputation as a skilled classroom practitioner who might be able to offer useful suggestions or even supervision. You might ask for an opportunity to observe a senior colleague's teaching, or under certain circumstances, go so far as to offer to team-teach a course for the sake of the learning experience involved. Conversely, you might ask one or more senior faculty to observe and critique your teaching, to review instructional materials and exams, to evaluate a course syllabus, to contribute a guest lecture, and so on.

If answers to questions about initiating a research project are needed, inquiry will quickly reveal who is reputed to have the knowledge, skills, and experience required for getting a successful program started. There is nothing to prohibit you as a prospective mentee from volunteering to collaborate or assist with a research project already underway or to offer help in drafting a proposal for a new study.

The situation with respect to writing is much the same. More often than one might suppose, a long and fruitful relationship can evolve out of a situation where the original act of collaboration between two faculty members, one a novice and one a seasoned veteran, began with the shared authorship of an article for publication. Ad-hoc faculty pairings for any such specific purpose may very well serve to lay the foundation for an enduring collegial relationship, one that carries with it much valuable mentoring. The same holds true when two naïve faculty members pair off to engage a common task.

Sometimes it is an administrative superordinate such as a department chair who is the logical choice to field questions about policies and procedures within the academic unit. Alternatively, a senior faculty person who has completed many years of service can provide a unique perspective on some problematic issue or difficulty. The important consideration in all cases is for you to extend yourself, to reach out and meet others more than halfway.[39]

Bringing questions on a particular topic to a specific individual, naturally, does not necessarily furnish the basis for a longer-lasting mentoring relationship with a more experienced colleague. On the other hand, some collegial exchanges of lasting duration begin in precisely this way. When you demonstrate your willingness to ask questions, to seek out information, the door is opened, as it were, for a relationship to develop. In many cases, the best mode of entry to informal communication networks that carry vital professional information is afforded by the newcomer's simple act of raising questions and asking for advice.[40]

Implications for Action

Obviously, as a faculty member, you have no control whatever over whether your institution sponsors a formal mentoring program or not. However, there are possible lessons to be learned from the literature on the topic, implications applicable to you as an individual even when there are no support programs in place:

First, at the risk of being unduly repetitive, in the absence of any formal program for new faculty, acknowledge the probability that it is still possible to receive mentoring and that you can benefit from having one or more colleagues who will serve in that role. Then assume responsibility for seizing the initiative in actively seeking them out.

Second, begin immediately. Do not wait to seek counsel until you have more "free time." It will never happen otherwise.

Third, do not hesitate to look for help from someone in a different academic discipline or specialty area. It is less important than it may appear that you share a common field of interest with whoever serves as your informal advisor. The more important consideration is the ability to feel comfortable with that person and the confidence that whatever advice is offered will be judicious and well considered.

Fourth, meet regularly (for lunch or over coffee, and so on) with a senior colleague willing to offer counsel, even though you may feel at that specific time there are no driving questions or compelling problems to discuss. Allow the discussion to flow naturally. It is almost inevitable that you will learn something useful just by listening.

Fifth, cultivate friendships with other new faculty and thus begin the process of building a support network among your colleagues.

Points in Review

- There is nothing wrong or inappropriate about seeking advice and counsel from your faculty colleagues. Reaching out to others can reduce the sense of isolation and estrangement many academic newcomers experience during their first few months on the job.
- Be open to the possibility of being mentored. Look for someone trustworthy to serve, perhaps informally, as a mentor. If a mentor is formally assigned to supply assistance and guidance, help nurture a working relation with that individual so long as the association is mutually agreeable and productive.
- It is incumbent on you as the academic newcomer to take the first step in getting to know your colleagues.
- Never hesitate to ask questions about how the system works (or fails to work).

PART II

FACULTY WORK ACTIVITIES

CHAPTER 3

TEACHING:
LECTURES AND DISCUSSION

Teaching and Traditionalism

The most immediate—if not the paramount—concern facing most new faculty members is doing well at teaching. Newcomers approach the challenge for the first time with a fair amount of anxiety and trepidation. As Wilbert McKeachie of the University of Michigan observes, faculty beginners want to avoid looking foolish or incompetent. They prepare their class notes with great care, but still dread the prospect of possible embarrassment if they cannot answer students' questions.

He goes on to comment, "We want to be liked and respected by our students, yet we know that we have to achieve liking and respect in a new role which carries expectations, such as evaluation, that make our relationship with students edgy and uneasy. We want to get through the first class with éclat, but we don't know how much material we can cover in a class period."[1]

Robert Boice of the State University of New York at Stony Brook claims that 20 years of observation have persuaded him that the felt need among beginning faculty to do well in the classroom is likely to provoke more anxiety and consume more time at the outset than any other single activity they are likely to engage in, including research and writing for publication.[2] Moreover, he alleges, only a relatively small percentage of new faculty members come to their first regular academic appointments with any substantial training or prior experience as teachers. Even among the more experienced, most are unable to recall whatever they might have learned about instruction in the sporadic hit-or-miss training they received as graduate teaching assistants.[3]

The almost inevitable result is that most new teachers tend to teach as they themselves were taught.[4] It is what they know. Because ostensibly it worked for their professors and mentors in the past, they invariably fall back on the same "tried-and-true" techniques to guide their own teaching. Most will be inclined, for example, to equate good *teaching* with good *content*, and will rely heavily on lecturing as their primary teaching strategy. In fact, if they have any plans for improvement, novice teachers will think mainly about further elaborating and reorganizing their lecture notes before even considering alternative teaching strategies.

First-timers teach defensively, playing it safe. Especially dreaded is doing anything to cause student complaints to be heard by senior colleagues. Acquiring a reputation as a bad teacher is a prospect to be avoided at all costs. Whenever problems arise, their inclination is to blame them on incompetent or lazy students. Where weaknesses are detected, they blame invalid instructional rating systems.[5]

Risk avoidance among new faculty members helps account in part for the pedagogical "conservatism" characteristic of academe in general. But even established faculty members, no less than their junior colleagues, often seem reluctant to depart from the methods to which they have grown accustomed over the years. They too are unwilling sometimes to embrace "high-risk" nontraditional teaching strategies. Hence, change comes slowly, grudgingly. At the risk of overgeneralizing, teaching methods in higher education may be said to have not changed overmuch since the midpoint of the nineteenth century when the medieval *lectio*—the familiar classroom lecture—began to supplant student recitation as a predominant instructional strategy in American colleges.

The great irony of much college and university teaching is that whereas professors have themselves excelled as learners when they were students, whatever insights they might have gleaned from their experience, as A. Alan Wright puts it, "are often abandoned as soon as the instructor ascends the classroom podium." Rather than reflecting critically on the conditions conducive to learning and then seeking to organize their own instruction consistent with those conditions, he claims, "many faculty base their approach to teaching upon an uncritical adoption of the model that comes most readily to hand—their old professors."[6] And once a teaching pattern has been set, it tends to persist thereafter.

Today, collegiate instruction as a rule still emphasizes a didactic model. Especially among new faculty and those who have never given their teaching much thought, students are often thought of as "empty vessels" to be filled up with knowledge, as "blank slates" on which the teacher writes, or as passive objects to be molded by a master sculptor.[7] Teaching is viewed, it has been said, as an "information transfer" process whereby learning flows from the professor's mouth, courses like a river until it reaches the ears of the student, and then funnels into an empty cranium.

Not only does the traditional lecture epitomize conventional wisdom about what teaching should be, it remains the most widespread instructional format in use on campuses across the country. Reasons for its popularity are obvious. The lecture allows for a cost-efficient ratio of students to instructors. Fewer teachers can instruct more students. It places the lecturer firmly in control of both instructional content and presentation, thereby minimizing chances of making mistakes. It allows the teacher to "cover" more material than alternative approaches. Finally, many students reportedly *prefer* listening to a good lecture, if only because (apart from taking notes) it demands minimal involvement or participation on their part.

It may be the case that some professors have never seriously considered doing anything else other than "telling" students—lecturing to them. Even so, what is surprising, considering how teaching is a major component of most faculty workloads, is that the broader topic of instructional methodology itself is so rarely discussed among academics. Professors love to discuss endlessly the intellectual substance of what they teach. Yet in their own collegial discussions and conversations, they tend not to talk about teaching at all. Attention to matters of pedagogy simply is not a prominent feature of contemporary academic culture in most colleges and universities. Remarkably enough, the absence of discussion is apparent even within institutions that pride themselves on having a strong teaching mission.

Accounting for this seeming "conspiracy of silence" is not easy. It derives perhaps from a widespread perception that good teaching is simply a matter of trial-and-error experimentation, or an idiosyncratic expression of an individual's own unique personality style. Some faculty members simply assume there is little that can be said about a person's teaching likely to prove helpful to others. Equally widespread is the belief that teaching is an "art" rather than a "science," and therefore not susceptible to the reasoned analysis and dissection other rule-governed activities and behaviors allow. Finally, there is always the dampening influence on discussion reflected in the cynic's judgment, "Everything has been tried—and nothing really works well."

The upshot is that teaching comes to be viewed as a solitary enterprise, something conducted behind closed classroom doors. Visitors, especially faculty colleagues, are not welcome. Hence, in an environment where raising questions with peers or asking them for help with teaching incurs the risk of being thought inadequate, suggestions for improvement are neither sought nor accepted. Needless to add, faculty exploration of alternatives to established practice is limited.

Meanwhile, novices are mostly left to their own resources. The expectation is they should manage their classrooms and laboratories as best they can, on their own. Protestations to the contrary notwithstanding, seeking assistance is subtly discouraged or made to depend on the initiative of the person needing help. As one crusty old faculty curmudgeon once remarked of a new colleague who reputedly was having trouble with her teaching, "If she's too stupid to figure it out on her own or too stubborn to ask for help, she damn well deserves to flounder."

Good Teaching

Is there really any such thing as "good" teaching? Against what specific criteria should instruction be assessed? How does one gauge pedagogical excellence? Are there fundamental principles or specific rules that collectively define "best practice"? Is there any single model of exemplary teaching that everyone should strive to emulate?

Further, are some people natural-born teachers? Or are mediocre pedagogues capable of developing into better instructors through proper training? In other words, can the elements of good teaching be made explicit

---

THE OPEN COLLEGE CLASSROOM . . .

Would you be comfortable with an "open door" policy for your classes? May anyone drop in without permission or without notifying you beforehand?

Do you welcome visits by faculty colleagues? Or does the prospect of informal peer scrutiny threaten or intimidate you? What conditions, if any, do you set on faculty visits?

Have you ever considered asking fellow faculty members to observe your teaching? What about your department chair or some other administrator?

How do others perceive you as a classroom teacher? On what information must they rely?

If a system of peer evaluation of teaching is already in place in your institution, is its purpose primarily formative or summative? Do faulty members scrutinize one another's teaching for purposes of assessment and evaluation (assigning a rating to your teaching) or for the purpose of assisting you in improving your classroom performance? How formal and systematic are faculty reviews of teaching?

and conveyed to others in some useful way? Questions such as these—issues never authoritatively resolved—always plague academic discussions of teaching, if and when they occur at all.

Kenneth Eble, writing in *The Craft of Teaching*, offers a useful insight as a point of departure. "The more I have looked at teachers," he observes, "the more I come back to an old truth of human existence. We are both born and made. At most, some teachers may have certain natural advantages: high intelligence, verbal fluency, patience, a capacity for service, good looks, a pleasant speaking voice, charm, a mind for detail, a good memory, a head for generalizations." Eble adds, "Most of these skills are as likely to be acquired as inborn, and, when examined closely, all lose the aura of mysterious capabilities that some people have and others haven't or that some can develop and others can't."[8]

Concurring, Maryellen Weimer declares: "The assertion that nobody knows what makes teaching good is a myth."[9] The constituent elements of good teaching are known, she argues, and in large measure can be transformed into acquirable skills. Since the early 1930s, she points out, the question about what are the components of effective instruction has been intensively pursued by researchers. At least five or six characteristics have been attributed to good teachers, and, according to Weimer, show up consistently on list after list. They reportedly include personal enthusiasm (which tends to be contagious so far as students are concerned); clarity of discourse and presentation; preparedness and organization; an ability to stimulate and arouse interest from listeners; and knowledge (both competence with respect to the actual content of instruction and an evident love of that subject matter).

Some enumerations of factors allegedly associated with good teachers and effective instruction distinguish among the teacher's intellectual and cognitive characteristics; personal attributes; and instructional behaviors.[10] Examples of the first include thorough, up-to-date knowledge of the subject matter; clearly defined instructional objectives; and a genuine commitment to teaching.

Personal strengths cited almost always include accessibility to students; a sense of humor; open-mindedness; rapport; tolerance and patience in dealing with students; compassion and sensitivity; and a demonstrated capacity for careful listening.

Good instruction, it is often said, is marked by careful organization; provision for constructive feedback; varied teaching methods; fairness; flexibility; encouragement of questions; and, generally, a positive, nonthreatening classroom learning atmosphere.

Current research does seem remarkably consistent in identifying teaching techniques, behaviors, and attitudes that assist college students to learn with the greatest facility and retention. "Best practice" is said to encompass or reflect at least seven basic features:[11]

- a degree of rapport that at once encourages and facilitates student-faculty interaction, both during class and outside of it
- a focus on active learning activities rather than an emphasis on techniques that reinforce student passivity
- provision made for cooperative learning and collaboration among students in the pursuit of clearly defined tasks
- high academic expectations, clearly conveyed and periodically reiterated as necessary
- timely and frequent feedback on student performance
- consistent attention to time on task
- respect shown for students' differences (e.g., the use of teaching methods that take into account learners' strengths and weaknesses, their individual identities, and various ways of learning and knowing).

Despite a consensus about behavior that contributes to good teaching, most recent research falls short of establishing links between specific teacher behaviors and probable learning outcomes. Most studies focus *in vacuo* on what teachers should do.[12] A common assertion, however, is that interactive learning is preferable to wholly passive learning. Content acquisition is obviously important, but so is the promotion of critical, reflective thinking.

Instructional objectives, it is said, should be stated explicitly and shared with students. Learners should be supplied with alternative models, per-

---

EFFECTIVE TEACHERS

More than 10,000 studies have been published on one phase or another of teaching effectiveness, and from them we have gleaned some reasonably consistent findings about the general characteristics of good teaching. Briefly, these findings indicate that effective teachers are masters of their subject, can organize and emphasize, can clarify ideas and point out relationships, can motivate students, and are reasonable, open, concerned and imaginative human beings.

—Peter Seldin, *The Teaching Portfolio, A Practical Guide To Improved Performance and Promotion/Tenure Decisions* (Bolton, Mass.: Anker, 1991), 1.

spectives, or interpretations of material treated whenever possible and appropriate. They should be afforded multiple opportunities to discuss, summarize, or explain the significance of the subject matter content presented.

Finally, a repeated finding from the literature on superior teaching is that "demanding mental effort" should be required of students, even at the possible risk of weakening their short-term approval or how they rate the instruction offered.[13]

Some writers and commentators stress the importance of using a variety of instructional strategies within any given teaching situation, depending on the goal in mind. James R. Davis, for example, emphasizes how lecturing and explaining (presenting information so that it can be readily processed and easily retained) differ fundamentally from training and coaching (breaking instruction into steps and reinforcing learning progress). Inquiry and discovery call for still other instructional approaches (problem solving, group information sharing, demonstrations), as do experience and reflection as teaching goals (giving students opportunities to learn via internships, independent study, journal-writing, travel, and so forth).[14]

Classroom "climate" affords another way of looking at exemplary teaching practices. Louis Raths and his associates, for example, offer an interesting list of what teachers can do to create and sustain a learning environment that encourages higher-order thinking skills: listening carefully to what students have to say, emphasizing processes of inquiry rather than the goal of obtaining predetermined answers, open discussion, utilizing activities that require problem-solving techniques, communicating that it is "safe" to make mistakes, nurturing confidence (offering chances to be successful in trying out ideas), facilitating feedback, using heuristic inquiry, and so forth.[15]

Learner Complaints and Preferences

Students, presumably, are the intended beneficiaries of instruction. Ultimately, then, what learners like and dislike ought to influence how professors teach—where teaching is construed not as "throwing out information, regardless of outcome" but as an act of "helping someone else learn something."[16] In study after study, citations of students' "pet peeves" or complaints are as predictable as they are consistent. They are apt to include most of the following:

• The teacher assigns work as though his or her class is the only course in which students are enrolled, or acts as though he or she assumes it is self-evidently the most important class they are taking.

FURTHER QUESTIONS AND SUGGESTIONS

- Assuming you lecture from a written outline, how worthwhile would it be to supply your students with a copy of the outline in advance, either online or as a class handout, so they could follow along with you and better organize their own note-taking? Alternatively, if you asked your students to outline their notes, how closely would their outlines resemble your own?

- As an experiment, supply someone in your class with a stopwatch. Assign the timekeeper the task of keeping track of the number of minutes in a given class period that you as the instructor are lecturing. Then count the total amount of time taken up by students talking. Relative to your goals and objectives for the class, is there an appropriate balance between teacher talk and student talk?

- What message do you convey to your students if you show signs of fatigue, boredom, indifference, impatience, or a desire to be somewhere else while you are talking? Conversely, if you exhibit enthusiasm, involvement, engagement with the material, is it more likely your students will come to share the same feelings?

- In terms of specific behaviors, what is the difference between talking *to* and talking *at* a classroom of students? (*Hint:* Try talking before a very small audience as though their numbers filled a large lecture hall. Then try talking to a large number of students as though they numbered only three or four people sitting around a table with you.)

- Presumably, knowing the names of your students is important for establishing rapport with them. How long does it take you before you can call on your students individually by their names? How large must a class be before it is unreasonable or unrealistic to expect you can learn everyone's names? Meeting one of your students off campus, could you introduce that person to a third party? What measures suggest themselves as ways of facilitating the process of memorizing students' names as quickly as possible?

- Imagine one of your students has lapsed into some type of trance. How much time in class would elapse before you as the teacher would be bound to notice because of some class procedure or activity demanding student responses or interaction?

- How likely is it in one of your classes that any given individual student might pose a question, respond to an inquiry, offer an explanation, express an opinion, or otherwise engage in some type of brief dialogue with you or with another student?

continues

- You interrupt your lecture to pose a question to your students. Seconds tick by without anyone responding. How many different factors could be at work to help explain the classroom silence?
- Hypothetically, would it be possible for a student in one of your courses to satisfy all of the assignments and be awarded a good grade without ever having been obliged to interact verbally with you as the teacher or with his or her fellow students?
- As the weeks go by, how is a student to judge whether he or she is doing well in your course? Does the student's grade depend mainly— or even exclusively—on his or her performance on a midterm exam and a final?
- How predictable is your classroom behavior as a teacher? Can students forecast accurately how each class session will proceed? Is the routine fixed and unvarying? Or are you able to introduce elements of surprise and unpredictability? Can you be spontaneous? Or do you tend to fall into a rut? How many different teaching approaches do you typically utilize in your classes?
- Trying to connect with your students, you recount a humorous anecdote or tell a joke. The class sits impassively—no reaction. They do not "get" it. What do you do next?

- The teacher shows little flexibility and is unwilling to take special circumstances into account when stipulating deadlines and imposing assignments.
- The teacher assumes at the outset that students already possess all of the background information necessary for succeeding in the course.
- The teacher assumes his or her students are already highly motivated to master the course subject matter.
- The teacher presents material too quickly, refuses to slow down when requested to do so, fails to adapt his or her pacing to the students' rate of note-taking.
- The teacher fails to make use of, or refer to, required textbooks and other assigned materials.
- The teacher's visual aids are dense, crammed with too much text, are unreadable, or are not displayed long enough to be assimilated.
- The teacher professes to welcome questions but allows no time for asking them, or resorts to ridicule if he or she dislikes the questions students ask. The professor judges responses to questions posed in class harshly.

- The instructor demands that students' opinions and interpretations of the subject matter mirror his or her own view and uses the threat of grading to guarantee intellectual compliance.
- The teacher fails to revise or update his or her notes; the class is taught in the same way every term it is offered; the instructor's information is obviously out of date, incorrect, incomplete, or biased to favor one particular interpretation or point of view.
- The teacher comes to class late or fails to show up at all, without advance notice or apology, but also penalizes students for their tardiness or nonattendance.
- The teacher comes to class ill-prepared, is disorganized, strays from the point under discussion, or digresses frequently for no apparent reason. Class presentations are difficult to follow.
- The teacher's presentations are marred by unnecessary profanity, or by sexist or racist remarks.
- The teacher conveys the impression he or she is bored and would prefer to be elsewhere, lacks enthusiasm, fails to impart any sense of excitement or involvement with the material, speaks in a monotone, or fails to articulate clearly.
- The teacher reads to the class at length, without interruption.
- The teacher acts as though he or she is on an "ego trip" and fails to establish rapport or show interest in the students as individuals. He or she is "stand-offish," impersonal and remote, acts in an insulting or condescending manner, fails to show respect, resorts to intimidation, and proudly boasts he or she is "the professor from hell."
- The teacher is unapproachable, tends to be inaccessible, limits communication with students, fails to maintain office hours, and otherwise is unhelpful outside of class.
- The teacher fails to indicate what students will be held accountable for on tests; gives exams that do not correspond with assignments or lectures, offers little or no advance help to students in preparing for tests, poses "trick" questions, uses arbitrary or ambiguous grading procedures, refuses to review tests after they have been given.
- The teacher fails to return tests and papers in timely fashion yet perhaps at the same time is unyielding about accepting students' late submissions. The teacher offers little commentary on papers, if they are returned at all.
- The teacher "plays favorites" and gives certain students preferential treatment.

TEACHING IMPERATIVES

1. Resolve even before the first day of class to be in command of both your subject matter and your presentation of course material. This commitment will require that you search for material and for activities designed to motivate students and arouse their interest.

2. Try to identify what is unique about your course—and what is specifically and identifiably your own. Ask yourself: How can this class be different and unique? What can I alone contribute as the teacher of this course?

3. Reach out to your students. Establish rapport. Make yourself as accessible as possible. Be visible. Be in the classroom before the scheduled starting time for class. Talk to each student. Move around the room continuously. Pay attention to your students! If they are sitting there glassy-eyed, whatever you are doing may not be working effectively. Allow access after class. Show that you are willing to answer questions instead of rushing off once class is over.

4. Come prepared for class. Students usually can tell when you are faking it. You owe your students careful advance preparation for every class session.

5. Foster free and open inquiry. Encourage students to be thoughtful and reflective. Be receptive to divergent responses. Reinforce and model the idea of a safe classroom environment where it is acceptable to disagree and where all points of view will be heard respectfully.

6. Never forget that grades are not only a measure of student learning but also a measure of the instructor's teaching effectiveness. Test for what you teach.

7. Endeavor to provide constructive and prompt feedback on all student activities. Students are entitled to know how you are evaluating their performance.

8. Show respect for your students, just as you want them to respect you as the teacher.

9. Expect to fail sometimes. Keep a sense of perspective and balance: not everything you try out will necessarily work. Adjust accordingly. Try something else. A sense of humor helps.

—adapted in part and modified from
"Seven Ways to Make Your Class Great,"
The Professor in the Classroom 7 (September 1, 2000): 1–3.

Conversely, when students are asked what they most value from their teachers, their answers follow a uniform pattern.[17] Whereas they tend not to endorse any one given teaching style to the exclusion of all others, students report they learn the most from professors who (1) show respect and concern for their students; (2) take the time and effort to establish rapport; (3) employ a variety of creative and imaginative techniques and processes to stimulate learning in the classroom; and (4) provide timely, fair, and useful feedback on student work.

In the final analysis, teaching can be done poorly or it can be done well. Skillful teaching takes hard work, though it probably requires no more time and effort in the long run than does poor or mediocre instruction. So long as one does not attract unwelcome attention or become too conspicuous about it, it is perfectly possible to "get by" with minimal effort in the classroom. Only the most egregiously bad teaching carries with it serious consequences for the offender. But doing a good job in the classroom certainly is more enjoyable and satisfying, more conducive to high morale and professional self-esteem. And since teaching frames an important part of what most academics spend time doing, it is difficult to understand why any faculty member would set his or her sights on anything less than becoming the best teacher possible.

It may be valid to claim that how one teaches is at root a function of one's personal character, personality, and identity more than anything else. But beside native talent, exemplary teaching unquestionably does demand the application of skill as well. And, as it is often said, anyone intelligent enough to earn an advanced graduate degree or two ought to be bright enough to learn whatever it takes to teach competently.

Course Development and Preparation: Preliminaries

Preparing to teach a course for the first time, revising a course, or developing an entirely new one from scratch ought to involve a substantial amount of planning. Obvious first steps include finding out how a course has been taught previously (if it is not an entirely new course), reviewing old syllabi on file, referencing catalogue descriptions, identifying the function or place of the course within some broader curricular context (e.g., determining whether the course is required or an elective), confirming at what level it is to be taught (intended for beginning students, upperclassmen, or graduate students), whether the course carries prerequisites, and what is considered normal content coverage for the course.

Once you have found answers to basic questions, it is advisable to begin looking to the availability of appropriate instructional resources. Which textbooks, reports, or other materials might best serve to help carry the course? (Noting how leading textbooks in the field are organized and how they treat main issues and themes is also helpful for planning a new course.) On what basis are texts to be selected—how have published works been reviewed and evaluated within the larger academic community? Are the titles under consideration currently in stock or out of print? By what date must they be ordered to ensure their timely arrival? Are readings pitched at a level appropriate for their intended audience? What costs to students are considered reasonable and necessary? What other lab or library holdings are available for enriching or extending instruction?

A third planning step involves your becoming familiar with, and taking into account, relevant institutional policies governing course management and delivery (late enrollment deadlines, room assignment, credits, scheduling, auditing without credit, eligibility for enrollment, testing requirements, maximum or minimum class size, and so on). Equally important are informal expectations attached to the course, strictures having to do with its expected level of difficulty, evaluation procedures in common use, how exams are administered, reasonability of workload assignments, and the like.

Fourth, it is highly advisable for you as the instructor to preview the classroom where the course is to be conducted. What is the room's seating capacity? Are tables, desks, and chairs fixed or can they be moved around in various configurations? What is available by way of instructional technology (blackboard, whiteboard, VCR, a computer terminal, projection screen, overhead or slide projector, audio recorder) to help support the teaching of the course? Does the course already have a website that needs to be updated? Has the course ever been taught in a "distance education" format, or is there any pressure to begin doing so? If so, does the course, as planned, lend itself to being conveyed via electronic transmission to remote sites?

All of the foregoing may seem so trite and obvious as to not even be worth mentioning. Yet, as many college students will readily attest, nearly all have undergone experiences where the unmistakable impression fomented was that a given course had been thrown together hastily and in slipshod fashion; where there was little evidence of advance planning and preparation; and scant attention was given apparently to even the most basic logistical considerations.

Course Planning: Goals and Objectives

It is a regrettable fact of academic life that some professors take an extremely cavalier attitude toward writing course objectives. Suggestions that

THE PHYSICAL CLASSROOM

The physical classroom environment can affect student learning. Factors include physical comfort, room lighting, the seating arrangement, air circulation, temperature, aesthetics, and so on.

Consider, for example, how seats placed in fixed rows, all facing front, suggest a teacher-centered pedagogy. Alternatively, chairs or desks placed in a rectangle or circle evokes and facilitates a more collaborative instructional climate, one that is less teacher-dominated and more conducive to interaction among students.

Suggestions to consider: Play music before the start of class. Bring posters, maps, or other visuals to class, if appropriate to the course subject matter. Experiment with varying seating arrangements whenever possible.

the core purposes and expectations of a course should be laid out expressly are apt to be greeted with derision and scorn. Many dismiss the idea of making goals or objectives explicit as too pedantic or "mechanical."

The further suggestion that the teacher has an ethical as well as a practical obligation to specify what it is he or she expects from students enrolled in a course is apt to fare badly at the hands of skeptics. A history teacher, for example, might retort, "I'm teaching a class entitled 'History of Europe from 1848 to 1918.' If students can't figure out from the course title alone what it's about, they're so obtuse I don't even want them to enroll." Alternatively, someone teaching a large introductory course in psychology might assert, "The point of enrolling in my course is to *find out* what the field or discipline is all about. I'll *tell* them what they need to know as we proceed!"

An obvious rejoinder is to point out that every teacher needs a basic plan for what is supposed to be accomplished. The instructor without one, as James Davis phrases it, is "like a traveler without a destination; not only is to hard to get there, it is also difficult to know when you have arrived."[18] Or as Lawrence Peter and Raymond Hull point out, "If you don't know where you're going, you will probably end up somewhere else."[19] And if you *do* know where you are headed—why keep it a secret from your students?

Every professor needs to be able to identify and articulate his or her intentions—for each individual class session and for the class as a whole. When adequately conceptualized, objectives are indispensable for designing, implementing, and evaluating instruction throughout the course. Goals provide a sense of direction for you as teacher as well as a guide for your students—they serve as "navigational beacons" or signposts along the way, not simply as ending points for the journey.[20] Without them, it can be difficult to know when students are straying off track or how to adjust matters in order to bring them back on task.[21] It remains to observe that in most professional schools, external accreditation standards *demand* explicit objectives for all courses.

"Teaching often breaks down at the beginning," Davis observes, "when we have not clarified our primary goals and expressed them. . . . When we lack a clear sense of the desired outcomes of instruction, we often try to do too much and our teaching gives way to random (often frantic) activity. Effective teachers know what they are trying to achieve, and they consciously select and continually refine their objectives."[22]

A quite useful distinction for course planning cited by some writers is that drawn between general instructional goals and specific learning objectives.[23] The former are broadly drawn, global statements of intent or purpose. An instructional goal is a descriptive expression of what the instructor expects to accomplish in treating the course subject matter. An example might be, "This course will analyze efforts to reconcile relativity theory and quantum mechanics in late-twentieth-century physics . . ." or "A major goal of this course will be to examine the social and cultural impact of religious confessionalism on the political economy of seventeenth-century Europe. . . ."

Instructional goal statements, it should be noted, are written from the *teacher's* point of view. Once again, they serve to indicate what topics, issues, facts, or principles will be taught and emphasized. The overweening advantage of spelling them out is that they serve to draw attention to, and help emphasize, the most fundamental and ultimate purposes of a course (understanding, knowing, appreciating something). The problem, however, is that there usually exists no direct, straightforward way of ascertaining whether or not they have been achieved once the course is over.[24]

Learning objectives, on the other hand, are more precise and specific statements of what it is a student *will be able to do*—what performance outcomes will be possible—once learning has taken place. Learning objectives are written from the *learner's* point of view and employ concrete action words such as "identify," "solve," "construct," "compare," "estimate," "measure," "contrast," or "demonstrate."[25]

A statistics class treating elementary probability theory and inference, for instance, might have as a learning performance objective: "Students will be able to construct frequency distributions and histograms . . ." or "The student will be able to compute the mean, median, mode, standard deviation and coefficient of variance for both raw and grouped data. . . ." In a history course, a defensible outcome expectation might read, "Students will be able to identify at least three key figures in the events that led up to the outbreak of the Spanish-American War and explain succinctly their respective roles in those events."

Performance objectives, once again, are intended to indicate ways in which students can demonstrate that the requisite learning actually has occurred. (This general approach to writing objectives is variously referred to as "competency" learning, "mastery" learning, or "performance-based" learning.)

A good rule of thumb in course planning is to identify no more perhaps than eight or nine basic teaching goals for the course as a whole. You can then develop as many individual learning objectives (expected performance outcomes) as seems appropriate for each goal statement specified.[26]

Benjamin Bloom's well-known taxonomy of educational objectives affords a helpful way of thinking about performance outcomes for a course, most particularly because it encourages concrete measures for evaluating what types or levels of learning are supposed to occur.[27] His framework, it will be recalled, posits a hierarchy of six cognitive skill sets, moving from the "lowest" concrete process of recognizing and recalling information, through several intermediate steps, to the "highest," most abstract level of judging and assessing material learned.[28] Several revisions and elaborations have been put forward since Bloom first published his taxonomy, but the basic idea remains the same:

- At the lowest level (knowledge), students are expected to "list" or "name" factual information. Action verbs appropriate for expressing a projected performance outcome typically would include: annotate, compile, define, list, match, name, record, recall, recognize, and so on.
- At the next level (comprehension), learners are expected to be able to describe, summarize, discuss, explain, restate, identify, or otherwise show an ability to grasp the meaning of material and to reframe it.
- The next level (application) requires the application of material learned to new or concrete situations. Appropriate performance verbs might include: solve, apply, compute, calculate, illustrate, or demonstrate.
- The fourth level in the hierarchy is analysis. Performances at this level—breaking information into its component parts so as to understand its organization and structure—involve comparisons, criticism, differentiation, estimation, or discrimination.
- The level of synthesis (integrating the parts of something to form a new whole) invokes performances requiring the learner to arrange,

assemble, enumerate, extrapolate, formulate, generate, design, plan, and so forth.

- Evaluation—the act of judging the value and relevance of data for a given purpose—is expressed in requirements that the learner defend, evaluate, appraise, assess, judge, or revise something.[29]

A major attraction of delineating performance expectations by learning levels is that it serves to flag potential mismatches between desired learning outcomes and the focus of instruction. The professor who expends most of the time presenting factual material in class, for instance, is liable to be disappointed when he or she asks students to demonstrate skills of analysis and synthesis on an examination, yet has neglected to provide a foundation for any such higher-order learning.[30] With only minimal forethought, this mistake is easily avoided.

Attending to performance levels, it is said, greatly facilitates the drafting of good tests. In principle at least, it is a relatively straightforward task to devise questions that assess what it is that students are expected to *do* with the material.

Course Preparation and Design: The Syllabus

The typical professor probably does not spend nearly enough time and care drawing up a syllabus for every course he or she teaches. For novices in particular, *the process of creating a comprehensive course syllabus represents an invaluable opportunity to think through in advance all the details that go into a successful learning experience for students.* Writing a syllabus can and should be an integral aspect of your course planning process—not a hasty afterthought.[31] Students, for their part, benefit from a course guide that is complete and unambiguous, that anticipates most of their questions about the class, and makes clear what will be expected.

Traditionally, the syllabus is a document supplied to every member of the class in hard-copy form on the first day of class. Nowadays, increasingly, professors are discovering the advantages of placing it online as well, along with supplementary reading materials, old tests, announcements, and so forth. Either way, and at the risk of appearing overly prescriptive, a model syllabus should incorporate all of the following:

- Basic course data. Course number and title; number of credit hours awarded; the academic term for which the course is scheduled; class times, days, and location; course website address (if any)

- Instructor information. Instructor's name, title, office location, regular office hours, phone number, e-mail address (important for asynchronous communications), outside-of-class contact procedures; instructor's academic credentials and background experience
- Course description. Catalogue or other official course description; information about what curricular requirements the course satisfies (elective credit, core course requirement, required of academic majors in a given field); prerequisites, enrollment eligibility requirements, if any
- Course objectives. Statement of general instructional goals and specific learning objectives for the course or for individual course topics
- Reciprocal expectations. What you as the instructor expect from students (e.g., regular attendance, classroom attentiveness, compliance with assignment deadlines, and your policy on tardiness or absences from class); what students may expect from you (e.g., preparedness, accessibility, responsiveness to questions); course evaluation criteria; recommendations for achieving success in the course; advance indication of teaching methods to be employed and how class time will be utilized (lectures, discussions, student presentations, etc.)
- Policies and procedures. Requirements governing excused and nonexcused absences, tardiness and class attendance; penalties for plagiarism, cheating, and other forms of academic dishonesty; inclement weather policy and possible class cancellation procedures; policy on delayed grades
- Grading. Explanation of grading criteria and procedures (criteria-referenced or grading "on the curve," performance improvement); types of tests or quizzes (length and types of questions: essay, short-answer, true/false, multiple choice); your relative weighting of homework, projects, special assignments, class participation; extra credit; availability of make-up exams; penalties (if any) for late submission of assignments; detailed instructions governing the submission of papers or other written assignments (including how they will be evaluated)
- Study aids. Hints for studying; sample test questions or study guides for midterm and final exam; questions for discussion; lecture outlines; performance guides; copies of overhead transparencies; comments and suggestions from students previously enrolled in the course
- Texts and supplementary materials. Complete citations for texts, indicating whether required or recommended; availability; cost; optional recommended readings
- Course calendar or schedule. Weekly or class-by-class schedule, specification of dates for tests and exams, submission deadlines for assignments; topics to be treated
- Caveat/disclaimer. Statement clarifying circumstances under which deviations or departures may be made from announced policies, pro-

cedures and assignments specified in the syllabus. (The syllabus has been construed in some cases as akin to a formal contractual agreement between an instructor and his or her students. It is therefore especially important for you to build in "flexibility" as unanticipated circumstances may warrant.)

FROM THE STUDENT'S POINT OF VIEW: QUESTIONS TO WHICH THE COURSE SYLLABUS SHOULD BE RESPONSIVE

- Where and when does this course meet? Are there any planned variations or additions to the regular schedule (extra sessions, field trips, special assignments, etc.)?
- Why is this course important or significant? What is its focus and rationale? For whom is it intended? Are there any prerequisite requirements or other restrictions on who may enroll?
- What supplies and books will I need for this course? What materials are required? Which are merely recommended or optional? Are course materials available online?
- Who is the teacher? What are his or her qualifications and background? Where is his or her office? What are the teacher's office hours? If I need help, can I just drop by or will I need to make an appointment in advance? Can I communicate via e-mail?
- What are the basic goals or objectives of the course? What will we be doing to meet those goals?
- How will the course be conducted? How will class or lab times be used? Is there a definite schedule to be followed?
- What are the course requirements? What will I have to do to get a good grade in the course? What kind of grading will be used? What will grades be based on?
- What is the teacher's attendance policy? What happens if I have to miss a class or a test? Do I need to notify someone in advance? Are make-up tests allowed?
- Will the teacher offer "extra credit" assignments?
- If the weather looks threatening, how do we find out whether or not class will be held?
- Does class participation count? Will I have to talk in class?
- Does the teacher have any specific suggestions based on past experience about how to do well and how I can get the most out of this course?

The Lecture as an Instructional Strategy

The instructional method most commonly used in college classrooms (as has been noted) is lecturing. The lecture format remains popular, first and foremost, because it is the least costly way of teaching large groups of students. Nevertheless, as William Ekeler of the University of Nebraska notes, it is the lecture that is most frequently criticized: "More abuse is heaped on it than on all the other teaching methods combined"—chiefly, because it forces students to assume the role of "receptacles" of knowledge rather than interactive participants in the learning process.[32]

This particular complaint assumes that students cannot learn while sitting passively in a large, anonymous lecture hall. But that claim may be overstated. Learning obviously can and does take place when people are listening to a sermon delivered from a church pulpit, for instance, or are absorbed in an interesting television documentary or a talk show. The college lecturer, Ekeler argues, is not wholly unlike the cleric or the televised commentator. "And yet," he points out, "we know that many . . . are singularly effective for their abilities to convey knowledge without great participation on the part of their audiences."[33]

Several considerations contribute to the durability of the lecture format. A good lecture has a certain dramaturgical quality about it: it can be used to pique student interest and motivate listeners to learn. Like live theater, an expressive lecturer conveys enthusiasm, excitement, and a sense of immediacy in ways unrivaled by any other medium of communication.[34] The lecturer's role thus often combines the talents of the scholar, writer, producer, showman, comedian, and dramatist—all intended to provoke student involvement with the material at hand. Listeners who are stimulated and enthused, after all, are those most likely to learn.[35]

Second, lectures facilitate the presentation of large amounts of information, making possible extensive "coverage" of a body of material. The lecture likewise is an efficient option when the task is to convey information not otherwise available, or when the material needs to be organized or integrated to fit the needs and interests of a particular audience.[36] This ability to use a lecture to bring together sources of information otherwise inaccessible to students (out-of-print books, source materials still in press, unpublished reports, and so on) supplies a partial rejoinder to the sarcastic query sometimes posed, "Given the recent invention of the printing press, why do college professors continue to lecture so much?"[37]

Third, the lecture allows the instructor to focus attention on what is deemed most important. Or it can offer a unique perspective on the subject being examined, or to demonstrate in some special way how something works. Whether introducing complex terminology, tracing a chronological sequence of events, adapting and translating information, telling stories, or simply summarizing and pulling together disparate ideas, the lecture allows the speaker to make the material his or her own, so to speak, impressing upon it the stamp of that teacher's own unique scholarship.[38]

Looked upon in this way, lecturing can be a means to many ends, some of them entirely defensible and appropriate, many of them well suited to the style of communication a lecture encourages. In sum, lecturing is neither intrinsically "good" or "bad." Its success depends mainly on how well it is done.[39]

The many virtues of the format notwithstanding, the traditional style of lecturing does carry with it some significant limitations as well. Not the least of them involves the hard truth that inspiring lecturers are difficult to find, no matter how many professors harbor the conceit they themselves are outstanding classroom performers. Rare is the hapless student, obliged to endure some instructor's incessant droning at great length, who has not imagined a special place reserved in Dante's inferno where professors are condemned to listen to their own lectures for all eternity.

Complaints about dry, boring lectures have an extensive lineage. "Our teachers never stop bawling into our ears," Michel de Montaigne once complained, "as though they were pouring water into a funnel, and our task is only to repeat what has been told to us. I should like the teacher to correct this practice. . . ." He fumed, "Like birds which go forth from time to time to seek for grain and bring it back to their young in their beaks without tasting it, our pedants go gathering knowledge from books and never take it further than their lips before disgorging it. And what is worse, their [students] are no better nourished by it than they are themselves."[40]

A more fundamental objection is that students do not actually absorb nearly as much information from a lecture as is commonly supposed. Study after study has revealed much the same attention pattern.[41] A lecture typically begins with a five- or ten-minute settling-in period during which students are reasonably attentive. Students retain about 70 percent of the information imparted up to that point. But then as the lecture proceeds, they become increasingly bored, restless, and distracted. They start to lose focus, "popping" in and out at shorter and shorter intervals. Note-taking falls off significantly. Thereafter, very little knowledge is retained until the last ten minutes when, anticipating the end of class, students revive themselves enough to refocus briefly. But they still retain only about one-fifth of the material presented during the lecture's concluding moments.

Other drawbacks come readily to mind. The classroom monologue as usually conducted obviously does encourage learner passivity. It proceeds with the expectation that all students can learn at the same pace and achieve much the same level of understanding—an assumption manifestly untrue.[42] The format cannot be easily adapted to accommodate differences in intellectual ability, listening and organizational skills, or interest levels. Nor does lecturing provide immediate feedback or reinforcement for learning.

Although some research appears to indicate that the lecture is as effective as other methods in conveying purely factual (as distinct from conceptual) knowledge, it is less well suited to presenting complex, detailed, or abstract information. The traditional lecture format similarly fares poorly in comparison with other teaching methods in encouraging critical reflection and higher-order problem solving. When it comes to facilitating the application, transfer, synthesis, or integration of information, the lecture is decidedly inferior. Post-course retention of knowledge also is relatively low.

Finally, success in lecturing, as previously noted, seems to depend heavily on charisma, on the presence of a teacher who exhibits a dynamic, expressive persona coupled with a keen sense for rhythm, pacing, and articulation.[43] As one commentator phrases it succinctly, "A very expressive, enthusiastic instructor can ignite students' interest in the material, while a reserved, reticent one can douse it"[44] The work of preparing and delivering a first-rate lecture, unfortunately, demands a level of talent, energy and skill uncommon within the ranks of most faculties.

COMMON STUDENT COMPLAINTS ABOUT LECTURERS

"Our teacher starts talking all of a sudden, and doesn't help us remember where we were at the end of the last class session. Also, he doesn't explain the reasons behind whatever he's talking about."

"The teacher avoids eye contact—he might as well be alone in the room. He looks *over* or around us, not *at* us."

"The teacher writes on the board while she's talking and we miss what she's saying. Her nose faces the board, not the class. Then she erases what she's written and replaces it with something else before we've had a chance to write anything down in our notes. Or she stands in the way of what's she's written so we can't see it."

"The teacher works a problem on the overhead but then omits some of the steps needed for a solution."

continues

"The teacher drones on in a monotone. He sounds artificial. He never changes his style of speaking. It can drive you crazy. Is this a real human being up there?"

"Our teacher seems unprepared. Her train of thought wanders all over the place. It sounds disjointed, sometimes improvised. You can't figure out what's important and what's not."

"You can tell the teacher doesn't like to be interrupted. He hates it when we ask questions or offer comments. In fact, he mostly discourages people in the class from saying anything."

"Our teacher talks too fast. Or, just as bad, sometimes he'll read from written material for a long stretch of time. Borrrr-ing!"

"Our teacher mumbles, then, all of a sudden, he's practically shouting. We have to wonder, what's that all about?"

"The professor strays from his own material and gets off the subject. We get tired of irrelevant stories and examples. He talks about himself or his family as 'filler' material to use up the time, I think. A lot of what he lectures about doesn't seem to pertain to the main topic. Some of his comments seem pointless or completely irrelevant."

"If possible, the professor acts like he's even more bored by himself than we are!"

"We can tell the professor is new at teaching. He isn't very self-confident. He practically hides behind the lectern, hands clutching each side of the stand, and he never ventures out from behind it. What does he think we're going to do—assault him?"

"The teacher is rigid. You can tell he has a written outline and he never wants to deviate from it, not for any reason."

"Our teacher is always running out of time. He starts talking faster at the end of the hour and tries to hold us over. Some of us have to get to our next class right away. Then he gets irritated with *us* for having to leave!"

"Our teacher thinks he's doing a great job just because he has computer-based visuals for us. It's still boring."

Modifying the Lecture

Despite its liabilities, so long as economic considerations dictate large classes, dependence on the lecture seems destined to continue for the foreseeable future. The short-range challenge therefore is twofold. The first aspect is to help established and junior faculty members alike to lecture more skillfully. The second task is to encourage modifications to the basic format in ways that enhance its pedagogical efficacy. Neither task is insuperably difficult.

Entire books have been written on lecturing techniques. Basically, the "how-to" advice they offer is reducible to a handful of principles and suggestions likely to be included in any freshman-level course on public speaking. Inexplicably, these caveats are often ignored by those who ought to know better. For present purposes, a simple enumeration of (admittedly formulaic) suggestions will suffice:

- Plan or adapt the lecture to fit its audience. Be clear about the purposes for which the presentation is intended. Prepare an outline, consisting of an introduction, main body, and a conclusion. Supply your students with the outline or summary of the lecture so they can follow along as it proceeds.
- Decide on what points to emphasize, and in what order. Select multiple examples or illustrations for each idea. Organize the lecture in accordance with the old adage, "Tell 'em what you're going to tell 'em; then tell 'em; and afterward tell 'em what you told 'em."
- Bring only skeletal outline notes to class and do not allow yourself to be excessively dependent on them. Do not read at length from written or printed material. Speak extemporaneously.
- Avoid a stationary position. Stand; do not sit. Move about the room. Fill the physical space with motion and activity.
- Make eye contact with each and every student at some point throughout the class period.
- Converse *with* audience members; do not talk *at* them. Speak clearly and distinctly. Vary the pace and rhythm of your delivery. Speak slowly when necessary. Change voice pitch and volume. Remain attentive to voice modulation. Repeat important points and be clear about managing transitions from one topic or point to the next.
- Begin with an "attention-grabber"—a question, controversy, problem, joke, dramatization, story, or anecdote that serves to focus student attention. Hold another one in reserve in case the first one falls flat!
- Be enthusiastic and expressive.
- Use humor or drama when appropriate.
- Utilize well-designed visuals to enhance, extend, explain, or illustrate the material being presented. Text projected electronically or with an overhead projector should be oversized so that it can be read by students from the farthest point at the back of the room. Use color. Tables, charts, graphs, and diagrams should be prepared in advance and projected for the class as a whole.
- Avoid irritating and distracting mannerisms. *(The most effective if painful method of identifying mannerisms is to allow yourself to be videotaped lecturing and then to review the tape thoroughly!)*

- Solicit and be receptive to questions. Pose questions to students. Allow sufficient "wait time" (between 5 and 10 seconds *minimum* for responses).
- Use narrative pauses for dramatic effect, or to underscore a point, to effect a transition, or to encourage questions.
- Attend carefully to students' nonverbal cues (body language, facial expressions, postures) for feedback, and then adjust the presentation accordingly. (If your listeners are slumped over and appear to be sleeping or are occupied reading newspapers, you are probably in trouble, whether you are aware of it or not.)
- Conclude the lecture on time. Do not extend remarks past the assigned closing time. Your students are not listening by then anyway.

The basic idea underlying efforts to improve upon the traditional lecture format is to punctuate a lengthy presentation with other kinds of learning activities. One study reportedly found that if an hour's lecture was suspended briefly (for about two minutes) at least three times, at intervals ranging from 13 to 28 minutes, and students were instructed to compare notes during the intervals, their learning increased in a statistically significant way.[45] Variations on the theme include arranging two intervals for students to share lecture notes, to complete a very brief writing assignment based on what they have just heard, to break out in pairs or triads to discuss questions supplied by the lecturer, or to respond to a short quiz over the material.[46]

On the assumption that the typical student's attention span is relatively short, some lecturers recommend presenting two mini-lectures of twenty minutes each, separated by a demonstration or illustration, a small-group review session, or some similar type of assignment. Time left for review and a short examination at the end of a lecture also are said to enhance students' retention of the material.

Another strategy is to ask students to listen to a twenty-minute lecture without taking notes, then allowing them five minutes to record what they have remembered. Next, students form small groupings and reconstruct the lecture based on their collective recollection of the main points addressed. Still another alternative is to offer a series or succession of six short mini-lectures, each based on students' questions drawn from a previous reading assignment or the preceding mini-lecture.

In all cases, whatever serves to break up the usual attention cycle and keep students more actively involved collaboratively, or so it is claimed by advocates, is preferable to the passivity fostered by a teacher's monologue. The point to be emphasized is that it is not overwhelmingly difficult— even in a large auditorium with fixed seats—to create opportunities for active student involvement within a lecture setting.[47]

BREAKING UP THE
LECTURE LEARNING CURVE

Activities you can insert into your lecture:

1. Allow two to three minutes for students to review their notes and to fill in gaps or omissions in their respective transcriptions;
2. Have your students exchange notebooks with their neighbors and allow them time to review one another's notes for completeness and accuracy;
3. Instruct students to write out at least one question from the material most recently presented. Allow a brief period of time for students to solicit answers to their questions from peers seated nearby. Or allow yourself time as the teacher to respond to some of the questions;
4. Administer a short oral quiz, consisting of five questions over the material, and then supply the answers. Ask for a show of hands in order to determine which questions were missed by the most people;
5. Call on a student to summarize the most important points covered so far in your lecture. Ask other students to add to or modify the list;
6. Throw out a sample problem, illustrative application, question, or issue for discussion, limiting the time to no more than four or five minutes.

Discussion and Questioning

If one accepts the view that teaching is not exclusively a matter of dispensing information, it follows that students do need opportunities to sort through and make sense of what they are learning.[48] When pressed, most professors will concede they want their students to be able to do more than merely absorb, recognize, and recall the information presented. The goal is more far-reaching: to help students understand, integrate, apply, extend, and critique what they learn—in other words, to convert mere "data" into genuine "knowledge" and so make it meaningful. It seems reasonable, therefore, that students should have opportunities to practice higher-order thinking skills.[49] Students need to discuss the subject matter.

"The fundamental value of discussions," Peter J. Frederick asserts, "is that through them students develop a sense of ownership and responsibility for their own learning. Nearly every study of higher education in recent years has stressed the importance of participatory student involvement in enhancing cognitive and affective development." Frederick adds,

"Learning is facilitated by teaching strategies that involve active learning, an open and cooperative climate where diverse views may be safely expressed, and immediate and frequent feedback."[50]

Class discussion should promote critical thinking and problem solving. Properly conducted, it implies a directed exchange of multiple points of view and a collective exploration of ideas.[51] A good discussion, for example, should never be allowed to turn into a glorified bull session without structure or clarity of purpose. It is important to bear in mind too that meaningful discussion is impossible if students, lacking pertinent information, do little more than pool their collective ignorance, or are allowed to drift without direction.[52]

At the opposite extreme, an authentic class discussion should never turn into an extended "guessing game," an exercise whose evident but unacknowledged object is to discover what the instructor has withheld all along—namely, the "correct" answer. Setting students to the task of figuring out what you want by way of an answer is mostly a waste of time.

Unfortunately, framing good questions to guide discussion requires a good deal of skill on the instructor's part; and the techniques involved are acquired more effectively through habituation and practice than through didactics. Some teachers appear to have a natural knack for posing discussion questions. For others, the act seems painfully stilted and artificial.

As experienced classroom veterans will attest, sometimes a class fails to respond despite the teacher's best efforts to mount discussion. But just as often student passivity results from the professor's own maladroitness. The teacher extends a perfunctory invitation, "Are there any questions?" A pause ensues. The silence grows deafening. Students offer nothing but blank, impassive stares; or they fumble through their notes, carefully avoiding eye contact. Hearing no questions after just a few seconds have elapsed, the instructor resumes talking.

The second-best way to thwart discussion is to treat some student's question as an unwelcome interruption, as a hiatus in the flow of one's narrative. The message conveyed is unmistakable: answering questions is something to be treated as quickly as possible so the class can get on with the "real" business at hand. Close behind is feigned incredulity or exasperation, when a student's query or answer is met with a raised eyebrow or curled lip, confirming that what was said was unworthy of attention or serious consideration in the first place.

All this having been said, it must be conceded that questioning and discussing are difficult to manage under the best of circumstances, and almost—but not completely—impossible in a large lecture hall. In medium-sized and smaller classes, of course, it is much easier. Commonplace rules of thumb include the following:

- Ask only one question at a time. Wait for a response. If no answer is forthcoming or if the question is not understood, probe further. Rephrase, repeat, or elaborate briefly on a question, but do not offer an answer prematurely. Allow students time to consider each question carefully.
- Reinforce correct or perceptive responses with praise. Acknowledge, but do not be overly judgmental about, inadequate or incorrect responses, to the point of unintentionally discouraging interaction. Build on irrelevant comments instead of ignoring them, linking them where possible back to the main focus of attention. Connect responses when it serves to move the discussion forward.
- Keep the discussion focused, interrupting when it has moved off center.
- Encourage multiple answers to a question. Attempt to encourage broad participation. Do not allow a small number of students to dominate the conversation.
- Periodically summarize or reframe what has been said and only then redirect the class to the next topic.
- Attend closely to what is said. Listen carefully. Do not dominate discussion. Allow students to challenge or disagree with one another, but keep the talk on track.
- Protect the classes' comfort level. Be accepting and nonjudgmental when appropriate. Conversely, do not hesitate to challenge students to revise, reexamine, defend, or explain responses as necessary. But be respectful. Supply answers only to questions students have posed. Do not provide more information than has been asked for, and allow follow-up queries.
- Reinforce the dictum, "The only 'dumb' question is the question not asked."

Different types of questions serve varying purposes.[53] So-called convergent questions encourage students to relate, compare, or combine information. "Divergent" questions foster creative applications of information to new situations. "Open-ended" questions have indeterminate answers; while "closed" questions require determinate responses. "Evaluative" queries call for assessment and judgment. The logical "shape" of each type of question, in other words, calls for a particular kind of response and lends itself to furthering a particular instructional goal.

"Critical" questions ("Why X?"), for example, differ from those asking for clarification ("What do you mean by X?"). A question may ask for evidence or logical justification: "On what grounds do you base X?" Some

CLASS DISCUSSION

Advantages and Disadvantages:

Class discussion is an excellent way to "track" and informally monitor student learning. It is well adapted for fostering high-level learning, including analysis, synthesis, or integration, and application of cognitive material. Not all students are comfortable participating in class discussion. Some find it extremely threatening. Discussion can be extremely time-consuming as well. It tends to limit your ability to treat ("cover") large amounts of material within a finite time frame.

Good classroom discussions usually require careful advance planning. A major drawback is the decreased control you are afforded when most of the time is given over to students discussing a topic, issue, or problem.

Some guidelines:

1. Define the initial focus of discussion and later on intervene only as necessary to keep the class "on track" if participants stray from the main topic specified.
2. Control excessive talkers who tend to dominate the discussion. Conversely, solicit comments from nontalkers. Ensure broad participation by all class members. Reinforce individual contributions to the discussion.
3. Do not force or attempt to control the conversational flow. Allow for pauses and "thinking time." Intervene only as necessary and keep your questions open-ended. Build on responses by asking students to explain, expand on, or defend their views. Do not accept one-word responses. Require students to speak in complete sentences; do not accept fragments of speech. Ask for examples, illustrations, and specific instances.
4. Test for consensus whenever possible or help clarify major lines of disagreement.
5. Help discussants move toward closure by providing reiterations, summaries, clarifications, implications, and conclusions.

inquiries are linking or connective ("If X and Y, then Z?"), while others pose hypotheticals ("If X were Y, then Z?"). Some are used to draw out causal relations: "When X and Y, then Z?" Still others are intended to initiate or bring focus to a discussion ("What do you think about X?" or "So is the problem really about X?"). Others serve chiefly to summarize or conclude an exchange ("Having considered X and Y, what can be said about Z?"). Teachers successful in managing class discussion tend to be effusive in their praise for instructional approaches that emphasize questioning and an exchange of points of view. Classroom discussion, declare Stephen Brookfield and Stephen Preskill, is indispensable for helping students explore a diversity of perspectives. It increases students' awareness of and tolerance for ambiguity or complexity. Discussion is invaluable for helping students recognize and acknowledge their own assumptions. Learners also develop a new appreciation for differences, even as they expand their capacity for learning through collaboration and cooperative sharing.[54]

Discussion, they allege, is unsurpassed for developing the skills of synthesis and integration. Finally, above all else, discussion moves the center of attention and power away from the teacher and "displaces it in continuously shifting ways among group members. It parallels how we think a democratic system should work in the wider society. In this sense, discussions always have a democratic dimension."[55]

Points in Review

- New faculty members fresh out of graduate school tend to teach as they were taught.
- Antiquated, counterproductive views of the teaching process still prevail in academe.
- Academics do not pay nearly enough attention to matters of pedagogy as these deserve.
- Teaching is not always "telling."
- Mediocre teachers can improve.
- Characteristics of "good" teaching can be identified and defined.
- Good instruction entails student-teacher interaction, preparedness, rapport, variety, enthusiasm, organization, provision for feedback, high standards, and accommodation to learner differences.
- When planning a course, include and make explicit both general instructional goals and specific learning objectives.
- The course syllabus should be comprehensive and detailed; it should be designed to anticipate and respond to students' questions about the course. It is worth taking the time to construct it with great care.
- The classroom lecture, if done well, is a legitimate and useful instructional strategy.

- The lecture format has significant limitations. Punctuating the lecture with other activities brings better results.
- Passive learning should be minimized in favor of "active" learning.
- The class discussion is potentially a powerful tool for learning.
- Classroom discussions require thoughtful preparation and supervision.

CHAPTER 4

ACTIVE LEARNING AND OTHER INSTRUCTIONAL MANAGEMENT ISSUES

Non-Passive Learning

"Learning is not a spectator sport," declare Arthur Chickering and Zelda Gamson, coauthors of a 1991 work entitled *Applying the Seven Principles for Good Practice in Undergraduate Education.* "Students do not learn much just by sitting in classes listening to teachers, memorizing pre-packaged assignments, and spitting out answers," they argue. Rather, "they must talk about what they are learning, write about it, relate it to past experiences, apply it to their daily lives. They must make what they learn part of themselves."[1]

Group discussion is obviously one expression of so-called active learning—understood as the product of a still broader array of techniques aimed at getting students to talk as well as listen, to read and write, and to think critically and reflectively over a body of subject-matter content.[2] Active learning, so construed, is what happens when students engage in analysis, problem solving, synthesis, criticism, application, and evaluation of material.[3] Students simultaneously do things and think carefully about what they are doing.[4]

"Twenty five years ago when I first got into college teaching," a senior professor recalls, " . . . college professors lectured from bell to bell. That was what college teaching was all about and a good teacher was one who lectured eloquently. . . . Now we know more about how students learn and research tell us that students learn better not when they are passive recipients of information but when they are actively engaged."[5] The focus, according to the newer perspective, has changed from teaching to learning.

Correspondingly, your role as teacher must shift from that of the "talking head" or archetypal "sage on the stage" casting out pearls of wisdom, to that of facilitator, a "guide on the side." Only when you are willing to step out of the spotlight as necessary and allow students to assume more responsibility for what happens can active learning take place.[6] It should be added, simply having students make lengthy presentations of their own to the class only substitutes the source of a monologue, from you to your students. Otherwise, little has changed.

Active learning, as its proponents stress, is something that occurs most effectively in some type of group setting. It requires collaborative effort among students, shared discussion, direct participation, and hands-on experience.[7] Teaching and learning, according to this model, are interconnected, intrinsically social activities—which is to say, something jointly constructed by the teacher and students.[8] Throughout, the focus of active learning strategies must necessarily be less on the transmission of a fixed body of content material and more on the processing and assimilation of information.

Advocates of active learning are fond of pointing out that a teacher's rate of speaking always exceeds the rate at which students can listen and learn. Nor is listening always the best way of learning. One is reminded of the old Confucian dictum, "What I hear, I forget; What I see, I remember; What I do, I understand."[9]

Most people, notes Linda Nilson of Vanderbilt University, neither absorb nor retain material very effectively by reading it or hearing it alone. More enjoyable and memorable by far are settings that permit learning by doing, by acting out, by experiencing firsthand, or by "thinking through to realization."[10] To suppose otherwise is to fall prey to the mistaken notion that "telling is teaching and hearing is learning"—or, as a naive teacher might put it, "If I said it, they learned it, and if I didn't say it, they didn't get it."[11]

Whether called "cooperative," "collaborative," "student-centered," "participatory," "action-oriented" or simply "active" learning, using classroom activities and exercises aimed at enhancing or extending student involvement in learning is limited only by the ingenuity and creative imagination of teachers willing to embrace their use.[12] The range and sheer variety of approaches reported in the literature on instructional innovation are enormous.

Possibilities described by various writers include many different types of student presentations, panel discussions, symposia, group exercises, debates, dramatizations and psychodramas, role-playing exercises, simulations, case-method studies, guided journal-writing, independent study projects, game-playing, "icebreakers" for starting a class (posing a problem, think-pair-sharing, three-step interviews, and so on), open-ended and closed small-group discussions, competitions, "fish-bowl" discussions, conceptual puzzle solving, roundtables, mini-lectures, brainstorming, partnering, computer software development projects, polls and surveys, field trips, multimedia presentations, service projects, video productions, peer teaching, interviews, and much else besides. The list is almost endless.

What ties these approaches together and what they share in common is an underlying conviction frequently expressed that "learning" should be thought of as a verb rather than as a noun. Learning, properly considered, is an action process, with students doing and thinking.[13]

Novice teachers interested in exploring possibilities offered by learning activities presumably would be well advised to begin one step at a time, experimenting at first with a very few basic techniques before moving on to more ambitious innovations. A good point of departure, for example, might be simply that of attending to the physical setting where instruction occurs. As James Davis notes, "Classrooms consist of physical space, more or less adequate to teaching, which is probably more amenable to re-arrangement than we realize, if we are willing to overcome the inertia to change it. Classrooms also include arrangements of space for communication; they are micro-social settings where teachers and students take on and play out various roles."[14]

The simple act of moving seats around in a circle or square, for example, so they no longer all face a podium or lectern at the front of the room, serves as a signal that the focus of instruction in the class will not be on a lecturer dispensing information. Rather, it will be on face-to-face interaction and student discussion.

Second, a point stressed previously, you need to establish rapport with your students from the outset. The point cannot be overemphasized: *The level of comfort students feel in the class will depend directly on the trust and confidence they have in you as the teacher and how comfortable they feel with their classmates.* The better the working relationship between teacher and students, the more flexibility and cooperation the instructor will enjoy in experimenting with student-based learning activities. The more at ease students feel with one another, the more willing and able they will be to work with one another.

It makes sense, therefore, to reserve time on the first class day for teacher and students to familiarize themselves with one another, to build group cohesion, and otherwise start the process of creating a functional learning community. At an absolute minimum—except perhaps in the very largest classes—arrangements should be made for everyone to begin learning one another's names (using tent cards, name tags, or instant photographs, and so on). If there are fewer than, say, 20 or 30 students in a class, there is no excuse whatever for your failure to memorize everyone's names and to address them accordingly.

Time spent on these preliminaries is *not* wasted time! The first day of class helps establish a "climate" for the entire course and, to a significant degree, shapes students' attitudes and predispositions toward the course throughout its duration.

Third, it is highly advisable for you to expend as much time as necessary on the first class day previewing the course, explaining its goals and objectives, setting forth your expectations, responding to questions, and, above all, illustrating or modeling how class time will be utilized. To take an obvious example, if discussion is to play an important role in the course, it makes no sense for you to monopolize the entire period. Discussion should be initiated and pursued as much as possible right from the beginning. Again, if students will be working in groups part of the time, they should be grouped and assigned a task before the conclusion of the first day's class.

Finally, teachers resolved to minimize or reduce time devoted to traditional lecturing must acknowledge the likely trade-off between scope and depth of content. Active learning strategies of any sort whatsoever inevitably consume time. Course content coverage is necessarily circumscribed as a result. The strategic question is how to balance the breadth of material that can be treated against the prospect of students learning less, albeit perhaps in a more thorough or meaningful way. Much depends on the nature of the subject matter. As Meyers and Jones point out:

> Although it is not a hard-and-fast rule, we think that someone teaching a course in a technical subject, such as human physiology or inorganic chemistry, has less room to maneuver with active-learning strategies than someone teaching a course in humanities, such as American literature or ethics. In technical-scientific areas, students must gain mastery over specific data and techniques . . . [and] time for extensive active learning in the classroom, then, is necessarily limited.

However, they add, in most cases, if the teacher is willing to undertake a judicious review of whatever concepts and facts are deemed truly essential, it is usually possible to allow time for students to "work with" the information presented.[15]

Group Activities

- Divide the class into groups of no more than five or six members each. Supply each group with two or three specific questions over previously

ACTIVE LEARNING: HIGH RISK–LOW RISK

Several factors account for the seeming reluctance of many faculty members to embrace active learning strategies in their classrooms. One is the assumption that if students are talking and enjoying themselves while engaged in some activity, "serious" learning is not taking place—that is, they are not bent over their desks taking down lecture notes.

Some faculty have trouble accepting the inevitable trade-off involved when time is given over to conversation and interaction among students at the expense of linear, didactic teacher talk.

Possibly the biggest concern of all is fear of loss of control. When a teacher lectures, he or she is in control of the content of instruction, the mode of its presentation, and its pacing. When the shift is toward group work, collaborative learning, problem solving, or student-led presentations, the locus of control shifts to the learners themselves. The "rhythm" of instruction no longer belongs to—and is not dictated by—the professor's own behavior. It becomes less predictable. The information flow tends to become a function of whatever it is students have been set to doing:

"low risk"	*"higher risk"*
the teacher talks, students listen the teacher reserves a limited time for discussion and questions	students talk, the teacher listens; the entire class period is reserved for student's questions and discussion
class time is divided between the teacher's mini-lecture and structured student presentations	structured student presentations occupy the entire class period
the teacher sets up and referees a class debate	a spontaneous argument among students takes up most of the class period
the teacher leads a discussion over assigned material	students conduct a "fish bowl" discussion
the class is divided into groups and the teacher assigns discussion topics to each group	student teams design and implement activities in which the entire class engages

assigned readings or material covered beforehand in class. Each group is assigned responsibility for preparing responses to its particular questions and then sharing those answers with the other groups.

- The class is divided into groups of no more than four members each. You announce you will make a 20-minute presentation on a given topic. One group is assigned to make an outline of the presentation as its members heard it. A second group is assigned to list all of the important or significant points in the presentation. A third group has responsibility for preparing questions about the material presented. Each group is given five minutes to prepare its assignment and five minutes to report back to the class as a whole.

- The class is divided into groups for a role-playing exercise based on material previously provided. For a press conference, one group's members serve as panelists, another group's members as radio or television reporters, still another group's members as print correspondents, and so on. Some topics lend themselves to a trial or other type of judicial proceeding, with persons designated as prosecuting attorney, defense counsel, defendant, judge, witnesses, and so on.

- Six students are designated (or volunteer themselves) to give an impromptu speech, each lasting no more than two or three minutes. Each speech is devoted to an explanation of a technical term, a prominent theme, or an issue abstracted from a previous lecture, a handout or previously assigned reading. During a three-minute preparation period, each speaker solicits suggestions from a panel of peer advisors. Discussion and questioning follows each student's speech.

- Ask students to take out a blank sheet of paper. Pose a question over the material being treated and allow them no more than two minutes to respond. Either collect the papers for later review or have individuals read from their responses during class time and have others critique their answers. (This simple technique helps to furnish a check on students' progress, both in terms of comprehension of class material and their ability to respond to it.)

- Require students to come to class with at least three *written* questions or comments about previously assigned reading. Devote the first ten minutes of the class to discussing these inquiries and reactions.

- Play "The ball's-in-your-court." Bring a rubber ball (or a beanbag or soft stuffed animal) to class. Pitch the ball to (at) a student. He or she has one minute or less to pose a relevant question. The student then throws the ball to a classmate for an answer. The person who asked the question indicates whether or not the answer is satisfactory. If it

THAT FIRST DAY OF CLASS:
FIVE UNSPOKEN QUESTIONS

The first day of class represents an opportunity to get your course off to a good start. Don't merely write your name on the board, hand out the syllabus, announce the first assignment, and then dismiss everyone early. The opening session sets the tone for the entire course. It should be a time to anticipate students' unspoken questions and to address them directly:

1. *Who's the teacher in this course and is he or she any good?* Introduce yourself and indicate how you prefer to be addressed. Disclose *briefly* some basic information about yourself: your credentials and degrees, where you were educated, what you have done, your professional background. Mention areas of interest. Add something about your avocational pursuits. Share something about yourself as an individual human being.

2. *Who else is taking this course with me?* Take the time to have students introduce themselves to one another and, time permitting, to the class as a whole. (No one should leave the classroom at the end of the hour without having learned the names of at least three or four other students.)

3. *What's this course about?* Assuming you've prepared a comprehensive course syllabus, review it in as much detail as necessary with the class, explaining or emphasizing all salient points. This is the time to display enthusiasm: Show your students you are interested in the course. Indicate you hope they will come to share your excitement and involvement with the course subject matter too. (If you are not interested in your own course, do not expect your students to become involved either.)

4. *Will I enjoy this class?* Discuss your objectives and goals for the course. Be specific about how you hope to meet them. Explain what you will require of your students. Indicate when, where, and how students can get help when they need it.

5. *How do I get a good grade in this course?* Explain in detail what evaluation procedures will be used. Explain the basis for your grading. Offer concrete, specific suggestions on studying, preparing for class, and reviewing the material. Include test-taking tips.

is, the person who caught the ball and answered the question may throw the ball to someone else. Once again, the catcher must pose a question and, by throwing the ball, select someone to respond to it.

- In the midst of discussion, call on student B to summarize the salient points in student A's response to a question. (Having a student summarize some one else's contribution to a discussion encourages careful listening by everyone and serves to broaden participation.)

- Initiate a "fish bowl" discussion by arranging seats in a small circle inside a larger circle. Those seated in the latter are asked to observe, listen, and take notes on a discussion conducted among those seated in the smaller circle. Conclude the exercise by asking "outside" observers to query those in the "inner" circle about major points raised during their discussion.

- Ask students to pair off and to respond to a question, either in turn or as a pair.

- Supply "advance organizers" to the class in the form of questions about the material to be discussed during the class period. Notify the students that they should be able to answer each question by the end of the session. Solicit responses to the questions at the end of class.

- Involve the students in a concept mapping exercise. A concept map is a method for illustrating the connections that exist among terms or concepts covered in the course material. Students construct conceptual maps by linking individual terms with lines that clarify the relationships between or among each set of connected terms.

- Create role-playing situations where students are asked to "act out" parts as a way of dramatizing the theories and concepts under discussion.

- Present students with a problem (case study, videotape, written research summary). Students work in groups to organize their ideas and previous knowledge about the problem or issue presented and then either present differing views or are encouraged to work toward a consensus on a possible response to the problem under scrutiny.

- Hand out slips of paper at random to class members. Each piece of paper contains information essential for explaining or describing something. The class assignment is for everyone to "mill around" and then coalesce into separate groups when its members discover they have all the information needed for explaining or describing a given concept, theme, or term.

- Divide the class into two or more competitive teams. Each team is charged with assembling a coherent and logical account of something, using otherwise-isolated pieces of information appearing on strips of paper you have supplied. Each paper strip contains a single datum or fragment of information. Competing teams might be working on the same chronology or account; or they could each assemble a different account of something.

- Two teams of students are assembled to assume opposing sides in a debate on a given topic appropriate to the course. Students not involved on either team serve as judges to determine which team makes its case most persuasively. Time permitting, the protocols governing collegiate forensics are observed; otherwise, simply allowing each opposing team equal time to present its side is sufficient to bring relevant information up for discussion and debate.

- Bring a pair of dice to class. Randomly assign each student a number from 2 to 12. Roll the dice and announced the number. A student with a corresponding number must immediately respond with an example, application, summary, or identification of a concept treated previously in class or in an assigned reading.

- Supply each student with a 3 x 5 card, on which appears a pertinent question *or* an answer. Have students move around the room querying one another until all the questions and answers have been matched up correctly. Each student holding a question reads it aloud, followed by the student who has the corresponding answer. The class is invited to judge whether the match has been made correctly. There are many variations worth trying out—for example, have each class member generate a question and its appropriate answer before the exercise begins.

- Appoint a team of students to create a review of previous material utilizing the format of a television game show (for example, having competing contestants select from categories of questions of varying difficulty).

- Assign each student the task of drafting a set of questions for a test or midterm exam (with an "ideal" correct response for each question). Then have each set of questions critiqued by a second student, utilizing such criteria as item difficulty level, significance or importance of each question, clarity of expression, level of learning called for, and so forth. Discuss the questions in class. Consider including the best questions on the actual test or exam.

- In a laboratory setting, require students to replicate a demonstration or experiment previously conducted by you as the instructor. Require the students to explain why their effort was successful or unsuccessful. Ask them to identify what specific factors, conditions, or variables affected the outcome observed.

SOME GUIDELINES FOR ACTIVE LEARNING IN THE COLLEGE CLASSROOM:

The professor is "student oriented"

- The point of departure for the course is where the students are, not where the professor is.
- Although students are expected to be self-motivated, the teacher accepts shared responsibility for a learning experience that is supportive, structured, and effective in attaining course goals.
- Everyone treats one another with dignity and respect.
- Individual differences are expected, welcomed, and supported.

Students participate in establishing goals and objectives

- Broad objectives are provided by the teacher; students select or create additional objectives.

The classroom climate is supportive and interactive

- Discussion, group work, and active participation by everyone are encouraged.
- The professor takes up no more than half the time with talking and does no more than two-thirds of the decision-making for the class.

Activities are problem centered and student driven

- The course is structured around "real" issues and problems that relate to students' goals and interests.
- Whenever possible, students work at their own pace and on their own schedules.
- Students are encouraged or required to work together part of the time in groups and to provide suggestions and support to one another.

Assessment is continuous and supportive

- Formative feedback is emphasized over summative grading.
- The teacher's focus is on success and suggestions for improvement rather than on mistakes and corrections.

continues

- Students are expected to revise and resubmit work that does not meet expected standards, and summative grades are based on revised work.
- Assessment is criterion referenced rather than normative.

Teaching respects learner initiative and participation

- Students are viewed as active creators of knowledge, not merely passive recipients of information.
- The emphasis is on comprehension and application rather than on repetition and recall.
- It is accepted that there is rarely one single right answer to any given question.
- The teacher provides access to information; students assemble, organize, and use the information.
- Students are allowed flexibility and encouraged to become as self-directed as possible in their learning.

Multilevel learning outcomes are expected

- Factual information gathering is expected to lead to broader understanding, application, and critical reflection.

—adopted in part from *Some Guidelines for Active Learning in the College Classroom* at http://www.educ.drake.edu/romig/activelng.html

Learning Styles

A major argument put forth to support the use of multiple instructional strategies is that active learning better accommodates the differing ways in which individual students learn best. Some people, for example, are primarily auditory learners—they need to hear something in order to absorb it. Others are visual learners—they must see something in order to understand it. Tactile or kinesthetic learners do best when they touch, handle, or do something with a body of material. (Presumably, there are no "gustatory" or "olfactory" learners.) People are allegedly dissimilar, in other words, in terms of the sensory modality through which they most naturally prefer to learn.[16]

Problems arise, or so it is argued, when learning style and teaching method are incongruent. Most learners favor visual input (diagrams, pictures, maps, plots, demonstrations). Yet a great deal of teaching typically emphasizes verbal presentation alone. Inductive learners begin with data and observations and infer principles. Deductive thinkers prefer to begin with principles or generalizations and deduce implications—the far more common method of organizing instruction. Sequential learners are analytic; they process information in linear, connected steps. Global or "holistic" learners, however, take in large connected chunks of data and excel at conceptual integration and the identification of connections among things. Learners who are "field-sensitive" approach ideas globally, viewing ideas in some broader context; while those who are "field-independent" are more analytical and focus on particular aspects of a concept or idea.

Sensory learners focus on what is seen, heard, and touched. Sensors like factual data and real-world relations. Intuitive learners rely more on memory, ideas, and a sense for unexplored possibilities. They favor theories and models but dislike detail work. Again, reflective learners generally prefer to work alone and learn best independently; whereas active learners process information while doing something (talking, moving) and, characteristically, do well with group work.

Quantitatively oriented learners are most comfortable working with numbers. Qualitatively oriented students—in extreme cases—may absolutely abhor them. Some students are highly logical; others are more esthetic and artistic in processing information. Some people are comfortable with abstractions. Others are inclined to think in more concrete terms.

Some students thrive in a competitive learning environment; still others gain from a setting where cooperation and collaboration are stressed. Certain learners achieve more if allowed to work alone, with a minimum of direction and control. Some can accomplish just as much, but only if given a great deal of structure and supervision.[17] And so it goes, with a bewildering array of possible combinations of categories and learner types competing for consideration.

How much solid empirical evidence supports these various classification systems is open to question. (Some skeptics claim their construct validity is little better than that of astrological signs.) Among the most fully developed, however, the analysis of personality types outlined in the Myers-Briggs Type Indicator (MBTI) seems to offer promise.[18] Various psychological types are identified through scores on each of four bipolar scales: extroversion-introversion; sensing-intuition; thinking-feeling; and judging-perceiving. The MBTI posits naturally occurring personality tendencies or "types" in terms of patterns of attitudes, perceptions, approaches to the world, and decision-making styles people exhibit.[19]

"Extroverts" direct their attention toward the external world of people, things, and activities. They are gregarious, talkative, and energized by people and outside activity. They learn best through activity methods in social settings. "Introverts," on the other hand, give their attention more to the inner world of reflection, thought, and feeling. They prefer privacy, quiet, and intimacy. They do well processing conceptual information, but require time for thinking and reflection.

"Sensing" types are factual, realistic, conventional, practical, and down-to-earth. As students, they prefer facts and hard evidence, concrete examples, and structure. They tend to be visually oriented learners. "Intuitive" people, in contrast, have an affinity for concepts and abstract thinking. They are often highly creative and innovative. They favor discussion-based methods of learning.

"Thinking" types are logical, rational, often critical, and highly analytic. They do best in learning situations that favor precision, objectivity, and logical analysis. The "feeling" personality is warm, empathic, and sensitive. Decision-making tends to be based on personal values and likes and dislikes rather than on objective empirical considerations. Their preferred

---

MULTIPLE TYPES OF INTELLIGENCE?

Psychologist Howard Gardner, in a 1983 work entitled *Frames of Mind,* along with several other researchers since, suggests that students' preferred learning styles derive in part from different types of intelligence:

- Verbal or *linguistic* intelligence is reflected by the individual's facility with language.
- Logical and *mathematical* intelligence relates to problem solving, logical reasoning, and pattern recognition.
- Visual or *spatial* intelligence is linked with the ability to create or work with pictorial representations, maps, charts, and blueprints.
- *Musical* intelligence facilitates awareness of pitch, tone, melody, and rhythm, as well as a natural talent for playing a musical instrument, singing, and composing.
- *Kinesthetic* intelligence is shown by coordinated physical activity and by an individual's ability to convey ideas and emotions through body motion—dancers and gymnasts, for example.
- *Interpersonal* intelligence indicates a capacity to feel comfortable with others, to excel at communication and social interaction.
- *Intrapersonal* intelligence refers to the individual's self-understanding and insight.

learning style emphasizes human interest, human values and benefits, and personal applications of information.

High scorers on the "judging" scale have a tendency to plan ahead, to be well organized, and to prefer a high level of structure and organization. As learners, they profit from plans, outlines, and schedules. They flourish in a learning environment where promptness, punctuality, clarity, and predictability are stressed. "Perceiving" types tend to be flexible, spontaneous, and somewhat disorganized. They are open minded and adaptable but prone to procrastination. They flourish as learners if multiple options are provided. They like "open" approaches to learning that reward personal initiative and choice.[20]

Taking it all into account, what implications follow? Is it true, for instance, that differences in *personality* type can be linked empirically with preferred *learning* styles? And if, in turn, learning preferences make for significant differences in how well individuals learn—acquire knowledge— does the linkage mean learning achievement correlates not only with *teaching* styles (didactic, discussion-based, authoritarian, egalitarian) but also with various kinds of classroom learning environments (competitive versus collaborative)?

Again, what works for 18- and 19-year-olds may not be appropriate for more mature, so-called nontraditional students. Even generational differences may be important. Professors who have been teaching over the span of several decades profess to find real changes over time in the students they have taught. Today's collegians, it is alleged, are more comfortable with technologically mediated instruction than their predecessors, more accepting of hypertextual arrangements of subject matter. They tend supposedly to be less dependent on linearity and sequence, but are more easily distracted and have greater difficulty staying on task compared with learners of a generation or so ago. Most noticeably, or so it seems, their attention span is considerably shorter than their forebears.

If it is valid to claim that there is no such thing as "one-size-fits-all" in teaching, what mandate follows for a "real-world" instructor facing a class of several dozen college students? If they actually differ as learners, what are you as the teacher supposed to do? How do you aspire to accommodate students' differences in some meaningful way? So far, current research offers few hard answers.

Possibly the best that can be hoped for, first, is that college teachers will develop enhanced sensitivity to the fact that students do appear to differ in how they learn, even if the variability cannot always be fixed with scientific precision. Second, so far as learning modalities and age-related characteristics are concerned, faculty must learn to eschew reliance on any

DO PROFESSORS AND STUDENTS LEARN DIFFERENTLY?

A professor commenting on teaching: *"My classroom would be a much better place if students were more like me!"*

When comparing the preferred learning patterns of faculty to those of students, researchers are finding that the "typical" faculty member is most likely to evidence an "abstract reflective" or "introverted intuitive" learning preference. Abstract reflective thinkers (about 10 percent of the population) reportedly tend to be thoughtful, innovative, introspective, scholarly, and interested in knowledge primarily for its own sake. They value ideas, theories, and thoroughness or depth of understanding.

Intuitive learners are "global picture" types who are most comfortable with concepts, ideas, and abstractions. They seek a high degree of autonomy in how they acquire learning. Intuitives value critical thinking, independence, depth and originality of thought, and the ability to grasp abstract ideas.

A majority of the new breed of college students descending on the nation's campuses nowadays allegedly tends to reflect a "concrete active" or "sensing perceiving" learning pattern, the preference most broadly distributed within the general population at large. The learning styles of those who are oriented toward sensing are characterized by a preference for direct, concrete experience; moderate to high degrees of structure; linear, sequential learning; and, often, a need to know why before doing something.

In general, students who prefer sensing learning patterns prefer the concrete, the practical, and the immediate. They are uncomfortable with abstract concepts, and evince discomfort with complex ideas. Their tolerance for ambiguity is low. Perceptual learners are less independent in thought and judgment, more dependent on authority, and profit from immediate feedback and gratification.

As R. M. Felder comments, "When mismatches exist between learning styles of most students in a class and the teaching style of the professor, the students may become bored and inattentive in class, do poorly on tests, get discouraged. . . . Professors, confronted by low test grades, unresponsive or hostile classes, poor attendance and dropouts, know something is not working. They may become overly critical of their students (making things even worse). . . ."

—Consult R. M. Felder, *Learning Styles,* available online at:
http://www2.ncsu.edu/unity/lockers/users/f/felder/public/
Learning_Styles.html. Refer also to Charles C. Schroeder, *New Students–New Learning Styles,* at: http://www.virtualschool.edu/mon

single teaching approach—for example, on "talk and chalk" alone, to the virtual exclusion of a broad range of other possibilities.

Multiple ways of imparting information do need to be explored even within the confines of a given course. Teacher talk must be supplemented or integrated with visual presentation, lecturing with discussion, passive learning with group activity. Rigid structure must be leavened by flexibility, planning with improvisation, and predictability of classroom routine with spontaneity and elements of the unexpected. In class no less than outside it, variety *is* the spice of life.

Assessment and Evaluation

Evaluation of student performance is an unavoidable feature of academic life. Unfortunately, nothing else contributes so much to tension between faculty members and students or so materially sets them against one another as adversaries. Teachers, for their part, are obliged to hold students accountable for their learning (or the lack thereof), usually expressed in terms of grades. Students, on the other hand, function in a highly competitive environment. Rewards associated with good grades are considerable. Conversely, the penalties for failure or mediocre attainment may be equally pressing (threat of the possible loss of a scholarship, the prospect of being denied admission to graduate school, endangered athletic eligibility, and so on).

Greatly exacerbating matters is the widespread tendency among faculty members to overestimate vastly their own expertise in constructing tests, quizzes, and examinations. For present purposes, no good purpose would be served by engaging in a lengthy, detailed discussion of test-construction theory and, more generally, the particulars of measurement and evaluation. It is sufficient perhaps to suggest that most faculty members, even those of long experience, probably do *not* give nearly enough thought to the work of designing assessments of student performance. Nor do they always appreciate the importance of timely feedback, no matter what sort of testing is conducted.

Ideally, testing should serve to reinforce the process of learning. Examinations should assist students to concentrate on what the instructor believes they should be learning.[21] This is to say that testing should be "formative," that is, should afford guidance and direction for improved performance, even if the underlying purpose is "summative," that is, is intended to help form the basis for a judgment about learning (in the student's case, a number or letter grade).

Two corollaries follow. The first and most obvious is that what is tested for should be fairly congruent with the goals and objectives set for the course. Evaluation should reflect more or less closely whatever material the teacher has previously identified as most important. (Extraneous information should be removed from consideration or deemphasized for testing purposes.) Assessment also should test as nearly as possible at the level of learning the preceding instruction was intended to produce. (Simple recognition or recall of information, it should be stressed once again, does not automatically give rise to the ability to analyze, apply, or solve problems with that same information.)

Second, brief quizzes administered at intervals throughout a course are almost always preferable to a single midterm and final exam. Frequent testing allows more opportunities for success, while reducing the penalty for any single poor performance.[22] When a person's grade depends primarily on an end-of-course assessment, it is obviously too late for that student to seek remediation or demonstrate improvement.

In matters of testing, quite frankly, the best counsel for inexperienced faculty members is to anticipate that *not everyone will be fully satisfied, no matter what is done.* This dictum applies with force when the choice must be made, for example, whether to grade "on the curve" or against a set of predetermined criteria.

Assessment based on relative achievement ("norm-based" grading) carries the advantage that a given student's work is assessed within the context of norms established collectively by the class as a whole. The disadvantage is that even if the class distribution of scores is high, a fixed percentage of scores must be considered low, relatively speaking. Conversely, if the class as a whole performs poorly, scores at the high end of the distribution must still be considered acceptable.

The attractiveness of criterion-referenced grading is that any given test score takes its meaning from the magnitude of its difference from a "perfect" or "highest possible" score. The drawback, of course, is that, hypothetically, ranked scores could all cluster at the top of the scale, thus precluding any meaningful discrimination between outstanding achievement and comparatively poor performance. Conversely, if all of the scores fall far short of the upper limits of a scale, everyone must be judged to have done poorly relative to the criteria set forth.

A "compromise" solution of sorts is to grade in terms of a percentage achieved of the maximum possible score, where an "A" is assigned a priori to a score at the ninetieth percentile or above, a "B" as the grade corresponding to any score falling between the eightieth and eighty-ninth percentile, and so on down. Percentile cut-offs, of course, can be stipulated in advance, or altered ex post facto to take into account where the scores turned out to be more broadly distributed across the scale than the examiner anticipated.

Testing formats lend themselves to numerous variations, whether of the "constructed response" type (short-answer questions, essays) or so-called objective items (matching, true/false, multiple-choice). The former is best adapted for testing at higher cognitive levels, while the latter are better suited for lower-level assessment. Either way, there are pitfalls to avoid.

Good essay questions are deceptively difficult to construct. Some are unjustifiably ambiguous or crafted in such a way as to be nearly impossible to evaluate against a set of objective criteria: "Identify and explain what you consider to be the most important factors involved in X." Or they are too complex to be responded to succinctly, within the time allotted for an answer: "Summarize the relevant research that supports or contradicts the Smellfungus theory of cultural entropy, with specific references to all of the relevant research conducted since. . . ." Or a question may be slanted to favor a particular ideological bias: "Explain why dialectical materialism offers the most cogent explanation for X, Y, and Z."

Crafting a good objective test is no less challenging. Ambiguous or confusing phrasing (using double negatives, as a case in point), multiple-choice "distracter" items that fail to distract, true and false items that are neither unequivocally true nor false, test questions that unintentionally penalize overinterpretation on a student's part, items that focus on the trivial or irrelevant—all are hazards to be avoided. Whether objective or subjective, tests must be assembled thoughtfully and with care.

If you lack extensive test-construction experience, you will find it advisable to do several things: pilot a test whenever possible; allow an exam to be scrutinized and critiqued in advance by your colleagues; and conduct an item analysis of an objective test after it has been administered so that its weaknesses can be corrected for in a future edition.

Guided peer grading in class or having students discuss the answers to test questions once the exam is over is something many professors assiduously avoid. Admittedly, the exercise can be both tension producing and time consuming. Yet nothing less is apt to suffice, as the old cliché has it, to transform test taking into an authentic "learning experience."

If grading is to fulfill a formative function, students must be given a chance to review, analyze, and discuss their test papers at length, and in detail. Teachers and students alike stand to benefit from the experience. The ideal, ultimately, is a general acknowledgement (regardless of any given individual's dissatisfaction or disappointment) that testing *has* been conducted in a way that is demonstrably fair, valid, and unbiased. And if it has not, there is nothing like a test "post-mortem" to show up its inadequacies.

Assigned essays and course papers pose special problems of their own. It almost goes without saying, the assignment itself should be clear and explicit. Evaluative criteria need to be spelled out in advance. These should include a requirement that any paper submitted be free of typographical, grammatical, and spelling errors—basic writing mechanics *ought* to count in assessment.

Students appreciate it when you make plain in advance the criteria by which their course papers will be graded. Whether you include them in the course syllabus or hand out a list of standards separately, your students are entitled to some indication about what considerations will apply when you assess their efforts. Consider the following, for example, extensively modified from a set of 1997 guidelines produced for scoring Graduate Record Examination essays by the Educational Testing Service of Princeton, New Jersey (*GRE Essay Scoring Guide: Perspectives on an Issue*):

Superior, Outstanding: Offers a cogent analysis of the issues entailed and demonstrates mastery of the elements of effective writing. Develops a well-reasoned position on the topic or issue; sustains a well-focused, well-organized narrative; expresses ideas clearly and precisely; utilizes language fluently, with varied sentence structure and appropriate vocabulary; demonstrates facility with the conventions of proper grammar, usage and mechanics; is free of flaws and errors.

Good: Presents a well-reasoned analysis of a thesis or position and shows strong control of the elements of effective writing. The paper is focused and well organized; shows clarity of expression; utilizes varied sentence structure and appropriate vocabulary; demonstrates facility with the conventions of good English and is marred by only a very few minor mistakes or flaws in style, grammar, syntax, and punctuation.

Satisfactory/Adequate: Presents an analysis of the theme or topic treated and demonstrates adequate control of the elements of good writing. Explicates a coherent position using relevant arguments and examples; exhibits a fair degree of organization and appropriate structure; expresses ideas clearly; lacks complete control in matters of style, grammar, syntax, and vocabulary.

Marginal: Demonstrates limited competence in structure, organization, and development and is flawed in matters of style, grammar, spelling, punctuation, and syntax. Paper is vague or unclear in narrative development; is generally not clearly reasoned, is poorly focused or poorly organized; indicates author's limited facility in the use of language and sentence structure; contains numerous errors.

Deficient/Unsatisfactory: Exhibits serious weaknesses in analysis, structure, organization; essential elements missing or poorly developed and contains numerous errors in usage, grammar, and writing mechanics. Paper is ambiguous, poorly focused, or unorganized; fails to show proficiency in standard written English; is flawed to the extent that the argumentation is obscured or unintelligible.

Will your students read through such descriptors and govern themselves accordingly when they draft their papers? Probably not. But at the very least, you have something to fall back on and to refer to if you are obliged to explain your grading once papers are returned.

Circumstances permitting, papers should fall due well before the end of the academic term so they can be evaluated and returned before the course concludes. When possible, in order to increase learning, provision should be made for rewriting and possible resubmission at the student's discretion. Your feedback should be detailed enough so that students profit from your comments and criticisms.

DESIGNING MULTIPLE-CHOICE TEST ITEMS:

1. Pose questions that require more than simple knowledge of facts. For example, require the selection of the best or most adequate answer when all of the options are partly correct—the test item is apt to be more discriminating and challenging.
2. Eliminate superfluous verbiage within the text of a question: make the "stem" simple and straightforward. Likewise, exclude superfluous or distracting information in the options.
3. Avoid response options such as "none of the above" or "all of the above" or "both B and C."
4. Maintain parallel construction throughout all of the response items for a given question. Check for grammatical consistency between stem and options.
5. Varying the number of response options from question to question is perfectly acceptable from a psychometric point of view.
6. Avoid double negatives and negative options following a negative stem.
7. Do not repeat wording from the stem in the options.
8. Avoid trivial, unimportant questions.

(Adapted from Testing Memo 10: *Some Multiple-choice Item Writing Do's And Don'ts,* Office of Measurement and Research Services, Virginia Polytechnic Institute and State University [Blacksburg, VA, n.d.]. See also Robert B. Frary, "More Multiple-choice Item Writing Do's And Don'ts," *Practical Assessment, Research & Evaluation* 4 [11]: available on-line: http://ericae.net/pare/getvn.asp?v=4&n=11)

CONSTRUCTING ESSAY QUESTIONS:

1. Be clear in advance about the level of learning you want to test for in an essay question, e. g., recall, interpretation, integration, application, and so on. Employing an essay question to test for simple recall of information, for example, is "overkill." Essay questions are best suited for assessing higher levels of learning.
2. Essay questions should be open-ended—that is, they should admit of a variety of valid responses.
3. Avoid drafting questions that allow for the unsupported expression of student opinion; there is no fair and objective way to assess them. Questions that *do* ask for supporting documentation or argumentation on behalf of a particular interpretation of the material avoid the trap of excessive subjectivity and can be very revealing.
4. Allow sufficient time for students to organize themselves and to respond thoughtfully to your essay questions. Placing severe time constraints of students practically guarantees inferior or incomplete responses. Speediness of response is not necessarily a good indicator of how much learning has taken place. Adjust the number and scope of questions you pose to the time available.

Instructional Evaluation

College teachers who feel secure about their teaching (and have valid reasons to justify their confidence) may or may not necessarily welcome feedback on their instruction. Others definitely do not—either because of a deserved lack of confidence in themselves as teachers or by virtue of simple inexperience. As a novice teacher once confessed, referring to student course evaluations, "The pressure of my department for good evaluations has put enough pressure on me that I often find myself thinking of my students as the enemy and these forms as the weapons they use in a thoughtless way to damage me. The last time I handed them out I nearly got sick to my stomach before class."[23]

Some seasoned teachers (even among those whose instruction is meticulously planned and brilliantly executed) are apt to be skeptical about the value of having students assess their teaching. Either they resist being given advice on what they think they already know, or they remain unpersuaded that course evaluation forms completed by students produce useful information. "I must say," observes one teacher, "that I have learned little from these evaluations. It is good to know that one's teaching is appreciated, of course, but even the most gushing praise does not allay self-doubts about not being as good on the job as one ought to be. In fact, in my own case, the only aid I have received from student evaluations is the single-sentence comment 'He jiggles the change in his pockets.' As a result of this penetrating criticism, I now put all my change in my briefcase before stepping into a classroom."[24]

Differences among faculty members in terms of willingness to work for instructional improvement has been alluded to previously. For some, teaching is akin to a sacred calling, an all-consuming vocation, something that demands constant refinement. For others, it is simply an unwelcome distraction from other, more attractive professional activities. The less time spent on it, the better. Willingness to accept feedback further depends on how a faculty member thinks about the nature of teaching itself, whether intensely invested in it or not. As Robert Menges astutely observes, not all faculty are willing to reflect on their beliefs and practices:

> Some cling to a holistic, vaguely romantic notion, as if teaching were too delicate to withstand examination: Because teaching is ephemeral, it eludes analysis. Like love, teaching can be experienced, contemplated, and celebrated, but it can never be understood. At the other extreme are technologists who relish analyzing and even dismembering teaching into components, factors, and flowcharts. They regard teaching as little more than a process of specifying objectives, developing teaching activities consistent with those objectives, engaging learners in the activities, assessing outcomes, and planning revisions for the next teaching occasion. The views of most college teachers, somewhere between these extremes, imply that while teaching can withstand examination, it is never fully understood through reductive analysis.[25]

Many colleges and universities now mandate the use of student course evaluations. Some instruments—especially those that allow the teacher to select statements with which students may agree or disagree—yield an illuminating if imprecise picture of what students think about the teaching done in a course. Unfortunately, while they are purportedly intended to help teachers improve and are defended as such, the results of student assessments more typically are employed in institutional decisions affecting annual faculty salary increments, promotions, and tenure.

All things considered, a better source of feedback information comes from narrative comments written out by students. Vaguely worded or open-ended questions (*"What did you like or dislike about the course?"*) are not apt to generate helpful responses. The more specific and precise the questions, the more useful will be the answers received. The most fruitful types of queries ask directly about the workload and level of difficulty of the course, the value derived from reading assignments, the use made of class time, the fairness of grading, what specifically should have been done differently, and so on. Even more revealing oftentimes are comments included in letters of advice written by students to peers who will take the same course in future: "How to succeed and get the most out of this course."

Examples of open-ended questions that might generate useful information:

- Compared with other courses in which you have been enrolled this term, how much time and effort did you invest in this course?
- If you had it to do over again, what would you do specifically to improve your performance in this course?
- What specific suggestions or advice would you offer students enrolling in this course in future? In other words, what would you tell them about how to get the most out of the course?
- Do you feel the instructor's expectations and standards were made clear and unambiguous? Why or why not?
- Compare the level of difficulty of the material treated in this course with those of other courses in which you have been enrolled this term. Was it higher, lower, or about the same? Explain.
- Were you conscientious about completing all the reading and assignments required in this course? Compare the amount of reading (and other assignments) with that demanded in your other courses. Did this course require more time, less time, or about the same amount of time?
- Do you anticipate receiving the same grade you originally hoped for or expected at the beginning of the course? Why or why not?
- Do you feel that help with this course was available if needed? Did you have occasion to seek assistance from the instructor?
- What specific suggestions do you have for the instructor in terms of future improvements in the course? What, if anything, should be done differently and why?

Note that these questions are not designed to elicit information on the popularity of the instructor or on how well the student "liked" the course as such. Rather, the focus is on what the student did or did not do, on what changes the instructor might effect in future, and on the student's perception of how the course compared with other courses—practical information you as the teacher can utilize in redesigning or revising the course as necessary in the future.

AGAINST STUDENT COURSE
AND TEACHER EVALUATIONS

Complaints about the misuse of numerical scores drawn from students' evaluations of courses and instructors are commonplace in academe. Consider the following allegations advanced recently by a professor of English at Montana State University:

1. No scholarly consensus exists as to what constitutes effective teaching. Hence, numerical data aggregated from "bubble" sheets cannot provide an adequate measure of the quality or effectiveness of classroom instruction.
2. What numerical forms measure is the degree to which students are satisfied with the instructor (personality), the course (requirements), and the outcome (grade). Such forms are thus only "consumer satisfaction" surveys.
3. The validity of most evaluation forms (ability to measure what they purport to measure) is largely unproven. They are likewise unreliable and inaccurate. (Students are not consistent or reliable evaluators of classroom behavior.)
4. The use of numerical forms to reward or punish teachers' classroom behavior encourages instructors to "dumb down" their teaching. If faculty raises, tenure, and promotion depend on high marks for teaching, professors will do what is required to obtain good scores. They give students what they want: easier assignments, less work, lower expectations. One result, among others, is rampant grade inflation.
5. Narrative evaluations, self-evaluation, peer visitation and review, and intensive focus-group interviews are more than adequate for monitoring a teacher's classroom performance.

Source: Paul Trout, "Flunking the Test, The Dismal Record of Student Evaluations," *Academe* 86 (July–August, 2000): 58–61.

Most research on student ratings of teachers does not indicate that the ratings measure the effectiveness of teaching, good teaching, intellectual achievement, nor understanding of basic concepts. The ratings appear to be measuring student satisfaction, the attitudes of students toward their teachers and classes, the psychosocial needs of the student, and the personality characteristics, popularity, and speaking quality of the teacher.

—M. C. Wittrock and Arthur A. Lumsdaine, "Instructional Psychology," *Annual Review of Psychology* 28 (1997): 417.

continues

Students, by definition, do not know the subject matter they are studying, so they are in a poor position to judge how well it is being taught.

—Steven M. Cahn, *Saints and Scamps, Ethics in Academia*, rev. ed. (Lanham, Maryland: Rowman & Littlefield, 1994), p. 39.

Hoary tradition works against another potentially valuable source of information for assessing and improving teaching, namely, faculty peer review. As noted earlier, professors usually are reluctant to intrude upon one another's classroom privacy unless expressly invited to observe a colleague's teaching firsthand. Likewise, the person whose teaching is to be evaluated may feel more than a little intimidated and self-conscious at the prospect of having faculty peers look over his or her shoulder and pass judgment on what they observe.

Nevertheless, so long as the exercise is conducted for formative purposes, there is much to be gained from having one's peers observe and garner "snap-shot" impressions of the instruction going on. Especially when some structured observation form is utilized to guide peer observation, the insights and suggestions of other faculty can be extremely revealing.

Ethical Considerations in Teaching

A Committee on University Ethics was one of the original standing bodies of the American Association of University Professors, established at the AAUP's inception in 1915. A "Statement on Professional Ethics" first adopted in 1966 and approved by the Committee, won formal endorsement in June, 1987. It reads, in part, as follows:

As teachers, professors encourage the free pursuit of learning in their students. They hold before them the best scholarly and ethical standards of their discipline. Professors demonstrate respect for students as individuals and adhere to their proper roles as intellectual guides and counselors. Professors make every reasonable effort to foster honest academic conduct and to ensure that their evaluations of students reflect each student's true merit. They respect the confidential nature of the relationship between professor and student. They avoid any exploitation, harassment, or discriminatory treatment of students. They acknowledge significant academic or scholarly assistance from them. They protect their academic freedom.[26]

A 1990 AAUP document entitled "Freedom and Responsibility" further addresses the ethical responsibilities of faculty with respect to teaching. "Students," it is observed, "are entitled to an atmosphere conducive to learning and to even-handed treatment in all aspects of the teacher-student relationship. Faculty members may not refuse to enroll or teach students on the grounds of their beliefs or the possible uses to which they may put the knowledge to be gained in a course. . . ."

"Evaluation of students and the award of credit," the document continues, "must be based on academic performance professionally judged and not on matters irrelevant to that performance, whether personality, race, religion . . . or personal beliefs." In teaching, "it is improper for an instructor persistently to intrude material that has no relation to the subject, or to fail to present the subject matter of the course as announced to the students and as approved by the faculty. . . ."[27]

Elsewhere, the AAUP stipulates that "the professor in the classroom and in conference should encourage free discussion, inquiry, and expression. Student performance should be evaluated solely on an academic basis, not on opinions or conduct in matters unrelated to academic standards. . . . Students should be free to take reasoned exception to the data or views offered in any course of study and to reserve judgment about matters of opinion. . . . Students should have protection through orderly procedures against prejudiced or capricious academic evaluation."

The document goes on to say, "Information about student views, beliefs, and political associations which professors acquire in the course of their work as instructors, advisers, and counselors should be considered confidential. Protection against improper disclosure is a serious professional obligation."[28]

Many of the same strictures are set forth in the professional code of ethics of the American Psychological Association, not to mention similar statements from other professional organizations. The APA's code affirms, "The teacher should encourage students in their quest for knowledge, giving them every assistance in the free exploration of ideas. Teaching frequently and legitimately involves a presentation of disquieting facts and controversial theories, and it is in the examination of perplexing issues that students most need the guidance of a good teacher."

"Disturbing concepts should not be withheld from students simply because some individuals may be distressed by them." When issues are relevant, they should be given full and objective discussion so that students can make intelligent decisions with regard to them. However, presentation of ideas likely to be difficult for some students to accept should be governed by tact and respect for the worth of the individual.

"Differing approaches to one's discipline should be presented to students in such a way as to encourage them to study the relevant facts and draw their own conclusions. Free expression of both criticism and support of the various approaches is to be encouraged as essential to the development of individual students. . . ." In dealing with an area of specialization other than his or her own, a teacher should make it clear that he or she is not speaking as a specialist.

"A teacher should respect students' right to privacy and not require students to give information which they may wish to withhold; neither should the teacher reveal information which a student has given with the reasonable assumption that it will be held in confidence."

"A teacher should require of students only activities which are designed to contribute to the student in the area of instruction. Other activities not related to course objectives . . . should be made available to students on a voluntary basis."

The APA's code concludes with caveats about sexual harassment, against conduct that interferes with an individual's academic or professional performance, and the necessity of avoiding behavior that might contribute to the existence of "an intimidating, hostile, or offensive" environment.[29]

Most of these themes have been sounded elsewhere. Conwell Strickland and associates, for example, cite six ethical imperatives governing collegiate teaching: (1) the student's right to be recognized as an individual and to be treated, by name, as such; (2) the student's right to learn from a faculty member who evinces interest and enthusiasm; (3) the right to receive instruction that exhibits careful preparation and planning; (4) the student's right to express opinions and to challenge those of the instructor without penalty or fear of possible retribution; (5) the student's right to have access to the teacher at times outside of class; and (6) the student's right to be informed about the system under which his or her work will be graded.[30]

Among the prescriptions and proscriptions cited in the literature on ethics in teaching, several derive from the comments of college students themselves. The following items seem especially interesting or noteworthy:

- The teacher has an obligation to intervene to control disruptive behavior in the classroom, but he or she must try to do so without unnecessarily humiliating or demeaning offenders.
- A teacher should never resort to intimidation as a method of exercising control in the classroom.
- The teacher should encourage rather than discourage questions from students.

- The professor has an obligation to avoid being chronically late to class. He or she should make provision for substitute instruction in the event of an unavoidable absence.
- Locking a student out of the classroom who is chronically late to class is an unacceptable way of dealing with the problem of tardiness.
- The privacy rights of students must be respected.
- Prejudicial comments made by students in class should not be ignored. They should be challenged, though always handled as diplomatically as possible.
- The use of profanity that is likely to be found offensive by some in a classroom, whether uttered by students or by the teacher, is unacceptable and improper.
- The teacher should always refrain in class from making negative comments about colleagues or criticizing the merits of another disciplinary specialty.
- Professors are obliged not to engage in "oral plagiarism," that is, misrepresenting the ideas or findings of others as their own within the body of a lecture or lesson.
- Video and audio recordings, films, and computer-based presentations should not be relied upon excessively, and under no circumstances should be made to serve as surrogates for the teacher's live instruction and presence in the classroom.
- The teacher has an ethical responsibility to adhere to the course syllabus as much as possible, and to conduct the course in a manner consistent with its published description.
- Professors should offer students timely feedback on performance, and should never resort to so-called one-shot or weed-out grading.
- Students should be treated equally and respected as individuals.
- No professor should appropriate a student's ideas and represent them as his or her own.
- Teachers hold an obligation to make themselves reasonably accessible to students at times other than those of the class.

Undoubtedly, there is room for legitimate disagreement when it comes to the ethics of teaching. Specifics are sometimes problematic in the extreme; and the circumstances of any given situation must always be taken into account. Certainly there are "gray" areas where black and white judgments cannot easily be applied. Notwithstanding, it is worth emphasizing that the act of teaching is inherently a social undertaking. In the final reckoning, it must be guided by the same normative considerations of equity, reciprocity, and consideration for others that govern other forms of social interaction.

Dealing with Troublesome or
Inappropriate Student Behavior

Working with college students is mostly a joy. Instances of troublesome or inappropriate student behavior calling for intervention by an individual faculty member, thankfully, do not occur often, and most of the time can be handled amicably, without rancor or conflict. Anticipating volatile situations before the fact and taking steps to prevent the likelihood of their occurrence simply makes good sense.

The usual sources of tension or disagreement between students and faculty, of course, are grades and grading practices. Disputes over grading are also the easiest to prevent, assuming: (1) you have a clear, explicit set of reasonable standards for assessing student performance; (2) you have made those criteria both explicit and intelligible to all your students; and, finally, (3) you have adhered scrupulously to your announced grading practices and standards—which is to say, you have awarded grades consistently and equitably.

If indeed you have fulfilled each of these requirements in good faith, you have eliminated or at least reduced to a minimum substantive grounds for student complaints. No matter how disgruntled or disaffected the student, if you as the teacher can refer back, or appeal to, a prior explanation of your grading at the very outset (as discussed on the first day of class, as summarized on the course syllabus, or as set forth in a class handout), and if you can show clearly how it was applied, you have, in effect, undercut the legitimacy of whatever complaints might surface.

If you have prior experience as a graduate teaching assistant, you probably are already familiar with some of the less-defensible grounds for student disaffection. A common complaint, for example, equates effort with outcome: *"I've worked really hard in this course, so I think I deserve a better grade."* Another equates need with entitlement: *"You don't understand, I have to get a good grade in this class or else I'll lose my financial-aid package and have to drop out of school!"*

One argument confuses an explanation of factors contributing to poor performance with its justification: *"I work a full-time night job and there's been sickness in the family, so I didn't have enough time to study."* Another ploy from the desperate offers the suggestion, *"Can I have an 'incomplete' and do an extra paper or something for a better grade?"* The argument from excessive subjectivity—there are countless variations—runs: *"I read my friend's paper and it wasn't all that much better than mine, yet she got a higher grade. How come?"* Similarly difficult to respond to (at least in a way likely to satisfy a grievant) is the allegation of instructor rigidity and inflexibility: *"My overall score*

QUESTIONS ABOUT PROFESSIONAL ETHICS

1. A student confides to a former teacher that she has a "problem pregnancy." The professor informs the student's faculty advisor that the student should be urged to seek counseling. The student reacts with shock and dismay. She accuses her former professor of betraying a confidence. He defends his action, claiming he was simply trying to get help for her. The distraught student refuses any further contact either with the teacher *or* her advisor. Should the teacher be rebuked or disciplined for having violated the student's confidential disclosure, even if the violation of privacy was well intentioned?

2. A departmental audit reveals that no African American student has ever earned an "A" in any course taught by Professor Y. Confronted by her department chair, the teacher emphatically denies racist bias in her grading. Word leaks out that Professor Y has been questioned about her grading practices. Moreover, unconfirmed rumors persist that she has been heard making racist remarks in private. A disgruntled black student, who was formerly enrolled in one of the teacher's courses, now threatens to file a grievance or lawsuit. What should be done?

3. A graduate student uncovers a journal article authored by his major advisor. It is apparent that part of the text is adapted—without acknowledgment or credit—from a seminar paper the student himself previously submitted to satisfy a requirement in the professor's course. What, if anything, should the student do? If the student's charge of plagiarism turns out to be well founded, what should be done with the offending professor?

4. Professor Z repeatedly pokes fun in his class at feminist literature and ridicules what he disparagingly refers to as the "pseudo-intellectual pretensions" of Women's Studies as an academic discipline. Some students object. His rejoinder is that anyone is free to defend feminism, and that his remarks are only intended to provoke discussion and controversy. However, his attacks continue. Several of his students claim to be feeling intimidated. How should the situation be handled?

5. A student enrolls in a course taught via "distance education." He has been led to believe the course will be offered on campus and simultaneously broadcast via compressed interactive video to remote sites elsewhere. Instead, at the first class meeting, the instructor announces that *all* of the course content will be posted online. There will be no live synchronous interaction between students and teacher. Nor will

continues

there be interaction among students. No scheduled class sessions will convene. Basically, the course will offer an electronic version of a correspondence course, utilizing an auto-tutorial format. The student objects, claiming he pays tuition for "a real live teacher." Is his complaint justified?

6. Professor X, a renowned authority in his field, is scheduled to teach a given course. At the last minute, having just been awarded a major research grant, he "buys out" his time in order to pursue his research. A qualified but unknown part-time adjunct professor is hired to teach the course in his place. A student delegation drafts a protest, claiming they paid to hear Professor X, not some substitute instructor. What should be done?

7. Professor X teaches a class on the history of American foreign policy since 1945. The entire course, according to disaffected students, amounts to one long diatribe on the professor's part against what he terms "U.S. fascist imperialism." Assigned readings in the course reflect the same point of view. The professor allegedly does not allow students to defend alternative, more charitable interpretations of American foreign policy in the postwar period. Professor X is an acknowledged expert in his specialty. He makes it clear that agreement with his views is prerequisite to students' success in the course. Complaints mount. The professor retorts that his right to advance a particular view is protected by academic freedom. What should be done?

8. Professor A is notorious for his combativeness, rigidity, and authoritarianism in class. He is widely perceived to be rigid and overbearing. He reportedly scares and intimidates his students. No one in class dares to challenge anything he says. But, as he points out in response to faculty critics, he is consistently successful in getting his students to achieve at a very high performance level. Does the end (high achievement) justify the means (harassment and intimidation)?

9. It is discovered that a young, single instructor has been involved in a clandestine, romantic relationship with one of her former students. Both parties claim the relationship has always been totally consensual. Records indicate the student was once awarded an "A" in a class taught by the instructor. Although conceding the "appearance" of a possible conflict of interest, both the student and the instructor insist the grade was well deserved; and they rebuff suggestions that they terminate their relationship. How should the institution respond, if at all?

fell only one point below the cut-off between an 'A' and a 'B'—I think I deserve the benefit of the doubt and should get the higher grade."

There are few hard-and-fast rules for dealing with student complaints over grading. In time, with experience, one learns how to defuse or deflect most criticism. But it is still important to deal with situations where in fact there may be legitimate grounds for changing a grade. A major consideration to bear in mind, whether the student has a valid argument or not, is the importance of treating the claimant with respect and dignity.

No good purpose is served by your becoming overly defensive or belligerent, as some faculty are prone to do when under challenge. Feigned commiseration with the student serves no good purpose either. Nor does a flat refusal to listen to what a student has to say. A matter-of-fact explanation of why a particular grade was awarded is—or should be—sufficient. And above all, having laid out the rules at the very beginning of the course, you as instructor have afforded yourself the best protection against charges of arbitrariness or unfairness later on.

Minor irritants in the classroom can be dealt with in much the same way—that is, by rehearsing your expectations and requirements well in advance. Typical situations that sometimes need to be addressed include chronic tardiness, distractions caused by students engaged in whispered conversations while class is underway, excessive absences from class, students using cell phones during class, failure to turn in assignments on time, students who constantly interrupt the instructor with questions or who monopolize class discussions, eating and drinking in class, and so on.

It sounds simple, and it is: Decide beforehand what policies and procedures you intend to enforce; discuss them with the class or include a statement on your course syllabus; and stick to your guns so long as your rules are manifestly reasonable.

Only in extremely rare cases do instances of unacceptable student behavior escalate to the point where some third-party intervention is required. A new faculty member experiencing difficulties should not hesitate to ask for help and advice from senior colleagues or from the department chair, if or when the need arises. Instances involving a student's cheating on a test or documented plagiarism afford cases in point—in such situations it is highly advisable to bring in disinterested outside parties to mediate and determine an appropriate response.

Infrequent but not totally unheard of are situations where a student intimates he or she might be willing to exchange sexual favors for a better grade. If ever a situation called for tact and diplomacy, this is it. No teacher should even consider entering into any such Faustian bargain. Yet neither can an offer be wholly ignored, no matter how subtle the intimation. First, the possibility always exists that signals were misread, by either party, and that the person's intentions were misconstrued. Second, the offer must be declined without turning it into a personal rejection of the individual involved. Third, there is always the temptation to overreact with shock, scorn, indignation, or anger, any of which can serve only to exacerbate matters.

Depending on your personality style and confidence level, there are several possible responses. You can try to brush off the overture as a jest. Or you can pretend not to understand and move on quickly to other matters. Or, in a low-key, nonjudgmental way, you can politely reject the advance, explaining that it would compromise your own professional integrity. Much depends on the specific circumstances and individuals involved. At best a sexual advance makes for an awkward situation devoutly to be avoided if at all possible.

Sometimes new faculty members need to be reminded, you are no longer a student, nor are you one of your students' peers. You can be a friend without trying to be a "buddy." You can be helpful to a student as a mentor or advocate without becoming an "enabler." You can serve to a limited extent as a student's confidant, but never with the same emotional intimacy enjoyed between equals. Professionalism, whatever else it may entail, demands of faculty in their dealings with students that a certain subtle distance be preserved. On the other hand, in today's increasingly impersonal, bureaucratized institutions of higher learning, it must be said, the problem between professors and students is not too much comradery or intimacy. More characteristically, it is the remoteness and lack of interaction between the two groups that should prompt concern.

Points in Review

- Students learn more not when they are passive recipients of information but when they are actively engaged in its acquisition. Learning is an action process.
- What happens on the first day of class sets the tone and defines the character of the entire course.
- So-called high risk instructional strategies require that the teacher relinquish a measure of control over how and when students learn.
- Problem solving, group work, and collaborative learning exemplify effective strategies to promote active learning.
- Students differ in their respective learning preferences and styles.
- Faculty typically overestimate their ability to conduct evaluations of learning that are both valid and reliable. Many academics fail to give

careful consideration to the work of designing cogent assessments of student performance.

- Feedback to students should occur early and often.
- Testing should serve to reinforce the process of learning.
- Teachers should be familiar with the advantages and disadvantages of norm-referenced and criterion-referenced grading.
- Essay questions testing at high learning levels should be conducted with the same care as multiple-choice exams.
- Faculty peer assessment of teaching can contribute to instructional improvement.
- Ethical considerations govern practically all aspects of professional conduct.

CHAPTER 5

ADVISING STUDENTS

Undergraduate Student Advisement

Responsibility for mentoring students is not something most new faculty actively seek out, give much consideration to in advance, or for which they spend much time preparing.[1] Yet in one way or another, most faculty members are called on to counsel and advise students, both informally and formally, in several different contexts or settings.[2]

As a matter of ordinary institutional routine, advising students is usually a humdrum affair. Under some circumstances, it can alter a student's life forever.

The most common faculty-student interaction occurs as a natural extension or outgrowth of instruction. A student enrolled in a course comes to the professor with an inquiry about an assignment, a complaint about a test, or, occasionally (though perhaps not nearly as frequently as the teacher might like), questions relating to the substantive content of the course itself. The ensuing exchange is likely to be both brief and narrowly focused, even adversarial in tone at the outset, depending on the issue at hand. It happens most often when the student has a specific problem with the course material, is dissatisfied with a grade, needs extra time to satisfy a requirement, or is called to account for having missed too many classes, and so on.

Even when precipitated by some sort of crisis or difficulty, however, the encounter always carries with it the potential for becoming more than a discussion about a course-related issue. If some degree of rapport has been established and the student feels comfortable disclosing personal information, the entire interaction can shift in a different and positive direction. This is especially true when the student senses the teacher is genuinely interested in his or her welfare and seems receptive to pursuing non-course-related concerns. Most students appreciate a good listener.

What began as a problem may evolve into a conversation ranging across a broader array of topics: questions about the student's academic area of specialization, possible difficulties in other courses, study skills, future career choices, employment prospects after graduation, and so on. The faculty member who is willing to take the time has an opportunity to offer suggestions and ideas that a student may find helpful. Out of such casual conversations, sometimes, lasting friendships between teacher and learner are forged.

Equally important is the working relationship that develops between a faculty member and a student advisee. In a majority of cases, perhaps, whatever interaction takes place tends to be confined to questions about course schedules and academic degree requirements. But occasionally a simple advisor-advisee consultation expands into an exploration of larger issues or concerns—the student's long-term goals, career aspirations, personal interests, future plans, and so forth. As many faculty will attest, assisting students in planning, choosing, and clarifying their objectives or priorities can be a rewarding experience, apart from whatever benefits accrue to the advisee.

How individuals are assigned to advisors, and what sort of advising takes place, varies from school to school. Where an institution offers postbaccalaureate degree programs, the time-intensive task of mentoring and advising graduate students rests with the faculty or their representative, a divisional or departmental coordinator of graduate studies. Undergraduate majors in a department are usually assigned to individual faculty advisors within that academic unit. In a small department with few baccalaureate majors, it is customary to designate a single faculty person as an academic advisor. In larger units, advisees are distributed among all (or nearly all) of the department's faculty members.

The particulars of how pre-baccalaureate student advising responsibilities are distributed between faculty and full-time staff advisors differ from one institution to another. Few if any colleges assign all incoming students directly and wholly to the faculty for advising. Nor, at the opposite extreme, are there many schools where all student advising is conducted from first to last by a staff of nonfaculty advisors and counselors. The more common arrangement is to split advising duties between the two groups.[3]

One approach taken by some colleges and universities relies on a campus-wide advising office staffed by nonfaculty professionals to apprise entering students of general academic requirements, rules, and regulations. All actual transactions must then be approved by each student's designated faculty advisor. Closely related is the arrangement in which an advisement office offers consultative services only to underprepared students, those admitted under probationary status, and those who have yet to declare a major. All other students are assigned directly to a faculty advisor or to a particular academic unit for further assistance.

Some schools employ a "dual" system under which each student has two advisors. Staff working within a centralized facility advise students on general requirements, polices, and procedures, while all academic considerations pertaining to a major are handled by the appropriate faculty unit. More common by far is the "total intake" model whereby advisory staff provide services to all students throughout some specified period of time on campus, after which students are handed over to the instructional faculty for whatever further advising may be needed.

A variation on the same theme is afforded by the so-called satellite system, where there is no centralized advising office, but each college or division within the university supports its own advising staff for students, up to a stipulated point in their undergraduate careers. Thereafter students are assigned to individual faculty advisors within the division.

The hand-off point may be defined by how many credit hours the student has accumulated, or by class rank attained (for example, the end of the student's sophomore year), or by some other appropriate criterion. The feature shared by most comprehensive advising systems is the progression from initial program planning, conducted with help from a full-time staff advisor, to academic consultation with an instructional faculty member throughout the latter phase of the student's campus experience.

Faculty Attitudes Toward Advising

While some faculty profess to enjoy student advising and many of them strive to do a competent job, many do not.[4] The explanation is simple—people tend to concentrate on what they get rewarded for doing. Unfortunately, for a whole complex of reasons, there exist few extrinsic faculty incentives for advising. Notwithstanding, there are those who, even in the absence of much recognition accorded their efforts, are generous with their time and energy in counseling students. But these individuals are rare. Among larger institutions especially, faculty reward systems governing annual salary increments, tenure, or promotion tend to give no more than perfunctory attention to how well an individual faculty member functions as an advisor or how much time they spend at it. Not surprisingly, in these settings conscientious undergraduate faculty mentors are hard to find.

Like the category of faculty service, advisement is an activity that, even when done well, tends not to be weighted proportionately compared with publishing or teaching performance. Two-year community colleges and most liberal arts colleges probably do a better job of emphasizing the importance of student advising than do larger public institutions where faculty workloads are more diverse. In research-focused schools, unfortunately, the work of undergraduate student advisement is likely to be regarded by most faculty as an unwelcome chore and a distraction from other more pressing duties.

Even among those who do appreciate the importance of helping students choose their academic programs and move in timely fashion through them toward graduation, many faculty members still are inclined to feel their time is better expended elsewhere. Academic advising is a purely clerical function, runs a not uncommon if short-sighted claim, a workaday exercise that entails little more than checking off courses completed against degree requirements listed in the catalog or on a computer screen.

Helping students navigate their way through the institution tends to be time consuming. "Much of my time," one respondent from a study of faculty attitudes toward advising is quoted as having declared, is "helping students find their way through the frustrating and unnecessary maze of red tape at this university, getting information that snotty secretaries and pompous professors will not provide."[5] Most of it, some faculty allege, could be done by "an astute secretary" or a trained staff person.[6]

"I think academic advising is largely a waste of time," opines another faculty member. "Students of college age and ability should be able to choose their own courses and should have the responsibility for doing so on their own." He continues, "Most advising functions are concerned with treating the students as though he [or she] were still in high school. This is demeaning to the student and deprives him of the opportunity to be responsible for his own well-being."[7]

A widespread perception among faculty is that those who excel at advising are penalized by being asked to do more of it. "On bad days," one faculty member muses, "I think . . . advising is like dishwashing. Actually, advising does have a lot of the characteristics of dishwashing: it's neglected; it causes a great deal of problems; and . . . if you get good at it . . . [you] end up doing it all the time."[8] But on good days, most faculty will concede that while they may not enjoy the work of advising itself, they prize the interaction with students that periodic consultations or conferences afford.

Advising: Why It Matters

If faculty oftentimes are less than enthusiastic about the task of advising students, students in turn tend not to think highly of the quality of academic advisement they are apt to receive. As two recent commentators on advisement issues aptly phrase it, "Next to limited parking and food in the residence hall that doesn't compare to home cooking, academic advising has been on the top ten list of student concerns for many years."[9] When undergraduates are asked to rate the quality of various student services on campus, advisement is almost always maligned.[10]

As plenty of disgruntled students will testify, for instance, there are times when, passed from one office to another, they find it nearly impossible to get an authoritative interpretation of rules and policies governing degree programs. Straightforward information on curricular requirements for graduation can be just as elusive. Apparently, the faculty's collective capacity to create a curricular labyrinth, almost Byzantine in its complexity, far outstrips the capacity of most of its individual members to lead students through the resulting maze en route to the degree. (From an actual college catalogue: "The student must complete three semester-credit-hours in each knowledge domain listed under sub-sections 1 through 5 in Section III, unless the student has previously completed nine or more semester-credit hours from any combination of two or more of the general core requirements listed in Section II. . . .")

Considering what is known about the importance of advising relationships, one might suppose all institutions of higher learning would assign more support resources and pay more attention to student advising than is usually the case. Virtually all relevant research serves to underscore the same point: Academic advising is the single most important factor determining students' academic success and overall satisfaction in college.[11] More specifically, the likelihood of a student persisting in college is closely related to nonclassroom contacts with faculty. Regular faculty-student interaction, it has been shown repeatedly, increases student academic success, satisfaction, and retention. Moreover, it is a leading factor affecting student achievement as well as academic skill development, not to mention expressed satisfaction with the collegiate experience in general.[12]

Students who report frequent and high-quality interaction with faculty members tend also to experience a greater sense of "fit" between themselves and the institution they attend. Not only are they are more involved with academics and more focused on success, they are more likely to be active participants in co-curricular activities on campus. In short, they are fully involved in the life of the college or university and report a higher sense of affiliation with it than students who lack satisfying faculty contacts.

Conversely, several studies over the years have found that students who dropped out of college were dissatisfied with or had received limited academic advising. The clear implication is that attrition and retention rates among collegians have much to do with the quality of relationships students are both able and willing to develop with faculty and staff. As Margaret King observes, once a student enters an institution, a great deal depends thereafter on the quality of that student's interaction with peers, staff, and faculty. If the interaction is positive and serves to help the student integrate within the campus community, then that individual will be more likely to persist at that institution. But if it is limited or negative in character, the student will be more likely to withdraw.[13]

With unimprovable brevity, Alexander Astin, writing in *Four Critical Years*, sums up a consistent pattern revealed through years of research:

> Student-faculty interaction has a stronger relationship to student satisfaction with the college experience than any other involvement variable or, indeed, any other student or institutional characteristic. Students who interact frequently with faculty are more satisfied with all aspects of their institutional experience, including student friendships, variety of courses, intellectual environment, and even administration of the institution. Finding ways to encourage greater personal contact between faculty and students might increase students' satisfaction with their college experiences.[14]

Faculty who have given the matter thoughtful attention tend to sense as much. "One thing I believe to be essential," observes George Douglas of the University of Illinois, "is that every student . . . have a 'real' adviser, that is, a full-time faculty member who is acquainted with that student, who knows at least something about his or her interests and peculiarities of mind." He deplores how the advising function on all too many campuses is a "perfunctory" administrative chore. "I have known places where the 'adviser' does nothing but rubber-stamp a student's program card—sometimes not even doing an adequate job of checking to see whether the student is fulfilling graduation requirements," Douglas notes. "I have even known students who have found the adviser's function so useless that they forge his or her signature . . . rather than wait for an appointment."[15]

Equally candid if somewhat exaggerated is an assessment offered up not too many years ago by Robert and Jon Solomon in *Up the University: Recreating Higher Education in America*. Student advisees, they allege, "get little advice, and most of it is useless or worse. University advisers rarely know particular professors or specific courses and are wedded to the official requirements instead of the students' needs and interests." As academic advisors, they argue, faculty "have proved themselves notoriously inadequate for the job." Professors, they further allege, "are often ignorant of courses and quality even within their own department—and in the name of 'professional courtesy' they will often not tell the truth anyway. They are typically ignorant altogether of what goes on across campus."[16]

How much truth resides in the Solomon's harsh indictment of faculty advisors remains open to challenge. Certainly there are individuals on every college campus who advise desultorily and who invest no more effort in the task than absolutely necessary. But in fact not all academic advisors are ill informed, incompetent, or dishonest. Many in fact *do* try to make themselves as accessible as possible, to offer accurate and reliable information to their advisees in conference, to communicate requirements clearly, and, as the situation demands, to offer students whatever support and encouragement they need in order to succeed.

So far as new faculty members are concerned, most department chairs or unit heads know from experience that it is unwise to assign advising duties to a faculty member who has just arrived on campus and is still struggling to get acclimated. Hence, a "grace period" of a year or so is usually allowed before the person is assigned student advisees. Nevertheless, sometimes exigent circumstances require even the rawest faculty recruit to help shoulder advising duties. Two commentators' terse advice: "For a beginner it's particularly tough: there's a lot to learn about being a student on your campus. Consider it an important responsibility . . ."[17]

Working with Student Advisees

Specialists in the field of academic student advising have long lamented the relative scarcity of training programs, workshops, and other types of in-service training designed to help faculty function more effectively as advisors.[18] Most institutions make some cursory provision for orienting faculty, though whether what is commonly offered is sufficient for the purpose remains a topic of disagreement on many campuses. Overcoming faculty antipathy or indifference to special training also poses problems. In any event, it is not terribly difficult to identify some of the major elements that make for effective advising and the skills or attributes advisors must acquire:[19]

- Knowledgeability about academic curricula and degree program requirements. A good advisor is well informed about current degree program requirements within the department, the division, and the institution as a whole. This is no small task. Even in an age of computerized degree program audits and online information, the advisor must have a thorough command of information to monitor students' progress and to interpret authoritatively program and graduation requirements.
- Knowledgeability about institutional policies, procedures, and facilities. Student advisees expect their advisors to be well informed about rules

and regulations, deadlines, schedules, and institutional procedures. They are liable to become extremely irritated when professors rationalize their ignorance with the excuse, "I just don't have a good head for all these details." Information items needed usually include the following:

—Important dates: when students may register for classes, the last day to add or drop a course, the last day to withdraw, when classes start, when classes end, when midterms and finals are scheduled.

—Withdrawals: what procedures govern withdrawals and what constitutes legitimate grounds for doing so without penalties.

—Costs: current tuition costs and miscellaneous fees.

—Support facilities: the location of psychological counselors (a counseling center); staff advisors (an advising center); where students can seek assistance with writing problems or study skills (writing center or academic support office), find a tutor, apply to graduate school, or get career counseling (career-planning center); where the GRE, MCAT, and LSAT exams are administered; what office handles grievances; where to go to petition for grade changes; how to obtain or send an official copy of a student's transcript.

—Graduate admissions: application process and requirements for admission to graduate school.

—Declaration of a major: when and where students may declare or change a major, or obtain information about eligibility requirements (grade point average).

• Referrals. An advisor who is well informed is more likely to be responsive to students' questions and can more accurately refer advisees to other agencies, offices, and on-campus facilities as individual circumstances warrant. The mark of a conscientious advisor is his or her willingness to make phone calls on the spot on a student's behalf rather than simply suggesting that the advisee embark on a hunt for needed information on his or her own. Students appreciate having a "proactive" faculty advocate who is able and willing to ferret out the information and instructions they lack.

• Organization. A good academic advisor is well organized. Basic information is kept close at hand—brochures and flyers, catalogs, addresses, and phone numbers of campus facilities and services, names of resource persons, student files, worksheets, and advising records.

• Record keeping. The advising process is greatly facilitated when the faculty member maintains an up-to-date file for each student advisee.

Every file folder should include basic information on the student and a running record of decisions made at each conference.

- Preparation. Most advisors find it helpful to review an advisee's record immediately prior to a scheduled conference. It is important to be familiar with each student's academic track record, career goals, and progress to date.
- Listening. Advisors need to maintain an open, caring attitude toward advisees. Careful, active listening and sensitivity are called for in order to understand each student's unique needs and perspective.
- Accessibility. Academic advisors must set aside time to make themselves available to students, both for scheduled conferences and more casual drop-in meetings.
- Patience. The single greatest source of frustration for a faculty advisor oftentimes is the indecisive advisee: the student who passively waits to be told what to do, who is entirely undecided about what courses to take, who is uncertain about his or her long-term goals, and who appears either unwilling or unable to assume responsibility for making academic choices. The least useful response is for an advisor to accede to the student's indecision and to take charge. The more appropriate response is to do whatever is necessary to help the student work through the issues involved and arrive at his or her own conclusions. Ultimately, the student must be encouraged (or compelled) to assume ownership of whatever choices and decisions are made.
- Advocacy. An effective faculty advisor willingly takes on the role of advocate or ombudsman for his or her advisees. The student may be confused or frustrated, caught in bureaucratic red tape, feel that he or she has been treated unfairly or victimized by institutional policy and procedure. The task of the advisor in such situations is to act on the student's behalf, not necessarily always accepting the student's side of a dispute at face value, but seeking in an even-handed fashion to resolve the difficulty, to cut through the red tape, or otherwise to assist the advisee in resolving whatever issues may be at stake.
- Respect for confidentiality. Legal liabilities aside, an academic advisor needs to be sensitive to issues of privacy. A student advisee is entitled to expect that his or her records will not be shared indiscriminately, and that confidences shared with a faculty member will not be betrayed. Nothing undermines an advising relationship more quickly than a perceived violation of trust.

A CLASSIFIED ADVERTISEMENT
FOR THE IDEAL FACULTY ADVISOR:

Wanted: A thoughtful critic who is also a constructive counselor and mentor, a stringent taskmaster who is also a supportive friend, a thoughtful intellectual who is also an effective tutor, a principled bureaucrat who knows how to work the system, a productive scholar who is also a charismatic teacher, and a respected authority in the field who is also available to students at any time. The successful candidate will be a paragon of virtue, an effective communicator, an individual of infinite patience with a good eye for detail, and a person who has both an uncompromised commitment to the welfare of students and unlimited time for advising them.

—adapted in part from Roger B. Winston, Jr. and Mark C. Polkosnik,
"Advising Graduate and Professional School Students,"
Developmental Academic Advising, ed. Roger B. Winston, Jr. et al.,
(San Francisco, Calif.: Jossey-Bass, 1984), 287

Advice to New Faculty Advisors

Recent literature on student advising appears to offer few suggestions tailored specifically for new faculty advisors. A survey conducted by Matthew Morano of George Mason University sought to identify the biggest "challenges" faced by beginning advisors nationwide. His poll ultimately identified three major concerns cited most frequently by respondents: the imperative to master a vast amount of detailed information in short order; the problem of preserving the distinction between "advising" and "enabling" students; and difficulties associated with telling students what they do not want to hear.[20]

New advisors polled consistently reported their most urgent problem was the amount of detailed information they needed to master even at the very beginning. "I was overwhelmed by the amount of information I needed to know in order to be effective," one advising neophyte disclosed.[21] For many, the task of knowing whom to contact and when, coupled with the perceived inadequacy of the prior training they had received, posed the single greatest difficulty they faced.

Practical solutions offered included seeking out an advising colleague for advance mentoring; taking time to explore service offices around campus to which students might need to be referred; organizing catalog information for easy access; developing a contact list of resource persons;

and soliciting student-generated information about specific professors and courses.

The second challenge cited was difficulty in setting limits. Many faculty novices reported feeling uncertain about how much should be done on a student's behalf and when it was more appropriate to require the student to take action on his or her own behalf. "I never know how much customer service is too much," one respondent confessed. "When I am helping a student, I want the student to be able to eventually do this work for herself, but I don't want her to go away feeling [as though] I did not help her."[22]

Suggestions mentioned included setting boundaries (for example, not staying late with a student, not working though lunch); learning when and to whom to refer a student for counseling; brainstorming solutions to problems with a student rather than supplying directive answers; and showing advisees how to access their own records instead of doing it for them.

The third-ranked challenge cited by Morano involved telling students things they did not want to hear—for example, informing a student about the inadmissibility of transfer credits for course work completed elsewhere, explaining why an anticipated graduate date might be unrealistic and would likely be delayed, or correcting misinformation supplied by someone else. Proposed advice included assisting a student to identify alternative solutions to a problem, learning how to defuse a confrontation with a belligerent student, and conveying empathy and understanding even when obliged to serve as a bearer of bad news.

Morano concluded his report on an upbeat note: "Although new advisers face a myriad of challenges when they go from the classroom to an advising session," he remarked, "it is important to keep in mind that . . . problems, while difficult at times, can be overcome."[23]

A recurrent theme is the role of the advisor as a resource person. Academic advisors should be thoroughly conversant with the school's rules, procedures, time tables, and operating policies. When the rules change, the advisor must keep abreast of them and alert students as necessary.[24]

Knowledge of current employment demands, positions available in a given field, and job market trends is also desirable. Faculty members who are approached for the first time about serving as advisors are entitled to have access to the training they will need in order to be able to field such questions once newly assigned advisees begin appearing on their doorsteps.

As previously noted, advisors also serve as advocates for students. In his or her advocacy role, the advisor may be called upon to negotiate on a student's behalf with unbending or capricious faculty, administrators, and staff personnel; to "clear the way," so to speak, when a deserving student seeks an exception to normal procedures or rules; and to point the student in the right direction when he or she needs assistance. Again, advisor and advisee alike are ill served unless provision has been made to familiarize the faculty member with all of the major components of the campus's administrative and student support systems.

One function entails another. An important aspect of advising is knowing when and where to refer a student to other professionals as circumstances warrant. This referral role is particularly important when there are serious physical, mental, emotional, or spiritual issues at stake. Finally, advisors, ideally, are friends. As Petress expresses it, "Students typically enter college fearful, lonely, away from home, confused in a strange environment, and in need of an anchor, their advisor, to provide stability, assurance, consistency, an outlet for frustrations, someone to hear them out and to answer questions, and a source of confidential guidance, affirmation, and support."[25]

The Educative Potential of Academic Advising

It is often said that faculty members should view the work of student advising as an extension of their teaching. In a sense, this is a valid injunction. Consider, for example, the common situation where a faculty advisor is helping a student complete a projected plan of study. Frequently, the process is undertaken mainly in order to check off boxes on a sheet of curriculum requirements. Very little consideration is given by either advisor or advisee to the logic or rationale for the courses selected in order to satisfy general education requirements.

Thereby neglected are educational opportunities to help students understand how the general education or liberal-arts component of the undergraduate curriculum is intended to enrich, broaden, and extend their learning. Never having had the importance of subject-matter scope and breadth explained to them or emphasized, many students (lower-division undergraduates in particular) simply go through the motions, unknowingly suffering from a kind of curricular myopia. Consequently, it is not uncommon to find students resentful of the time and effort needed to satisfy general-education requirements, who view them as obstacles to the narrower courses of study they otherwise would pursue. As Carol Ryan emphasizes, "We need to be prepared to talk about the connections between disciplines or courses and also to discuss why certain courses are part of general education or core requirements or why other foundation work may be necessary. . . ."[26]

The faculty advisor's attitude is all-important. Nothing serves more effectively to discredit or undermine the legitimacy of general learning in the student's mind than the advisor's subtle reinforcement of the student's own

AN ADVISOR CHECKLIST:

Advance Preparation:

____I have posted my office hours and other times that I am available for advising.

____I have reviewed the catalogue, schedules of classes and advisor handbook and am familiar with basic academic policies.

____I have reviewed the names of my advisees, and I have updated their files.

Notes of Meeting with Advisee:

____We have reviewed the student's academic plan.

____We have reviewed progress made toward realizing the plan.

____We have discussed potential academic difficulties and possible remedies.

____We have reviewed specific requirements for graduation.

____We have discussed future course selections.

____We have discussed the student's involvement in other campus activities and his or her job demands (if any).

____We have discussed any additional concerns the student may have.

____We have set a future meeting time and have outlined what tasks need to be accomplished by then.

Follow-up Notes for Future Reference:

—adapted from Thomas J. Grites, "Techniques and Tools for Improving Advising," *Developmental Academic Advising*, ed. Roger B. Winston, Jr. et al., (San Francisco, Calif.: Jossey-Bass, 1984), 215.

resistance. The message may be conveyed by nothing more than a shrug, a rolling of the eyes, or the tone of voice assumed. The faculty member's behavior may be an attempt at commiseration with the student, or an implicit effort to be ingratiating. Or it can be overt, as when the advisor becomes defensive over the fact that the student's program has to fulfill certain requirements whose relevance is not apparent to either party (*"I don't know why you have to take all these courses either, but you can't fight the system."*).

A faculty member certainly is entitled to his or her own personal views about the propriety of certain curricular requirements, whether they have to do with general learning or the detailed requirements that must be satisfied to complete a particular academic major. But either way, it is the faculty member's professional obligation to be clear about what is appropriate when he or she is serving in an official capacity as a representative of the institution and its faculty body as a whole.

In dealing with students, one might argue, every faculty member has a responsibility to uphold institutional policies in good faith and to clarify their rationale if called on to do so. And if, as in the example of general learning, the faculty advisor happens to be a fervent advocate of liberal education, certainly the opportunity to communicate to a disaffected advisee why distribution requirements exist in the first place ought not to be missed. Academic advising affords many such "teaching moments."

There are other ways in which teaching and advising merge into one another. When a student's academic performance is unsatisfactory and assistance is sought, it is only natural for the advisor to begin suggesting intervention techniques. The advisor's inclination is try to work with the student, for example, in terms of improving time management, note taking, study skills, problem solving, or planning and organizational techniques.[27] Here too the advising function is as much a matter of instruction and coaching as it is anything else.

The line between academic advising, strictly speaking, and personal counseling is not always distinct either. The fact of the matter is, students do bring "baggage" with them. Personal concerns—financial worries, health problems, relationship issues, family pressures and responsibilities—clearly serve to impede academic performance. Yet so far as the student looking for help is concerned, there may be no clear demarcation in his or her mind between faculty "advising" and professional "counseling."[28] It therefore falls to the advisor to decide when the student would be best served by working with a trained, professional counselor. The actual referral itself must be handled with the utmost tact and sensitivity. Otherwise, a troubled, anxiety-ridden student may interpret the advisor's suggestion that he or she seek counseling as a form of rejection or even a betrayal of trust.

Deciding when to intervene and when the wiser course of action would be to refrain from becoming directly involved is an important judgment call. As Robert Berdahl astutely observes in a related connection, advising is a communication process that under some conditions or circumstances combines career planning, crisis counseling, and surrogate parenting, all rolled into one.[29]

INSTITUTIONAL GOALS
FOR ACADEMIC ADVISING

1. Assistance to the student in clarifying his or her life and career goals
2. Collaboration with the student in the development of educational plans
3. Identification of appropriate courses, consistent with the advisee's academic goals
4. Interpretation of institutional requirements, policies, and procedures
5. Enhancing student awareness of educational resources and academic support facilities
6. Evaluation of the student's academic progress toward established goals
7. Fostering the development of the student's decision-making skills
8. Referral to and use of institutional and community support services, where appropriate
9. Collection of student data regarding a student's needs, preferences, and performance for use in institutional policy making.

—modified from Council for the Advancement of Standards, *Standards and Guidelines for Student Services / Development Programs* (Iowa City: American College Testing Program, 1986), 11; reproduced in Susan H. Frost, *Academic Advising for Student Success, A System of Shared Responsibility* (Washington, D.C.: School of Education and Human Development, George Washington University, ASHE-ERIC Higher Education Report No. 3, 1991), 62.

Advising Graduate Students

Mentoring graduate students tends to be considerably more labor intensive and time consuming than advising undergraduates. At the master's degree level, the presumption is that candidates are somewhat more mature and more self-reliant than baccalaureate-level students. Moreover, there are additional complications not applicable in the case of undergraduates: preparing advanced students for matriculation or comprehensive examinations, orals, and, of course, the drafting and execution of a thesis.

Much the same considerations apply to the advising of doctoral students, who, although they are regarded more nearly as autonomous peers and "junior colleagues," do require extensive individualized attention. Especially at the outset, much "hand holding" is called for. Supervising a doctoral candidate demands time spent in assisting with the planning of an individualized course of study, assembling an advisory or dissertation committee, ensuring that residency requirements are properly interpreted and fulfilled, helping the student prepare for comprehensive written and oral examinations, and, ultimately, working up plans with the candidate for a dissertation.

Graduate-level advising demands that the faculty mentor be thoroughly conversant with all pertinent graduate school rules and regulations as well as with whatever degree-program requirements govern a student's course of studies. Although it is true that the degree candidate must take primary responsibility for compliance with policies and procedures, no graduate advisor can be effective unless he or she can provide precise guidance and direction. An additional responsibility for an advisor is to anticipate problems before they occur and help the student avoid them when possible.

It may seem absurd that a professor who has been hired on the basis of mastery of the details of a complex body of subject matter should be allowed to claim he or she is incapable of keeping graduate-degree program requirements straight, or that attending to "petty details" is beneath his or her dignity.[30] Still, it is a sad fact of modern academic life that there are times when students are pretty much left to their own devices, when advisors fail to advise, or when they make themselves so inaccessible that hapless students are left to fend for themselves or to seek counsel elsewhere.

Graduate advising, it must be said, differs in several fundamental ways from its undergraduate counterpart. The most significant difference is the role played by a faculty member in helping to "induct" the student neophyte into a body of professional knowledge or an academic discipline. Graduate school, ideally, is a time and place where academic apprentices learn how to become full-fledged scholars and work productively within a field of knowledge. As they grow in competence and proficiency, they begin to assume a new identity as academic professionals in their own right, especially at the doctoral level. The advisor's task is to facilitate, support, and guide that transformative process.

As former Harvard dean Henry Rosovsky puts it, the faculty advisor is a mentor, an intellectual surrogate parent, someone who will "extend a hand while crossing the dark valleys" on the way to graduation. Rosovsky recalls fondly one of his own advisors who was a "paragon" and exemplar throughout the long, tedious process of writing a dissertation. "All my letters were answered by return mail, typed with two fingers on an ancient typewriter. He made me feel that my work was important and that he enjoyed learning from me! During a difficult period he put me up at his house for a week, while we discussed my results for many hours every day." Rosovsky asks, "Do they still make them this way today?"[31]

New faculty who have accepted appointments at colleges without post-bachelor's - level degree programs obviously will not have graduate advising duties to assume. For those hired at colleges or universities where master's degrees are offered, graduate advisement may become a significant part of an assigned workload. At doctoral-degree-granting universities, a new faculty member hoping eventually to achieve tenure almost certainly will need to become involved sooner or later in the mentoring and advising of advanced-degree candidates.

Procedures and policies governing graduate education differ considerably from school to school. As a rule, it is the individual faculty member who must exercise the initiative to acquire eligibility for graduate-level advisement and achieve the proficiency to serve effectively. Useful steps for you to consider:

- Take the time early on to review the school's catalog and other materials pertaining to graduate education. Special attention should be paid to whatever descriptive literature and forms are made available to students seeking admission to graduate-degree programs. Some people find it helpful to develop a graphic "flow chart" or other schematic representation of the steps that take a student from initial application for admission to a degree program all the way through to graduation.
- Become thoroughly conversant with the major rules, regulations, policies, and procedures of the graduate division, graduate school, or other administrative body responsible for superintending graduate studies. Seek additional information, when necessary, from ranking administrative functionaries at the college, divisional, or departmental level whose responsibilities include graduate-studies administration.
- If admission to a graduate degree program requires a personal interview at the divisional or departmental level, sit in on an interview as an observer—learn what implicit or "unofficial" criteria, if any, actually govern a student's admission, above and beyond published standards. Try to develop a feeling for what senior colleagues are looking for in prospective program applicants. Ask to see and review students' written admission applications.
- Request a "walk through" of departmental degree requirements from an experienced colleague who currently advises graduate students. Particular attention should be paid to options and alternatives within a given set of degree requirements—what is allowed in terms of transfer credits, course substitutions, graduate work completed prior to a student's formal acceptance into a program, and so on.

- Ask to be allowed to attend and observe a program-planning conference of a new student advisee and his or her faculty advisor.
- Review back files of comprehensive or matriculation examinations to determine what type of information students are held accountable for and what format is used for evaluation purposes.
- Attend oral testing sessions (e.g., the oral defense of a dissertation, an oral review of a written comprehensive test, and so on); learn how they are conducted and what etiquette is customarily observed.
- Make a point of reviewing copies of recent master's theses or doctoral dissertations approved by colleagues in the department. Become familiar with the format, scope, and length, and the level of performance expectations from faculty to which such studies are approved responses.
- Be clear about what requirements or conditions govern a faculty member's eligibility to serve as a full-fledged graduate advisor (e.g., graduate faculty status). Since graduate advising is likely to be considered an element of any faculty member's assigned workload, progress toward achieving eligibility within some reasonable time frame may be considered important.
- Once eligible to do so, volunteer to serve on a student's advisory committee or to codirect a master's thesis with a more experienced colleague.
- Begin developing a resource list, consisting of the names of specific individuals (not simply offices) to contact when help with a particular issue or problem is needed. Learn who is responsible for what.
- Make a strong effort to learn the name and status of each assigned advisee. Request that each student schedule a conference for an initial orientation. Consider having the session over coffee or lunch. Give some thought to the possibility of holding group advisement sessions, if possible.
- Devise a personal record-keeping system for advisees that allows each student's academic progress to be documented and updated as necessary.
- Take time to explain to each advisee as early as possible a typical progression through the degree program; encourage them to ask questions; and be accessible to students on a regular, scheduled basis. Do not hesitate to ask students to share their perceptions of the institutional culture or environment and their reactions to it.
- Maintain an advising log documenting time spent on advising. Save the documentation for later reference when the time approaches to assemble a dossier for tenure review.

RECOMMENDATIONS FOR ADVISING GRADUATE AND PROFESSIONAL SCHOOL STUDENTS

1. Strive to build relationships with students based on trust, openness, and shared commitment to the student's success and the advancement of the discipline or profession. Convey confidence in the student's ability to succeed.
2. Make yourself accessible to students both for dealing with academic concerns and for informal social interaction.
3. Research, write, and publish with students.
4. Make the effort to remain current on rules, regulations, and policies that affect graduate students. Communicate needed information to advisees.
5. Make joint presentations with students at scholarly and professional meetings.
6. Give students specific feedback about their work. Lessen ambiguity about expectations, evaluations, and grades. Offer praise and positive evaluations to students whenever possible.
7. Assist students as they near graduation in preparing for the job search and in securing positions.
8. Confront students who lack the ability, attitude, or personal attributes necessary for completing the graduate program. Candor is important. Assist them in exploring alternative career options.

—summarized and adapted from Roger B. Winston, Jr. and Mark C. Polkosnik, "Advising Graduate and Professional School Students," *Developmental Academic Advising*, ed. Roger B. Winston, Jr. et al. (San Francisco, Calif.: Jossey-Bass, 1984), 309–311.

Unmentioned so far is another important mode of interaction between faculty members and graduate students, namely, that pertaining to the supervision and mentoring of graduate teaching assistants (GTAs). In larger institutions where enrollments in a basic lecture course may sometimes number in the hundreds, it has long been customary to utilize graduate students in an instructional support role. The well-established pattern is to assign leading responsibility for lecturing to a regular faculty member. (More often than not, this type of teaching assignment is handed over to a faculty newcomer, thereby freeing up senior personnel for the upper-level, specialized seminars they presumably prefer to teach.) To the weekly lectures of a large class delivered by that faculty member are then added multiple "lab" sections or discussion groups conducted by graduate students.

The assumption behind this shared arrangement is that the professor is best qualified to convey the main content of the course via standard lecture presentations, perhaps twice weekly for a three-hour-credit class. Graduate TAs, on the other hand, are entrusted with the work of extending, explaining, discussing, or applying the material within smaller class sections meeting separately from the lecture.

A variation on the theme is to assign responsibility for an introductory course to graduate teaching assistants exclusively, all of them working under the nominal supervision of a faculty coordinator, but left largely to their own devices so far as the actual delivery of instruction is concerned within their own respective classrooms. Freshman-level English and entry-level courses in such fields as biology or psychology at some institutions are commonly taught almost entirely by graduate students—economic considerations, if nothing else dictate their use as low-paid teaching staff. If it is possible to generalize, it must be said most of these academic apprentices strive diligently to do a good job with their teaching. Some end up doing quite well; unfortunately, others do not.

Responsibility for serving in the capacity of coordinator of graduate teaching assistants is liable to fall to a junior faculty member—for the same reason that newcomers tend to be assigned to teach the larger introductory courses within a given department. While the coordinator's role is an important one, it can be extremely demanding and time-consuming if carried out conscientiously. Logically, the challenge of mentoring novice pedagogues ought to be handled by senior faculty members with the most teaching experience. In practice, the task frequently falls on the least experienced faculty neophyte.

As the newest faculty member, you may conceivably find yourself placed in charge of a large lecture course, assisted by graduate teaching assistants. Or you may be assigned as coordinator for all of the graduate teaching assistants in the department. Your first move is to identify what amount of help and support is available for GTAs. In some schools, there is a campus-wide teaching support center or office charged with providing some type of instructional training for new assistants. You can build upon and extend whatever assistance such a center affords. At other universities, each school, college, or department mandates participation in a credit-bearing seminar geared to the needs of novice classroom instructors. Again, more informally, the custom in many institutions is for the GTA coordinator to hold an extended series of "brown bag" luncheon seminars devoted to teaching issues and problems.

Whatever the specific arrangements, your goal ought to be to provide graduate teaching assistants with as much direction, support, and counsel as they require, especially first-timers. Specifically, they will need regular opportunities to share ideas, to report back on the results of their classroom experiments and the instructional innovations they may have tried out, to ask questions, and to garner help and advice from others. They must have the opportunity to learn from one another about what works and what does not. Above all, they must not be allowed to feel they have been "abandoned" or left to sink or swim on their own.

Group meetings, convened on a regular and predictable basis, offer GTAs a chance not only to coordinate their individual efforts, but to share experiences and to learn from one another in ways that are likely to prove immediately helpful. In any event, time must be set aside for college teachers-in-training to discuss classroom management issues and problems in some type of group setting, to compare performance standards with their peers, or to work together on constructing tests and grading student work, and so on—the possibilities are quite broad.

As coordinator you will find it helpful to arrange for individual conferences with your graduate assistants as well. It is wise to require periodic updates or progress reports from each assistant. Also, it should be your practice periodically to drop in and observe one of your assistants' classes in progress. So long as it is mutually understood that the purpose is formative—to help him or her improve rather than to render a judgment about his or her competence—your visit may precipitate, as the cliché has it, a valuable "learning experience."

Supervising graduate teaching assistants is a form of advising or mentoring, although of course it combines elements of teaching and coaching and counseling as well. Graduate students, after all, are "junior colleagues" of the faculty; and the relationship of a faculty mentor to a teaching protégé is very much akin to that between a master craftsman and an apprentice. Hence, while it remains true to observe that the relationship carries with it a certain potential for volatility, ideally the challenge of working with graduate assistants is one of the most satisfying tasks a faculty member may be obliged to assume.

Discontinuities and Connections
within the Academic Community

In some idyllic past, according to Kenneth Eble, author *The Craft of Teaching,* professors and students mingled personal and intellectual development so closely, there was no need for a special class of academic advisors or counselors. Counseling and advice giving were integral to the total educative process; and campus life and formal learning were indistinguishable aspects of a seamless whole. Today's radical discontinuities of learning, reflected by the separation of classwork from out-of-class activities, of one class from another, and of one discipline from another, had not yet poisoned the groves of academe.[32] In the closely knit collegiate community of yesteryear, everything worked together in the service of each student's holistic development—intellectual, physical, mental, moral, esthetic, and spiritual.

Of course, no such roseate past has ever existed. Only in imagination or myth, Eble admits, has there ever been a time when colleges or universities were true educative communities, places whose exclusive focus and highest aim were nurturing and cultivating the young men and women entrusted to their care. In the real world today, he judges, formal advising of students, although undoubtedly needed for program planning and ensuring students' compliance with degree requirements, serves to a far greater extent than most people realize as a surrogate for collegial intimacy—the goal to which institutions of higher learning once aspired, however imperfectly, but rarely attempt to realize in the contemporary world.

George Douglas judges that for a whole host of complex reasons, today's institutions of higher learning ultimately fail to provide a culture and a human setting in which education worthy of the term can truly flourish. Most colleges and universities, he avers, are too distracted, too full of activity, and too busy to be places of authentic learning or mentoring.[33] Faculty have too much to attend to; and despite their best intentions, the work environment on many campuses actively discourages their setting aside adequate time for students outside of class.

Eble, concurring, wonders what it would take to bring faculty and students closer together beyond enjoining the former to keep regular office hours and not to brush students off after class. "I have tried many of the usual devices: sponsoring clubs, taking students to lunch, having them into my home, arranging picnics and parties, worrying about formal counseling procedures and trying to find better ones," he reports ruefully. "I have drawn the conclusion that nothing works very long, that very little works without careful attention, and that students vary as widely as faculty in their need for enhancing institutional learning relationships and in their responses to ways of meeting that need."[34]

Historian Page Smith in his incisive critique of modern academe, *Killing the Spirit, Higher Education in America,* cites a telling anecdote recounted by Alfred North Whitehead's wife, Evelyn: "When we first came to Harvard, Altie's [Whitehead's] colleagues in the department said, *'Don't let the students interfere with your work!* Ten or fifteen minutes is long enough for any conference with them.'" But rather than heeding his colleagues' advice, Whitehead would often deliberately spend "a whole afternoon or a whole evening" in company with students. The traffic was two-way, for Whitehead felt he needed contact with young minds to keep his own springs flowing. "'It is all nonsense,' he said, 'to suppose that the old cannot learn from the young.'"[35]

Sustained interaction and exchange between professors and their students outside the classroom, Smith argues, are far more important than contacts within the lecture hall or laboratory. An ideal college or university, as Woodrow Wilson once insisted, should be a real "community, a place of close, natural, intimate association . . . of teachers with [students], outside the classroom as well as inside. . . ."[36]

The problem, of course, is that invocations of the old-time college with its greater intimacy and more leisurely rhythms—something already fast disappearing in Wilson's own time—fail to take into account the transformation of higher learning that has since transpired.[37] In an era of impersonal, complex mega-universities preoccupied with new, multifaceted missions, the likelihood that professors can find more time for their students is negligible.

Robert Berdahl, however, remains optimistic. He believes advising can and should be considered integral to the educator's role in academe, something that extends beyond but includes instruction, scholarship, and personal mentoring. "Not every teacher can, but the sum of our teaching must," he writes, "address the whole person if the classical idea of educating the whole person, of nurturing physical, spiritual, and intellectual development, is to be kept alive by the university. Teaching and advising need to be part of a seamless process, sharing the same intellectual sphere, informed by a relatively consistent educational philosophy. The vision of unity, the human unity, still obtains. A university which loses that vision," he concludes, "loses its only significant purpose."[38]

Points in Review

- Advising students is an integral aspect of faculty work.
- Advising tends not to be weighted proportionately or rewarded well compared with teaching and research.
- Faculty often feel intimidated and overwhelmed by the information load involved in advising students.

- Good advising increases student academic success, satisfaction, and retention.
- Faculty members who excel at advising students reportedly enjoy high job morale.
- Advising students requires thorough conversance with curricula, degree program requirements, and institutional policies and procedures. It demands a fair level of organization, preparedness, and conscientious record keeping.

CHAPTER 6

GETTING PUBLISHED

Teaching Versus Research: Pro and Con

Faculty in virtually all the nation's leading colleges and universities these days are expected to "do" research and to publish their findings. Even in institutions where teaching traditionally has been the primary mission, a faculty member's publication record is fast becoming a dominant consideration governing annual contract renewals, promotion, tenure, and salary adjustments. Recent trends at a growing number of four-year schools now clearly favor publishing as the assured route to career success.[1] The predictable result has been an outpouring of faculty-generated literature: a veritable avalanche of articles, research publications, technical reports, scholarly books, and new academic journals—the whole of almost stupefying proportions.

Critics of the "publish-or-perish" imperative allege that an exaggerated focus on research productivity—or, rather, on the frequency with which faculty publish in professional journals—has had a debilitating effect on higher education generally, and on college teaching in particular. Defenders of the new dispensation are just as insistent that publishing is by no means incompatible with teaching. In fact, it is said, the two serve to reinforce one another. True or not, nowhere else in academe perhaps (the possible exception being debate over faculty tenure) is dichotomous rhetoric of the "either/or" variety more vividly illustrated than in polarized debates over the relationship between teaching and research.

A characteristic rationale for faculty publishing is that it stimulates the flow of ideas, new information, and inspiration needed to keep classroom teaching both vital and current. The modern college professor, it is alleged, should not be seen simply as a disseminator or *transmitter* of received knowledge to students, someone who depends on others to advance a field of study or discipline without making some independent contribution of his or her own. Rather, today's academic is expected to *create* new knowledge, generating insights and otherwise furthering scholarship in ways that ultimately inform classroom discourse.

Denials and allegations to the contrary notwithstanding, defenders argue, teaching and research taken together should not be thought of as a "zero-sum" game where one must choose between them.[2] Conducting research does not—or need not—lead to a neglect of teaching, any more than attending to instruction vitiates a professional obligation to share in some public arena the outcome of one's scholarly and creative endeavors. These two interdependent aspects of a professor's duties are by no means antithetical to one another. What is called for, rather, is some sort of synergistic "balance" between the two.

Partisans on the other side of the argument concede that under certain circumstances teaching and research may enliven one another. But, they argue, the combination is, as one writer phrases it, "not always for anyone, not at all for everyone, not in the same proportion for every university."[3] Some go further. "To talk about the 'balance' needed between research and teaching," Benjamin Barber of Rutgers University observes, "is, at best, an exercise in wishful thinking. At worst it is a lie." What he calls the "dirty little secret" of American higher education, known to every faculty member who manages to gain tenure is this: "No one ever was tenured at a major college or university on the basis of great teaching alone; and no one with a great record of research and publication was ever denied tenure because of a poor teaching record."[4]

He might have added, what was once true exclusively of research-focused universities is now increasingly applicable to regional institutions as well, not to mention a substantial and ever-expanding number of private liberal arts colleges. Even among lower-echelon schools of modest size and local focus, faculty publishing, once strictly optional and pursued as a matter of personal initiative, is now becoming more and more an institutional mandate. In the competitive scramble for visibility and "standing," the evident tendency seems to be one of smaller colleges and universities striving to emulate their more prestigious brethren by expropriating their faculty incentive and reward systems.

As for the argument that published scholarship is the lifeblood of inspired teaching, critics concede merit to the claim that advanced graduate students benefit when their professors are doing "cutting edge" research and in other ways are dealing directly with the latest issues in the field. What is more problematic is the presumption that advanced specialized research has much at all to do with *undergraduate* teaching.[5] Connections between the ideas, problems, and findings of research studies and the subject matter of instruction in lower-level courses, more often than not, are apt to range somewhere between the tenuous and the nonexistent.

William Schaefer of the University of California-Los Angeles insists that the time and energy faculty expend on specialized research cannot help but encourage a certain neglect of instruction. The attention paid to generating publishable manuscripts, he feels, reduces the time that could and should be spent on preparing for classes and working with students. "As a profession we . . . are continuing to stress the less important—dissemination in print— over the most important—dissemination in the classroom—and in so doing are forcing our undergraduate students to pay a terrible price." As he sees it, "we are cheating not only our students but the society that innocently supports us that, or so I would argue, we have no other legitimate purpose than to serve."[6]

Despite repeated assurances from the leadership at large research universities that teaching is still valued and remains a top campus priority, the common faculty perception is that professorial rewards are far more dependent on published research and grantsmanship than on teaching.[7] And so far as claims and counterclaims about the linkage between teaching and research are concerned, evidence appears mixed. The preponderance of empirical data garnered from scores of studies conducted in recent decades indicate rather persuasively that claims about creative ties between the two have little basis in fact. Research and teaching appear to be only very loosely related—which is to say, there is scant evidence to support the view that research productivity predicts classroom performance, or vice versa.[8] Just as good teachers are not always skilled researchers, productive researchers do not necessarily make outstanding teachers.

Confusing the dispute somewhat is the fact that "research" is by no means a single, undifferentiated activity.[9] The prevailing paradigm, of course, is one of rigorous statistical analysis, controlled experimentation, and inquiry leading to the discovery of new empirical knowledge. But it is worth reiterating what should be obvious: that scholarship can and does assume many different legitimate forms, depending on the field or discipline involved. In other words, much of what is termed "research" is in fact critical and speculative, a matter of argumentation or exegesis, rather than the scientific experimentation, discovery, or invention popularly associated with the term.

Part and parcel of the mystique of faculty research is the notion of scholarly inquiry breaking through the boundaries of the discipline to uncover new truths or of validating novel ways of conceptualizing and organizing extant data. Engaging in the work of original research of this sort *is* undoubtedly an excellent means for keeping abreast of the latest developments in a field—indeed, a leading researcher may help create or define such developments within the discipline. But the argument that *all* faculty should be engaged in original research collapses, so dissenters allege, when it is claimed that the *only* way of staying current in the field is by pursuing a research agenda leading to publication.

The fact of the matter is, it does not necessarily follow that if one fails to publish, one will inevitably fall years behind and somehow be rendered incapable of conveying to students the latest information on a subject. Good teaching, it has been rightly suggested, may require only the enthusiasm, interest, and self-discipline to keep reading and going to conferences and perusing the latest research reported.[10] When all is said and done, currency in the discipline does not necessarily demand that each and every professor who teaches be directly involved in doing firsthand research and publishing in that field.

Scholarship at Gunpoint

Is the efflorescence of faculty publishing justified on any other grounds? Jacques Barzun for one thinks not, terming it "scholarship at gunpoint."[11] Historian Page Smith is equally acerbic in his characterization of today's mushrooming professorial literature as "busywork on a vast, almost incomprehensible scale." Much of what appears in print, he estimates, never should have been written in the first place, much less published. What it all really amounts to in his view is a corpus of verbiage "as broad as the ocean and as shallow as a pond."[12]

No more charitable in his estimation is George Douglas of the University of Illinois who professes to find most academic writing afflicted by a ponderous and nearly incomprehensible argot, writing that by any measure is overspecialized beyond legitimate disciplinary needs. Much of it, he claims, consists of microscopic analyses of narrowly drawn topics far removed from issues of larger public import. Compelled to publish when they have little to say but who nevertheless must make their writing seem significant, faculty "miniaturists" serve up, at best, as he phrases it, a "weak gruel of dead abstractions occasionally seasoned with obscure pomposities."[13]

Making much the same point, the former editor of the major journal of the Modern Language Association reports he and his editorial board were unable to identify more than two and a half dozen or so articles from a total of 1,200 submitted over a two-year period that could be deemed both well written and of sufficient general interest to warrant acceptance for publication.[14] Small wonder then that many faculty members themselves, in moments of candor, privately concede the whole publishing enterprise has become an absurdly inflated boondoggle, an undertaking of dubious worth and even less cultural or intellectual utility. Hence, a great pall of cynicism descends on the untenured. The talk in offices and in the hallways is not about ideas or teaching. It is about the need to "produce," to "get something into the pipeline," to "turn out" or "crank out" an article or two each year, regardless of whether one has something worth sharing with the world. (The mechanistic metaphors to which faculty typically resort when talking about writing are revealing.) The first few years of a faculty member's professional life are thus spent in a frenzied paroxysm of activity—or in brooding over inability to generate that activity—whose real purpose is not to advance scholarship in a field so much as it is to produce a record of individual "productivity."[15]

All the while, piles of unsolicited manuscripts collect on the desks of journal editors. Most of the submissions—not all of them, happily—reveal themselves to be "hackneyed, hastily conceived, turgidly written, deficient in clarity and perception."[16] Some few, the best among them, are eventually accepted. Most of the others are returned for revision or are rejected outright. The search for other publishing venues continues—fortunately, possibilities abound. University libraries, already hard-pressed to keep up with the cost

ACADEMIC RESEARCH

Promotion, tenure, salary, esteem in universities are all closely associated with research and publication. . . . We write, study, and publish not only selflessly to share our ideas with the international community of scholars, but also to advance from assistant to associate professor or to get a 7 percent salary increase when the average raise is 6 percent. No doubt these pressures can lead to adverse consequences usually associated with the slogan "publish or perish."

—Henry Rosovsky, *The University, An Owner's Manual*
(New York: W.W. Norton & Company, 1990), 88.

The university is not "paying us to do research." The university is paying us to teach, and doing research is, in part, what we must do to master our subjects and teach well. The luxury of time that it takes to do research is one of the best "perks" of the teaching profession, but it is not, as such, our job.

—Robert Solomon and Jon Solomon, *Up the University, Re-Creating Higher Education in America* (Reading, Mass.: Addison-Wesley, 1993), 14.

of maintaining literally thousands of periodicals, remain under relentless faculty pressure not to reduce their holdings. The point after all is not to have the journals to read; it is to maintain them as publishing outlets.[17]

Second Thoughts

No matter how harsh or widespread the criticism surrounding faculty publishing, for a new faculty member on appointment at a university with a pronounced research orientation, the whole publish-or-perish issue is moot—if not the former, then most assuredly sooner or later the latter. Anyone strongly adverse to writing is therefore ill-advised to attempt to build a career based on teaching or service, for example, in an environment where the lion's share of rewards clearly goes to those who are prolific researchers. As a novice faculty member, you need to ask questions at the very outset about your institution's publishing expectations as they affect tenure, promotion, and salary.

Unfortunately, getting straight answers is not easy. No institution wants to appear too rigid about how much published research is enough. For understandable reasons, individual academic administrators are not anxious to be pinned down precisely either. Yet without hard answers, you may come to feel you are obliged to play a strange Alice-in-Wonderland game, one whose rules are never adequately clarified or explained, but where the penalty for not following them is quite real. As an approximate rule of thumb—the formula is never reduced to print—research universities tend to expect (all things being equal) that a faculty member will publish an average of two or more peer-reviewed ("refereed") research articles per year in reputable journals. Elsewhere, an occasional article in any reputable journal—perhaps no more than one or two every five or six years—may be considered sufficient when the time comes for a decision about tenure.

Knowing *how much* published scholarship is expected is important. Knowing what *kind* of publishing record will buttress the case for tenure is equally critical. With due allowance for differences among academic disciplines as well as institutions, an informal status hierarchy determines how a particular contribution to the scholarly and professional literature is apt to be weighed. In approximate descending order of significance:

- An original scholarly book published by a leading academic press
- A scholarly monograph or a major (published) technical report
- A research-based article appearing in a leading refereed journal within the field

- A critical essay, research analysis, or interpretive study published in a refereed scholarly journal
- An edited anthology or collection of essays released through a well-known academic press or a major trade publisher
- A contributed chapter (refereed or invited) in a scholarly book
- A major invited essay in a leading academic or professional journal
- A journal article of multiple authorship (name placement is sometimes considered important; multiple-authorship of research articles in most scientific and technical fields is the rule rather than the exception and, accordingly, would be ranked higher)
- An original textbook published by a reputable trade press (the importance assigned to the writing of "pedagogical works" differs greatly from school to school)
- A refereed paper appearing in a published collection of conference proceedings
- An article or essay appearing in a nonrefereed journal
- A publication appearing in a semi-professional or general-circulation magazine
- A book review (unless it is an extended or invited essay, in which case it might rank higher)
- Newsletter reports and articles; data-base abstracts
- In-house papers, reports, and articles.

WHAT ABOUT CYBER-JOURNALS?

The economics of publishing are such that hard-copy journals and academic serials may soon become a thing of the past. So-called electronic journals ("cyber-journals") already exist in profusion, and their numbers are growing. Subsisting only in the peculiar netherworld of cyberspace, taking on conventional hard-copy form only when downloaded off a computer, they offer the best hope of continuing to supply viable outlets for faculty writing on the scale now prevailing. Whether soft-copy publishing can serve as a credible and satisfactory substitute for the more traditional placements for academic research, in effect successfully challenging the mystique of the printed word, still seems uncertain.

—Christopher J. Lucas, *Crisis in the Academy, Rethinking Higher Education in America* (New York: St. Martin's Press, 1998), 202.

ACADEMIC PUBLISHING:
THREE POINTS OF VIEW

I won't tell you publishing hasn't advanced my career. It has. But I've never felt under any particular pressure to write for publication. It was something I wanted to do. A few entries on my vitae have helped when it came time to decide on salary raises—no question about it. . . . Our president is proud of me as a published scholar. But [publishing] isn't something I've empha-sized over teaching or advising my students. . . . I'm proud I've had papers accepted at national meetings. I've also done a few good pieces—maybe not a lot, but some—over the years that appeared in reputable journals. Still, I can keep up in my field without trying to make original contributions to the world of scholarship. I like the freedom to decide whether to do my own research or not.

—a senior professor from a
small, private liberal arts college

They've made it very clear we're supposed to get grants, do research, give papers, publish. There's no way I'll get tenure without doing these things. Yet right now I feel swamped with classes and students and committees. . . . There aren't enough hours in the day. I'd like to be more productive. But somehow priorities at my institution seem all screwed up. Research and publishing are emphasized above practically everything else. I admit it, I have trouble sleeping at night, thinking about it.

—an untenured associate professor in a
medium-sized, comprehensive university

When I give a paper, do research or publish something, I am legitimating myself and my right to get paid to teach something. I validate my position both as a scholar and as [a] member of an academic community. I put my work out there for my peers to judge.

—a tenured assistant professor in a
medium-sized, comprehensive university

Practical issues of job security and tenure aside, there are any number of reasons why making the effort to become an accomplished, published scholar is an act of prudence, depending on your individual circumstances and your specific institutional situation. Among the more cogent consid-erations frequently cited:

- A successful academic career in today's competitive environment is enhanced when the scholar becomes known for his or her work. Teaching, although important, remains a "local" phenomenon. A faculty member may acquire a reputation as an accomplished teacher, but very rarely does that repute extend beyond the boundaries of the person's own home campus. Publishing is far more likely to attract national attention—with the added attractiveness of bringing recognition to the institution with which the author is affiliated (a prospect the school's leadership is likely to appreciate).[18]
- Writing for publication is a generative, thought-provoking process. Good writing is a form of discipline. The regimen entailed demands creativity, originality, analysis, and thoughtful reflection. The process of writing lends clarity and precision to thought.[19]
- Writing for many people serves as a creative outlet akin to painting, sculpting, building, inventing, composing, or performing. Writing can be a genuine form of self-expression and development.[20]
- Published research and scholarship, unlike teaching and many other professorial involvements, generates a tangible artifact as its outcome.
- Large-scale research supported with external funding brings needed resources to the host institution.
- A good publishing record has portability and enhances one's potential job mobility.
- Refereed publishing is a form of self-validation. It attests (although in a very circumscribed way) to the caliber of one's scholarship and academic standing within a community of scholarly peers.
- Writing for publication demands—and furnishes an occasion for—in-depth familiarization with an otherwise-unexplored body of academic literature.
- Compared with teaching, advising students, and professional service, research productivity tends to be disproportionately valued and rewarded. As common adage has it, "Publications are counted; and publications count."

Getting Started

Making writing a professional habit early on is advantageous to your professional career. Evidence indicates that academics who begin writing and publishing early in the game are more likely to stay productive than those who defer writing until later on. Compared with peers who delay getting involved, early starters are both more proficient and more prolific in their research and scholarship; they publish more of higher quality over the long haul; and reportedly derive more satisfaction from their writing than do authors who write only occasionally.[21]

Needless to add, all things being equal, writing for publication enhances prospects for tenure. An extensive publishing record likewise confers a distinct advantage over nonpublished competitors later on when seeking academic employment elsewhere. Not without good reason, the author of a guidebook for new faculty in liberal arts colleges warns, "Your first college may be [a place] where there are neither overt pressures nor subtle enticements to enter a life of research and professional vigor. . . . But down the road—and not very far down the road at that—the faculty member who has . . . built a vitae that reveals a continuing record of scholarly vitality, will have a professional currency and a set of options that are slipping quickly away from the faculty member who chose at the start to shelve his or her dissertation, pick up a textbook, and eschew active inquiry and creativity forever."[22]

Writing has a uniqueness about it within the triumvirate of professorial responsibilities. Teaching must be done on schedule. Service responsibilities come with their own timetables and deadlines. But writing begins as a solo performance, usually without a specific time frame or date for completion.[23] Because there are no immediate or obvious penalties for putting it off, it is easy for a prospective author to procrastinate. Faced with the daunting challenge of making words march across the page (or computer screen) it is tempting always to defer the start of writing indefinitely, or—what sometimes amounts to the same thing—to await a large block of uninterrupted time to devote to the task—perhaps at the end of the term, during summer vacation, on sabbatical, or possibly not until retirement.[24]

Lack of time is the most frequently cited faculty explanation for delays in their planned research and writing.[25] New faculty especially report feeling too busy, too overloaded with other responsibilities to contemplate writing for publication. The obvious if irritating rejoinder is that faculty, like everyone else, usually find time to do the things they want to do most. Ultimately, it becomes a matter of setting priorities, exercising self-discipline, and establishing realistic goals. Learning to reserve time for writing is not easy. But it is essential.

The fundamental mistake, most experts agree, is assuming that successful writing demands long, open-ended periods of time free of all distractions or interruptions. So-called binge writing works for very few people.[26] The myth of the author who waits for inspiration to strike and then in bouts of creative frenzy churns out page after page of deathless prose for hours on end is largely just that—a myth. Marathon binge sessions, in other words, rarely fulfill their intended purpose. They simply invite needless frustration and fatigue, and so make progress more unlikely.

A more realistic strategy is to set aside time for daily writing sessions ranging in duration from less than half an hour to no more than two hours maximum. These are much more time-efficient and far likelier to produce positive results. Experienced writers may gradually learn how to extend their writing time for longer periods (up to four or five hours perhaps) and still remain productive. But novices are said to do better by starting out with preset limits and working for much shorter intervals on a daily basis. A moderate regimen established early on works best for most authors.

Writing requires habituation. Successful authors set schedules for themselves and strive to adhere to them as closely as possible. Some prefer to work in the early morning hours when it is quiet and they are feeling fresh and alert. Others prefer late evening hours after time has been spent unwinding and relaxing. Some reserve chunks of time on weekends and during vacation breaks. Others keep writing as a workday preoccupation and refuse to allow it to intrude on leisure activities and family routines. Trying to sandwich writing time in between other responsibilities in midday, however, rarely works. In all cases, whenever time is set aside, the abiding

FROM UNTENURED FACULTY MEMBERS WHO ARE PUBLISHING . . .

"What could be more satisfying and fulfilling than completing a major [research] project, writing it up, and mailing off the manuscript—unless it's a letter of acceptance from a journal editor and, later on, seeing one's work in print?"

"I call the place I write my Sanctuary. It's a place of refuge as well as a place to compose. I probably spend too much time in there. My wife calls herself a 'logo-widow.'"

"Our eight-year-old daughter asked me why I was writing a book. As she pointed out, 'The library is already full of 'em!'"

"Writing for me is the single most intense, most challenging thing I do. Some of my most exhilarating and some of my most despondent moments occur while I am sitting in front of my computer."

"I write mostly because I need to in order to get tenure. However, I've done enough of it that I am starting to get good at it!"

"It never ceases to amaze me: writing is so much harder than talking. The act of putting words down on paper forces me to organize and clarify my thinking."

consideration is to get words down on paper and make progress, regardless of your mood or readiness to write at any particular moment.

Writing demands scheduled time. It also requires a physical place, inviolate and sacrosanct, a comfortable work area devoted exclusively to writing and nothing else (for example, returning phone calls, writing letters, reading the mail, and so on). Ideally, the work site should be entirely free of distractions and temptations (magazines, newspapers, correspondence, other work-related papers) and configured to reflect orderliness and organization. While some faculty members feel comfortable working in the midst of paper chaos and disarray, most find the writing process greatly facilitated by an environment free of clutter.

Selecting a Topic

Identifying a problem or topic to write about is a highly individual decision. Some prospective authors find it helpful to try out preliminary ideas in informal conversations with colleagues. Attendance at professional conferences and listening to others' papers may stimulate thought. Reading journals in order to become better acquainted with what are sometimes termed the "great conversations" in a given discipline is almost always helpful. Conducting a literature search in a specific area may provoke an idea or uncover productive lines of inquiry that warrant further investigation. Some people recommend carrying around a notebook in which to record thoughts as they occur—one never knows when good ideas for writing will pop up. Eventually an interesting research question or a project worth pursuing is bound to emerge.

Presenting a Conference Paper

Presenting papers at professional meetings can and should become an integral aspect of your scholarship, even if it is something you do only occasionally. The task of drafting a paper is not dissimilar from authoring a manuscript for publication, except that it is important to bear in mind that the paper will be heard—not read—and accordingly needs to be organized as such for its debut appearance.

Every scholarly society or professional association has its own rules, procedures, and requirements members must observe in responding to a call for papers. Chances of having your prospective contribution accepted for presentation are greatly improved if you already have attended meetings of the sponsoring organization in question, have listened to others' papers, and, generally, have gleaned a sense for the types of presentations judged worthy of inclusion on the convention program.

Curiously enough, very few presenters seem to give much thought or foresight to the presentation dynamic itself. First, typically, they run afoul of scheduling constraints by attempting to present too much material within the time allotted. Second, they read—literally—the paper in its entirety before the audience, more often than not to mind-numbing effect. Or, third, despairing of conveying the whole substance of what they have written, they offer a hurried summary notable for its evident lack of organization or structure, and refer prospective readers to a stack of manuscript hard-copies (which may or may not ever get read). In short, a common failing is neglecting to think of the presentation as a *pedagogical* act. Inattentiveness to the communication process inevitably results in bad teaching, even when conducted in the presence of, and for the benefit of, one's peers rather than students.

Conference papers vary tremendously in both form and intent. Some are intended to offer an interim report on research in progress. Some introduce preliminary findings from a study just completed. A few may be conceptual pieces, intended more than anything else to open up new lines of inquiry or to point in some novel direction for further research. Sometimes a conference forum is provided for commentaries and analyses of "the state of the field" in a given specialty. Still others are interpretive bibliographies or reviews of major works recently published.

Paper presentations also vary greatly in their formality. At its best, a presentation is akin to a speech or public address, delivered from an outline that allows for a modicum of spontaneity and flexibility, whatever circumstances demand. Others are more informal: something akin to a "conversation" or dialogue between a speaker and his or her listeners. In almost all cases, the preferred method of presentation is to work from an abbreviated outline and to utilize projected visuals to display major points, diagrams, formulae, equations, charts, graphs, or other similar materials. Whatever the nature of your presentation, you can enhance its impact by rehearsing its delivery and attending to how it will be heard. Once again, the mode of presentation ought to adhere to canons of good pedagogy.

Presenting a paper at a major conference serves as a first-rate "dress rehearsal" for publishing. It allows you to try out and polish an idea before committing anything to print. Comments and reactions from colleagues to a preliminary study described in a conference paper also may prove invaluable later on when it comes time for launching a full-fledged investigation or undertaking a larger-scale piece of research. It should be noted too that a well-received paper is a real confidence-builder, serving perhaps to encourage you to pursue some particular line of inquiry further. In short, it is helpful to think of the act of presenting a paper as a "trial run" before moving ahead with an effort to enshrine something in print.

Presenting a paper at a professional conference is thus an intermediary step on the way to publishing. Assuming the paper was well received upon delivery, the would-be author already has a rough manuscript in hand to rework and revise until it takes shape as a publishable journal article. Alternatively, if the original article was refereed, it might be submitted for possible inclusion in a published record of conference proceedings.

Identifying an Audience and Market

The sine qua non of successful academic writing for publications is having something of substance to say on a given subject. Next in importance is determining to whom the message is intended: academic peers, practitioners in the field, or laypersons at large. Identifying the audience for a journal article is tantamount to targeting a specific publishing outlet. *The single most common mistake writing novices make is failing to decide beforehand on the journal to which a manuscript will be submitted once it is completed.* Well before starting the actual crafting of the manuscript, it is absolutely imperative that you as the prospective author become familiar with similar articles that have previously appeared in print in a particular journal. Notice should be taken of length, reference style, types of topics treated, and other particulars of the general format followed. As one extensively published author advises, "Using the publication as a blueprint, craft your article so it reads [and looks] like those published."[27]

Would-be authors who ignore a journal's "Instructions to Authors" or fail to request a copy of an "Authors' Style Sheet" do so at their own peril. Most editors will refuse to consider your submission or send it out for review unless it conforms in all respects to the journal's own template. You must give attention to margins, headings and subheads (flush left, flush right, or centered, boldface or not, upper or lower case), footers and headers, margins, references and bibliography, writing style (passive or active voice, use of personal pronouns, and so on), and total word count (manuscript length). Especially critical is compliance with whatever citation format is used by the journal, whether it follows the Chicago Manual of Style, guidelines published by the American Psychological Association (APA), the Modern Language Association (MLA), the American Medical Association (AMA), the American Bar Association (ABA), or any one of several other sources.

As a rule, "juried" or refereed journals that make use of independent external reviewers are considered the most prestigious and desirable publishing outlets. Those lacking an outside review process are reputedly less distinguished. There are important exceptions, however, most notably journals that feature invited contributions from leading scholars in a field. In practically every discipline there are a few nonrefereed journals whose reputation for quality is high. Limiting your submissions solely to refereed journals may be unnecessarily restrictive and in the long run counterproductive.

Advice-givers disagree on whether it is wise for a novice writer to submit his or her manuscript to the most prestigious, refereed journal in a field before considering less distinguished alternatives. Some view the former option as a mistake, since the better journals tend to be more selective, and

---

ADVICE FROM A JOURNAL EDITOR . . .

As to what advice I can offer would-be contributors, please consult our web page where we offer specific, detailed instructions to aspiring authors. We also mail out the same material on request. . . . My main suggestions are these:

Check to be sure your topic is appropriate for the forum we provide. Common sense should prevail. It does not take much judgment to detect a potential misplacement. Familiarize yourself with the types of articles and reviews we normally run. If your manuscript in no way resembles what we have already published, it is unlikely we will consider it seriously.

Keep your cover letter short. Like most editors, I am much too busy and lack the patience to read through long missives explaining in great detail why we should publish your manuscript. Keep it straightforward and to the point. Your material should sell itself.

Submit clean copy. Never send a preliminary draft. Help us out by ensuring your work fits our format and style. . . . Manuscript length is always a big consideration.

Our reviewers can easily recognize term papers and dissertation chapters. Unless they have been extensively reworked, we cannot afford to bother with them.

Reviewers are notoriously slow. Allow enough time before badgering my office about a decision to accept or reject. We do the best we can.

Even if our reviewers like your submission, expect them to demand revisions. Do not write to me to explain why our reviewers are mistaken in their criticism. Also, I have no time to serve as a middle man by sending along your rejoinders to their evaluations. A good editor puts his [or her] faith in reviewers. As editor, I need their help. And my decision is always final.

—correspondence from the editor of a major social-science journal

the likelihood of having an article rejected is much higher (upwards of 95 percent in some cases). "Like moths drawn to a flame," one author remarks, "few beginning writers seem able to resist the temptation to send their manuscripts to the journals with the lowest acceptance rates."[28]

Given the uncertainty surrounding of the review process, on the other hand, the verdict (acceptance or nonacceptance) could easily go either way. The psychological toll exacted by likely rejection has to be weighed against the prospect of placement in a very desirable journal. A confidence-building alternative for any faculty neophyte is to publish initially in less widely circulated journals and then, with increasing experience, "work up" to more selective journals in the field.

Collaboration and Multiple Authorship

For writers lacking extensive publishing experience, collaboration with a senior colleague or colleagues on a research project intended for publication may offer a less intimidating prospect than going it alone. So far as journal articles and research reports are concerned, multiple authorship in the sciences and applied technical fields is actually quite common, whereas single authorship tends to be more nearly the rule in the humanities and certain other disciplines. Some institutions tacitly assign less "credit" to anyone other than the first-listed author of a publication. Notwithstanding, the advantage of having others with whom to collaborate may far outweigh the drawbacks involved and afford you a helpful learning experience.

Essential to the success of jointly authored work is a shared understanding among all parties involved about how the work should proceed. Faculty who intend to work together need to map out a specific set of assignments, establish a work schedule, decide on a division of responsibilities, and reach agreement on how name-authorship will be assigned. The most junior member of a research and writing team, with few if any publications to his or her credit, probably has the greatest vested interest in the project's eventual success. Correlatively, the novice has more at stake than anyone else in seeing to it that the terms under which the project is carried forward are clear and explicit.

Invisible Preliminaries

Behind almost every finished writing project are countless "invisible" hours spent conceptualizing an idea, conducting a literature search and researching references, collecting and analyzing data, note taking, outlining, revising successive draft texts, submitting the manuscript; the interval that must elapse—sometimes months on end—before an editorial decision is forthcoming; time expended on rewriting, and the additional lead time needed before an article appears in print. The unseen preliminaries that go before the actual appearance of a printed text are rarely apparent.[29]

Few guideposts exist to lead a beginning writer through this labyrinth preceding publication; and there are no hard-and-fast rules governing the actual writing process itself. What works well for one individual may not serve effectively for another. Some writers compose in fits and starts, relying on periodic bouts of inspiration for their progress. Others crawl forward methodically, sentence by sentence, paragraph by paragraph, rewriting, revising, and polishing endlessly before moving on to the next section. Still others find it preferable to "prewrite," that is, to block out ideas quickly either in outline or rough narrative form, going back to rewrite and effect revisions only after the whole has been laid out in its entirety. The latter approach has been aptly dubbed a "results-first" strategy.[30]

Inside every writer's head, it has been said, is a noisome, censorious editor. During the composition process, the internal critic is constantly throwing up blocks and finding fault: *This is a waste of time; the work will never see the light of day; the writing is fatally flawed; the exposition is unintelligible, the treatment derivative;* and so on.[31] Writing without revising, or freewriting, affords a way of silencing this critical internal editor. The objective is simply to generate ideas even when they are imperfectly formed in order to establish a flow and get something preliminary down on paper. Improvements, revisions, and rewriting can come later.[32] Once the negative fault-finding is suspended, a writer can start generating a more positive inner monologue: *This is only a rough draft; I am making progress; the writing is flowing well; ideas are coming together; the narrative is showing promise.* If for no other reason, prewriting is an attractive strategy for beginners.

Inexperienced writers and veteran authors alike sometimes use diagrams, flow charts, or outlines to guide composition. So long as an outline is used only provisionally, as a rough guide for enumerating points and establishing a sequence of essential elements (always subject to revision), it can be extraordinarily helpful. The challenge, of course, is not to allow a predetermined outline to control composition. Outlining is simply an expedient to prevent unintended digressions and to keep an exposition or narrative on track.

With practice a writer learns when finally to break off preparations and actually begin writing. At some point in the process of familiarizing oneself with the relevant literature, consulting pertinent sources, making outlines, planning and prewriting, the law of diminishing returns sets in. It is time—as a fitting if trite metaphor has it—to take the plunge.[33]

ON WRITING AND REVISING . . .

Blot out, correct, insert, refine,
Enlarge, diminish, interline;
Be mindful, when intervention fails,
To scratch your head, and bite your nails.

—Jonathan Swift

Back to Fundamentals

The typical new faculty member is a relatively inexperienced writer. He or she may have finished a thesis or dissertation, but usually has not completed any other major piece of writing apart from the occasional student seminar paper. Not surprisingly, when writing weaknesses begin to surface, nothing less will do than a return to the basics of prose composition. Most problems fall under one or more of three overlapping categories: organization, style, and grammar.[34]

Structural and organizational deficiencies are easily corrected once recognized:

- Purpose. Readers are entitled to know why an article was written. Its purpose should be made clear within the first paragraph or two—it should never be implicit, hidden, or assumed.
- Verbosity. Written prose should be reasonably succinct. A narrative should not ramble or meander aimlessly around its subject matter. Redundancies should be avoided.
- Structure. A good piece of writing exhibits a clear plan, a logical sequence, and an identifiable line of argumentation or exposition. The narrative has an introduction or strong beginning point, a midsection, and a conclusion. The narrative flow throughout is easy to follow. The text coheres; it has a unity about it.
- Clarity. Professional-level writing leaves no doubt about the nature of its subject matter, its focus, and the limitations within which the subject is to be treated.
- Argumentation. When appropriate, an author should take a position on the subject under consideration. While it is important not to overgeneralize, oversimplify, assume causal connections unsupported by data, or draw conclusions that extend beyond the evi-

dence presented, it is equally important not to overqualify, to equivocate, or to be overly cautious. The key is balanced exposition or argumentation.

Stylistic considerations are trickier to handle. Besides the usual warnings against the use of euphemisms, unnecessary jargon, quote-bound text, inadequate documentation, and so on, some standard caveats worth considering include the following:

- Paragraphing. Each paragraph within a text should include a strong key statement. As a general rule, if a paragraph runs on for two-thirds or more of a typed page, it is too lengthy and should be broken up. If a single run-on sentence occupies most of a paragraph, it too should be broken down into shorter segments.
- Transitions. Transitional phrases that carry the reader forward from one paragraph or section to the next facilitate narrative flow. The problem is, they can easily be overdone and consequently should be used judiciously.
- Headings. Heads and subheads break up a text into more manageable portions and facilitate reader comprehension. Subheads may also substitute for overt textual transitions and linkages between sections.
- Voice. Current usage increasingly favors the use of the active voice over the passive voice and encourages the use of personal pronouns ("I," "You," "We"), even in formal writing.
- Tone and color. Composition stylists increasingly urge the use of strong action verbs, colorful adjectives, and vivid figures of speech. Consistency of tone or "color" throughout is important.
- Formality and informality. Appropriate style is critical when writing for publication. Poetic metaphors, for example, rarely find a place in formal technical reports. Each writing format or genre tends to have its own stylistic features.
- Inclusivity. Gender-inclusive, nonsexist language is mandatory in professional writing.
- Rhythm and pacing. Authors control narrative rhythm or pace by varying the length of sentences and paragraphs. Long cumbersome sentences burdened by complex subordinate clauses slow things down. Short simple sentences pick up the pace. Emphasis is established by using a brief, free-standing paragraph that expresses a single idea in one or two simple declarative sentences.
- Fillers. Inexperienced writers tend to fall into the trap of relying on "fillers" that sound awkward or that serve only to belabor the

obvious: *"The purpose of this study was. . . ."* or *"Having looked at such-and-such, we turn now to a consideration of so-and-so. . . ."*

- Underwriting and overwriting. Every writer must steer a course between treating content at excessive length or in unnecessary detail and failing to allow sufficient space for the necessary development of the subject. Ultimately, the proper balance is a judgment call on the author's part.

Grammatical errors creep into even the most accomplished author's manuscript draft. Problems to look for include subject-verb disagreement; the use of "like" for "as" or "as though" ("She looks like she is confused."); faulty parallelism; ambiguous antecedents for pronouns ("John told Bill he was upset"); split infinitives ("to greatly and constantly admire"); dangling modifiers ("Having been shot in the stern, the commander ordered his vessel to break off the engagement."); misplaced participles ("Riding my bicycle, the vicious dog attacked me."); the use of "this," "that," or "which" to refer to the complete sense of a preceding sentence of clause ("I felt abandoned. This upset me."); inconsistency of tense; and inappropriate use of colons, semicolons, dashes, and commas.

Revising Text

Writing blocks are practically inevitable, lending credence to the rueful jest about the writing process being something akin to squeezing dried toothpaste out of a tube. Experienced writers suggest the following remedies:

1. Read the text aloud (or listen to its being read aloud by someone else). There is no better way to troubleshoot possible problems: organizational structure, redundancy, lack of clarity, narrative flow, style.
2. When a writing block develops, walk away for a while or revert temporarily to freewriting. Committing ideas to paper comes first; deciding how to develop and express them can follow later.
3. Copyedit in short spurts. An author should not get too "close" to his or her own text, or become too invested in particular constructions. It is preferable to "distance" oneself from the text as necessary, sometimes leaving it alone for a day or two.
4. Share draft text with colleagues. Ask specific questions. Be willing to respond to constructive criticism and suggestions, both substantive and editorial.
5. Exercise patience throughout the revision process. Even veteran writers rarely if ever get it right on the very first try. It is not at all

unusual for a manuscript to require upwards of a dozen or more revisions before it is ready for submission.

Submitting A Manuscript

The would-be contributor to a journal needs to pay close attention to
each and every requirement governing manuscript submission. Instructions will likely indicate how many copies should be supplied, whether
pages should be clipped or stapled together, whether a separate title
page or abstract is required, whether a computer disk will be called for,
whether a biographical sketch should be enclosed, how camera-ready
artwork (if any) should be handled, whether a self-addressed stamped
envelope must be included. (Some journals even specify bond paper or
the paper rag content preferred.) The finished manuscript should be free
of typographical errors or last-minute handwritten corrections and
other addenda.

The cover letter accompanying the manuscript should be written with
care: it can "sell" the submission. Essential elements include a concise description of the work submitted, its uniqueness or originality, the contribution it purports to make to the field of scholarship, and, if possible, how
the theme or subject matter treated builds on, or relates to, other articles
that have appeared in the journal within the recent past.

Common custom dictates that exclusive consideration rights be assigned over to the journal to which the manuscript has been submitted.
Under no circumstances should a copy of the same manuscript be sent to
more than one publisher at a time. In effect, the journal selected is empowered to hold the work "hostage" for however long its review process
requires—anywhere from two to six or more months in some cases.
(Elapsed time to actual publication after final acceptance, depending on the
journal's backlog, ranges from a few months to a year or more.)

The Manuscript Review Process

Every refereed journal has its own standards or criteria for reviewing submissions. Reviewers generally are asked to respond to the same basic questions: Is the subject matter of the article important and significant? How
does the submission fare in terms of readability and style? Is the argument
or exposition clear and unambiguous? How skillfully has the study been
constructed and carried out? Does the author's treatment of data omit or
ignore major relevant considerations? Is the content appropriate for the
journal's readership?

WHAT EXPERIENCED ACADEMIC AUTHORS RECOMMEND . . .

The vagaries of the writing and publishing process are such that even experienced authors disagree among themselves on the best way of approaching the task of crafting and submitting a journal article for publication. However, the following suggestions command broad assent:

1. Trial and error will reveal the work style that best suits you. Some academics favor a highly regimented approach that allows them to focus on their work for long periods of time, insulated from office distractions. Others seem to function best "as the spirit moves them," even if it means their writing time is punctuated by frequent interruptions.

2. Most seasoned writers concede that finding time for writing is challenging. It is not easy to deflect those who want "only a minute" of your time. Minutes lost to other activities add up. One useful suggestion is to *make an appointment with yourself* for writing. Keep that appointment as carefully as you do all others.

3. Select in advance—before you begin writing—the journal where you hope to submit your manuscript. Avoid any obvious mismatch between your topic or its treatment and the types of articles that have already appeared in the journal under consideration. Pick the outlet that publishes articles similar to the one you plan to write. In deciding whether to target a top journal in your field, weigh the prestige factor against the low probability of acceptance and the lag time required before a work appears in print.

4. Adhere conscientiously to a journal's *Instructions to Contributors* regarding length, style, headings and sub headings, citations, documentation, graphs, tables, illustrations, and so on.

5. Convince your intended readers at the outset that the topic of your paper is both interesting and important. Do not assume your readers already care anything about it.

6. Utilize—and refer your readers to—primary source materials or original data whenever possible.

7. Be sure your material is genuinely fresh and current.

8. Keep your writing style direct and simple. Write in such a way that any reasonably bright person would be both willing and able to understand, with minimal effort, what you have written. Your text should be concise and uncluttered with extraneous material.

continues

Wordiness and rhetorical overkill are common mistakes to avoid. Stylishness and verbosity are not identical—they are usually opposites.

9. Avoid unnecessary jargon and the use of faddish "buzz words." Confer on your ideas and findings the significance they deserve by using language comprehensible to the widest possible readership.

10. Learn from others. Circulate a draft of your manuscript among colleagues and students for help in making revisions. Accept assistance in clarifying and smoothing out the text. Have others look for redundancies or critical missing information. Do not be defensive. Be open to input and incorporate good suggestions when offered. Actively seek advice and include it in your work whenever possible.

11. Resist the temptation to mail out your manuscript right away once it seems complete. Put it aside for a while and only then reread it aloud to yourself to see how it sounds.

12. Never make multiple submissions of a single manuscript. Negotiate with one potential publishing outlet at a time.

13. Never submit a rough draft. The manuscript you submit to an editor should represent your best, polished work.

14. If an editor or reviewer requests revisions, follow through with a good-faith effort to correct whatever problems allegedly exist. Return the corrected manuscript promptly.

15. If your paper is rejected, move on. Success demands persistence in the face of discouragement. Do not take rejection personally—it's not about your worth as an individual. Revise and prepare the manuscript for submission to another journal. Mail it out again.

Sources: Louis J. Budd, "On Writing Scholarly Articles," in A. Leigh DeNeef and Craufurd D. Goodwin, eds., *The Academic's Handbook,* 2nd. ed. (Durham, N.C.: Duke University Press, 1995), 249–262; Boyd R. Strain, "Publishing in Science," in DeNeef and Goodwin, 263–272; Richard C. Rowson, "The Scholar and the Art of Publishing," in DeNeef and Goodwin, 273–285; Susan J. Ashford, "The Struggle for Meaning," in Peter J. Frost and M. Susan Taylor, eds., *Rhythms of Academic Life, Personal Accounts of Careers in Academia* (Thousand Oaks, Calif.: Sage Publications, 1996), 119–127; Kevin R. Murphy, "Getting Published," in Frost and Taylor, 129–134.

Once reviewers' comments have been returned, responsibility for making a final decision on whether the manuscript should be accepted, rejected outright, or returned for possible revision falls on the editor's shoulders. The judgment is sometimes a close call, considering how often reviewers tend to disagree with one another on the merits of a work or address entirely different points in their respective assessments.[35]

If the general consensus among reviewers is that a manuscript shows promise in spite of certain weaknesses or faults, the editor may invite the author to make specific changes and submit it for reconsideration. Some authors inexplicably fail to respond to an invitation to revise their work, thereby needlessly depriving themselves of a second chance at publishing in a preferred journal.

If an author's submission is rejected altogether, self-interest dictates that it be revised if necessary and then promptly reformatted to fit the requirements of the next journal in line. As Tara Gray of New Mexico State University breezily advises, "Kick it out the door and make 'em say no."[36] Rejection by one journal editor by no means predicts it will receive the same treatment at the hands of another.

The Book Proposal

Months, even years of labor go into the authorship of a book; and not all faculty are willing or able to take up the challenge. In one respect, preparing a book-length manuscript is easier than writing an article, in that the former allows more space for the full development and treatment of its subject. However, a work of larger proportions correspondingly demands more effort in planning, writing, and revising. There is a trade-off required, a personal sacrifice, in terms of time spent away from friends and family as well as diverted energy that could be expended on projects yielding shorter-term benefits.

Publishing a book is a major professional coup for any faculty member. It is a still more notable accomplishment for a faculty novice on a tenure-track appointment. Since the outcome is always uncertain until a publishing contract has been secured and the payoff is long delayed, embarking on the task of crafting a book is a somewhat risky undertaking. An author who already has compiled a solid record of scholarly productivity might do well to consider the possibility. Someone whose writing has been more circumscribed, by contrast, might defer a long-term project whose outcome is uncertain until he or she has acquired more publishing experience. A proven track record significantly enhances prospects for securing a publishing contract.

Since most publishers want to examine two or three sample chapters (not necessarily in their planned order) before considering whether or not to offer a contract, the development of a book manuscript should begin long before the author seeks a publishing outlet. As with writing a journal article (though on a much larger scale), the point of departure is picking a subject, identifying carefully the audience for which the book is intended, and settling on a strategy for organizing and developing the work as a cohesive whole. Once again as with article writing, the approach taken to an appropriate publishing outlet is all-important. Obviously, a house that specializes in technical works would be uninterested in a proposed work of literary criticism. A publisher whose list emphasizes humanities scholarship is unlikely to consider a work in the physical or biological sciences and applied technologies. Sending out a book prospectus to an unsuitable publisher simply indicates the author has not done his or her homework properly.

The tendency among a surprising number of novice authors is to imagine that the world breathlessly awaits their perorations on some topic of limited scope and negligible popular appeal. A volume devoted to an obscure Chinese poet of the Sung dynasty, for example, is unlikely to hit the national best-sellers' list, just as a technical discourse on the history of plate-tectonic theory is probably not going to attract a vast lay audience. The topic contemplated may be potentially important to the world of scholarship—in which case the work should be directed to an academic press—but not to a commercial trade publisher for whom "bottom-line" considerations of sales potential are necessarily paramount.

Before investing months or even years of labor polishing a work that is inherently unpublishable, you need to prepare a book prospectus or proposal and a query letter suitable for submission to an appropriate publishing house—that is, a publisher whose current listings include works of a similar nature. Elements incorporated within the prospectus should include: (1) a very brief overview of the subject; (2) a rationale for why the work deserves to be published (its novelty, uniqueness of approach, or intrinsic importance); (3) a discussion of similar works in print or books with which the proposed magnum opus might compete for attention or sales; (4) special features planned for inclusion; (5) a tentative outline or synopsis; (6) an indication of planned length; (7) an analysis of the likely audience for which the work is intended; (8) an estimate of the time required for its draft completion; (9) suggestions for marketing the work; and (10) a summary of the author's qualifications and previous publishing experience.

The accompanying query letter should be thoughtfully crafted and designed to arouse a publisher's interest in the project described. It is important to bear in mind that the average editor already has a hefty "sludge pile" of unsolicited manuscripts sitting around the office and an even higher stack of proposals awaiting attention. An infinitesimally small number of authors' queries actually lead to published works, a hard fact that underscores the importance of doing everything possible to beat the odds up front.

REVIEWING A BOOK MANUSCRIPT

The following composite, adapted from three different book publishers, serves to illustrate the questions typically posed by an editor to external reviewers of a book manuscript under consideration for possible publications:

1. To whom is this work addressed? What is its intended readership? In your opinion, is there a market for this work? If it were published, could this work find use as a textbook? In what courses, and at what level?

2. Has the author's intention been sufficiently well clarified and made explicit? What purpose would be achieved by the publication of this work? In your judgement, has the author succeeded in achieving his or her purpose in the writing of this work? In other words, how successfully has this project been carried out?

3. Assess briefly the significance or importance of the substance of this proposed work. How original is the treatment of the subject matter? Would the appearance in print of this work satisfy a genuine need in the world of scholarship?

4. Evaluate what you consider to be the major strengths and weaknesses of this manuscript. Please be specific as possible in your assessment.

5. Does the treatment of the substance of this work reflect high standards of scholarship? Is the use of source materials comprehensive and appropriate? Comment also on the adequacy of the author's documentation.

6. Evaluate the author's quality of writing, style, and organization.

7. With what other works in print could this manuscript be fairly compared?

8. What suggestion for revision and improvement, if any, can you suggest?

9. Which of the following do you recommend?
   —Accept with minor revisions as indicated?
   —Return with an expression of interest but suggest major changes before reconsidering.
   —Invite resubmission after specific required changes have been made.
   —Suggest another publisher to whom the manuscript should be submitted.
   —Reject.

10. Additional comments, suggestions for strengthening the manuscript, instructions, or criticisms:

Most publishers will not undertake a manuscript review without assurances from the author that a given editor enjoys exclusive reviewing rights and that the work is not under consideration elsewhere. Nevertheless, there is absolutely nothing to prevent an author from sending out copies of the initial prospectus to as many different publishing houses as desired. Here also, you can try to tip the balance in your favor.

The Review Process

An editor's willingness to receive and send out your materials for review is always a good sign. The amount of time required for feedback varies considerably, sometimes attaining scandalous proportions. Typically, many months elapse before reviewer's comments are finally returned. If reactions are negative, the editor may or may not choose to disclose whatever specific criticisms were supplied and the rejection is unequivocal. If the editor remains interested and outside reviews have been favorable or mixed, comments are usually sent on for the author's benefit.

Few book proposals garner immediate agreements to publish. More common by far is for an editor to offer suggestions for improvements and sometimes to request additions or deletions of material as a condition for further consideration. Unless it becomes evident that the editor wants an altogether different book from the one you intended to write, it is foolhardy for you as the would-be author not to follow through. Indeed, in many instances a book manuscript will go through several successive incarnations with a single editor before the much-coveted publishing contract is finally awarded.

If and when a formal publishing contract is forthcoming, it falls to you to comply with the editor's directions as the work moves toward completion. Among other things, you must show a good-faith effort in responding to whatever additional criticisms and suggestions are offered (although under the terms of the usual contract there is usually no obligation on your part to accede to each and every demand for specific changes). Problems and delays arise when an author fails to conform to deadlines, does not observe submission guidelines, or is unresponsive to copyediting suggestions. It has been said that authors naively assume a book has been completed once it is written. Experienced editors know better. Receipt of the manuscript is just the beginning of a long production process leading to its eventual appearance in print.[37]

Anthologies, Compilations, and Textbooks

Anthologies or collections of previously published materials pose their own problems and opportunities. Probably the single most troublesome aspect of trying to publish a compilation of other authors' writings is securing "fair-use" permissions, either from the respective authors or from the sources in which the content originally appeared, depending on the copyright holders. Reprint permission costs almost always are charged against the author's royalties.

The marketability of almost any anthology is problematic. Its viability depends to a great extent on how the materials included are assembled and whether they have some plausible editorial focus. If the work has potential for use as a textbook and is judged to cohere in an original way, there may be no major problem attracting a trade publisher's interest. Academic presses, for their part, rarely evince much interest in anthologies unless they fill an important niche in the scholarship associated with a particular theme or set of issues.

Collections of original, previously unpublished essays or chapters (for example, a Festschrift), each a free-standing piece by a different author, is perhaps not the most appropriate project for a junior faculty member to contemplate tackling—certainly not unless an express invitation to serve as editor has been issued by some sponsoring professional or academic body. (A better alternative is for the novice writer to contribute to someone else's collection!) As editor, the task of identifying contributors (usually well-known scholars in a field) and eliciting their cooperation is a time-consuming chore. Even when all contributors are lined up and ready to get to work on a volume, university presses are predisposed to avoid any such project unless there is a major tie-in between the institution and the subject matter or theme of the compilation—for example, a collection intended to pay homage to a distinguished member of the university's faculty, past or present. Mainstream trade publishers, with few and rare exceptions, cannot afford to take them on.

College textbooks present other publishing prospects. Curiously, however, the art of writing a good pedagogical work—compared with composing a scholarly tome likely to be read by a much smaller audience—has long been seriously undervalued. Creating a textbook capable of competing successfully with its established competitors is actually much more difficult than would-be authors commonly suppose. Publishers tend to favor proposals that have a uniqueness about them or that take a novel approach, but are wary of treatments that appear to stray too far from established norms and conventions. Special teaching aids such as review exercises, discussion questions, suggested activities, and topical bibliographies are highly valued.

Editors above all look for evidence that the prospective author is savvy enough to provide a comprehensive coverage of the field, while at the same time offering something new or features not present in competing texts. For these and other reasons, assembling a first-rate text may demand just as much creativity and originality, just as much time and effort, and at least as much scholarly acumen as that required for any other type of book.

Commercial publishers—for obvious reasons—prefer to invest in projects of the highest marketability—for example, an omnibus introductory text in a subject where student enrollments are largest (psychology, biology, world literature, sociology, or American history). Prospective textbook authors should not delude themselves that mainstream publishing houses are impatiently awaiting proposals to come across the transom promoting textbooks for advanced graduate seminars in semiotics, chaos theory, pre-Raphaelite esthetics, or Peruvian ethnography. Specialized works with potential for use as course texts do get published—they appear by the hundreds every year—but they are typically handled by small or perhaps regional and local presses that happen to be interested in addressing the needs of a particular segment of the marketplace.

Online Publishing and Vanity Presses

Electronic, or online, book publishing is a comparatively recent phenomenon. Basically, it is simply a way to use e-commerce technology to print a limited number of books on demand. As with so-called vanity or author-subsidized publishing (of which it is basically an extension), online production of a manuscript amounts to an author paying a printer to transform a manuscript into a printed volume. Expenses associated with design and layout (usually very rudimentary), typesetting, printing, and binding are all borne by the author. Vanity or author-subsidized publishing offers no independent editorial review of material, no editing, and no quality control of content. Only rarely does a vanity press produce a work genuinely deserving of regular trade publication. Sensible advice to faculty members seeking a publisher: Avoid the temptation of placing a work with a self-subsidy press, electronic or otherwise.

Publish-Or-Perish Reconsidered

No balanced assessment of American higher education can discount altogether the many harsh criticisms levied in recent decades by the likes of

AUTHORING AND PUBLISHING A BOOK

I have spent more time writing books, chapters, and the like than articles, but that is because books are more fun. . . . In writing a book, you can pursue a topic in depth, pursue tangents than seem interesting to you, speculate to your heart's content, and more, without the normal constraints of a journal article. . . . For the most part, book and chapter writing should be done because it is interesting, fun, and sometimes profitable. . . .

—Kevin R. Murphy, "Getting Published," in Peter J. Frost and M. Susan Taylor, eds., *Rhythms of Academic Life, Personal Accounts of Careers in Academia* (Thousand Oaks, California: Sage Publications, 1996), 130.

Major types of book-length writing projects:

- The scholarly monograph is usually undertaken by a university press and deals with a highly specialized topic. Normally the print-run is less than a thousand copies. A monograph tends to be relatively high-priced, and is likely to attract only a limited readership among fellow specialists in the field. A Festschrift consists of collected essays on a narrow scholarly topic, usually assembled to honor someone who has contributed significantly to the academic field at large.
- The scholarly study with a general readership potential may be handled either by a commercial, for-profit publisher or by a university press. The nature of the subject matter or its scope of treatment offers the prospect of a larger readership than that of the monograph. The typical print-run ranges from 1,500 copies to a few thousand. Variations include an anthology of previously published articles sharing common themes or an edited collection of original essays on a given topic.
- The textbook is usually published by a commercial house, with a print-run ranging from a few hundred copies to several thousand. If the work wins widespread acceptance as an instructional source within its market, the author's royalties can be substantial, depending on the size of the intended audience. However, a textbook tends not to be held in as high esteem by promotion and tenure committees as is a specialized "scholarly" work.
- The trade book appeals to a general readership and can command a print-run numbering in the thousands if public demand warrants. A successful trade book either involves the popularization of some topic or issue of general interest or it is a work of fiction. Professors do write popular books—after they are tenured.

continues

Practical Suggestions:

1. Select a prospective publisher who handles the type of book you are interested in bringing to print.

2. Never submit an unsolicited manuscript. Instead, send a prospectus (and perhaps an accompanying cover letter), consisting of a preface, an outline or table of contents, a rationale for the work, an estimation of your projected manuscript completion date and its length, and your curriculum vitae. Inform the publisher if your work is already under review elsewhere.

3. If sample material is requested, submit a consecutively paginated, double-spaced, one-sided copy of the text. Your material should be free of grammatical defects and typographical errors.

4. Review a contract to publish carefully. Make sure you understand all of its provisions before signing and returning it. A publishing agreement is a legally binding contract once signed by both parties.

5. Anticipate a request for revisions once the manuscript in its entirety has been submitted for editorial review. Be as responsive as possible to all suggested changes. Ultimately, the publisher is not bound to publish the final draft work until or unless it is deemed fully acceptable—by the publisher.

6. Once the final manuscript is submitted, include if requested a computer disk whose text matches the printed hard copy in all particulars.

7. Throughout the ensuing production process, respond to all queries promptly, expect to be asked to complete an extensive marketing questionnaire, and return page proofs (if any) on the schedule supplied by your editor. A delay of little more than a week during the design and production process can result in a much longer delay (possibly months) before your book finally appears in print.

8. Writing a book is an act of faith in a positive outcome, not to be realized until some indefinite point in the future. Crafting a book-length manuscript demands months of concentrated effort, and in some cases may entail considerable personal sacrifice. Sometimes the process takes years. Consider carefully how time spent on authoring a book (otherwise available to expend on shorter-range projects) will affect your academic career prior to receiving tenure or promotion.

Compiled in part from Kevin R. Murphy, "Getting Published," *Rhythms of Academic Life, Personal Accounts of Careers in Academia,* in Peter J. Frost and M. Susan Taylor, eds. (Thousand Oaks, Calif.: Sage Publications, 1996), 275, 279–283.

Martin Anderson (*Imposter in the Temple*), Charles Sykes (*Profscam*), Robert Worth (*The Velvet Prison*), Page Smith (*Killing the Spirit*), George Douglas (*Education Without Impact*), William Schaefer (*Education Without Compromise*), Stuart Rojstaczer (*Gone for Good: Tales of University Life After the Golden Age*), and literally scores of others whose diatribes have attracted so much public attention over the last few years. Despite their exaggerations and occasional lapses into hyperbole, these critics of modern academe have performed a useful service by bringing forward for discussion issues long ignored or papered over.

Notwithstanding, so far as their attacks on faculty publishing are concerned, fair-mindedness demands some serious qualifications. Certainly not all academic scholarship is conducted under duress, or for the sole purpose of securing tenure or promotion. Not all professors write and publish because they are obliged to do so (in fact, statistically, those who *do* publish still make up only a small percentage of the total professorate). Authors write because they want to, because they enjoy the creative process, and, above all, because they have something to say they wish to contribute to the world of scholarship.

Some—many—of the books published by academic presses in recent years address important topics and are extremely well written, as are scores of faculty-authored scholarly works released by trade publishers. The general quality and accessibility of college textbooks are probably much higher today than ever before—thanks to the labor of dedicated academics. And although it must be conceded that the journals in many fields are filled with a high percentage of poorly-written articles devoted to seemingly trivial subjects, there is undeniably much of great value out there as well.

Trends afoot that would make publishing mandatory for faculty working in teaching-oriented colleges and universities, in the final analysis, should be challenged and reversed wherever possible. There must always be places where faculty can devote themselves exclusively to the work of mentoring and teaching students, without the interference of extraneous pressures and constraints to limit their effectiveness. Those who do not wish to publish should never be obliged to do so.

As for new faculty members in institutions where research and publishing are major elements in the incentive system, the need for faculty mentoring, it would seem, is likely to become even more critical in the years ahead. New faculty must be afforded the support and encouragement they need in order to facilitate their development as productive researchers and competent writers. The institutions that employ them have a vested interest in their success, as does American higher learning as a whole.

WHY PUBLISH?

In my profession, I write because I want to say something: to create a message that is clear, pleasing to my ear, and meaningful to me and, I hope, to others. I write because I have an urge to create. I also write because my livelihood depends on it. The publication process is highly charged because it involves making my inner self tangible and opening it up for assessment of the adequacy of its products, It is also charged because my survival depends upon those assessments.

—Susan J. Ashford, "The Struggle for Meaning," *Rhythms of Academic Life, Personal Accounts of Careers in Academia,* in Peter J. Frost and M. Susan Taylor, eds. (Thousand Oaks, Calif.: Sage Publications, 1996), 119.

. . . A community of scholars in critical dialogue with one another is the sine qua non of any university. And to that extent, it can be argued that publishing is not only integral to the scholarly activities of the university, but constitutes an essential part of its organic wholeness.

—Richard C. Rowson, "The Scholar and the Art of Publishing," in *The Academic's Handbook,* ed. A. Leigh DeNeef and Craufurd D. Goodwin, 2nd ed. (Durham, N.C.: Duke University Press, 1995), 274

Points in Review

- Research productivity leading to publication greatly enhances one's academic career.
- Writing for publication is a generative process; and for some a major creative outlet.
- A good publishing record facilitates potential career mobility.
- Increasingly, as smaller institutions emulate larger ones, research productivity is disproportionately valued and rewarded. Publications count.
- Alleged lack of time for scholarly writing is the most common explanation cited by faculty to account for lack of productivity.
- Writing requires habituation. But you must discover for yourself an optimal work style, one that works best for you.
- When drafting a journal article, select a target journal first.
- Compliance with a journal's format and stylistic requirements enhances prospects for acceptance of a manuscript.

- Authorship of a book is a long, complex process, beginning with submission of a well-drafted prospectus and culminating in collaboration between author and publisher in carrying a text forward through the final production process.

CHAPTER 7

THE ART OF GRANTSMANSHIP

Pursuing Grants: Is It Worth It?

M ost faculty research and writing is done unsupported by external funding. Presenting and publishing papers, for instance, are usually considered integral aspects of one's work profile, at least in institutions of higher learning where scholarly inquiry and the pursuit of a research agenda are expected of every faculty member. Most of the labor involved requires only budgeted salary dollars. Hence, financial support from outside the institution is not a consideration. So too, much of the professional outreach and service work performed by college professors is conducted without external financial assistance.

Success in securing research grants or service contracts from an outside source is still highly valued by most colleges and universities, nevertheless, since the benefits that accrue to an institution are considerable. Among small private colleges and regional or local municipal universities, seeking grants is considered desirable, though—with certain rare exceptions— certainly not mandatory. Grant activity is strictly a matter of individual choice. But in major research universities (depending on one's particular discipline or academic specialty), pursuing external funding may turn out to be an imperative the newcomer ignores only at his or her professional peril. Indeed, in some instances obtaining grants or contracts frames an expectation to which new faculty members—especially in the sciences, applied technologies, and engineering—simply must respond if they are to have any hope of receiving tenure or promotion.

Determining the degree of importance attached to grants within your academic unit is not difficult. Your inquiries will soon reveal the extent to which your new colleagues are engaged in funded research, how much time and attention are given over to writing grants of one sort or another, and, generally, how important a role grantsmanship plays in decisions about tenure and promotion. (Presumably, you would want to seek out this information long before accepting an offer of an academic position at a particular institution.)

Beginning faculty members tend to be busy people. For understandable reasons, they often come to feel overwhelmed by their various work responsibilities. So much time is devoted initially to course preparation and teaching, advising students, and in some cases fulfilling service obligations, that it hardly seems possible to find time to seek external funding for anything else.[1] And the point needs to be emphasized at the outset: the process of applying for government or foundation grants, whether an elective choice or a mandated response, *is* unquestionably a major task. Generating viable projects, locating likely funding sources, writing successful grant applications, and then managing them once they have been awarded is almost always a labor-intensive, time-consuming undertaking.[2] Deciding whether or not to get in the game, so to speak, is therefore never an easy choice, given the demands on one's time and energy. On the other hand, assuming one has a say in the matter, there are powerful incentives within academeme for electing to do so.

Tenure considerations aside, an obvious advantage of seeking grants, for instance, is the prospect of an infusion of funds to support a particular research initiative, one that would be difficult if not impossible to carry out with only local "in-house" resources for support. Depending on its scale and how it is written, a major grant can provide significant monies to pay for graduate research assistants to help out with the project. A grant can make possible the use of specialized equipment otherwise inaccessible to an unfunded researcher. Funds from grants help pay for laboratory facilities, for the expenses associated with doing surveys and polls, for secretarial support, project-related travel, computer time, and a host of other amenities important to today's productive scholars.

A grant can make other good things possible—for example, supporting a partial "buy-out" of your work assignment so that you as the principal investigator are free to devote more time to a particular research endeavor. (Many academic studies, monographs, and other book projects would never have been written without support of this kind.) Finally, the point may be an obvious one but it bears repeating: funded research and other types of scholarly inquiry furnish the springboard for publications, since sharing the results of your work in some public forum is the natural culmination of that scholarly activity.

ON GRANTSMANSHIP:
FACULTY TESTIMONIALS

I had been working on a book manuscript for almost three years. My editor was pressuring me to wind things up. I simply couldn't find enough time to finish. A small "startup" grant awarded by my home institution made all the difference in the world. I was able to leverage that grant to attract additional funding from an outside source. . . . To make a long story short, I applied for and received a sabbatical, using monies awarded to help pay for someone to teach my classes for the semester. I finally finished the book. I couldn't have done it without the sabbatical. It in turn would never have been approved if I hadn't found a way to get my classes covered for an entire academic term.

—a tenured associate professor in a liberal-arts college

I can't say I'm exactly thrilled that I need to get grants just to cover my own salary. Also, I'm not very happy that my raises each year are tied more closely than I'm comfortable with to the total grant dollars I generate annually. I worry about monies drying up some year—what am I going to do then?

—an untenured assistant professor in a polytechnical school

Of course I think it's important to go after external dollars! I've got a new lab, a half dozen or so grad assistants, some new equipment—things my institution could never have provided if I hadn't gone out and found the funding myself. . . .

—a tenured associate professor in a research-oriented university

Chasing grants is a little like hitching a ride on a moving train. Once aboard, it's hard to get off without getting hurt.

—a tenured associate professor in a comprehensive university

There's an old cliché about people who live off grants. We're like hookers—we'll do practically anything for money.

—a tenured professor in a comprehensive university

I believe grants and contracts are good for society, good for business and industry, good for private philanthropy, good for higher education, and good for professors. Without external funding, there's no way I could remain a productive researcher or a published scholar in my field.

—a tenured professor in a research-oriented university

Getting Started: Funding Opportunities

Deciding where to begin is half the battle. "Most new beginning faculty," it has been observed, "hear a lot about how important it is to bring in research money. . . . It is easy to get caught up in this topic and feel that money is the only factor in selecting research topics." While the availability of funding is undeniably an important consideration, experts agree that "one should not lose sight of academic interest as the key driving force in choosing a topic. After all, one of the joys of being a faculty member is the freedom to work on research that is personally stimulating and rewarding."[3]

The catch-22 dilemma facing the neophyte academic amounts to this: Without a proven track record of successfully conducted funded research, prospects for success with those first few grant applications are somewhat problematic, no matter how interesting or potentially fruitful the research agendas proposed.[4] Kenneth Henson offers three practical recommendations to aid first-time grant seekers:

- First, develop an efficient system for collecting and analyzing the voluminous information inevitably generated as a byproduct of the proposal planning and writing process; you may need it for the next proposal.
- Second, learn to make effective use of computerized listings and descriptions of grant sources, not to mention websites that offer advice on developing proposals and data-management techniques.
- Third, begin cultivating good time-management skills, including setting priorities; avoiding or minimizing unnecessary time-wasters; observing specific deadlines; delegating routine chores to secretaries or graduate assistants; and, finally, keeping organized and on task at all times.[5]

Successful grant management demands nothing less than a high level of self-discipline and mastery of basic organizational skills. Disorganized people unable to budget their time and make it count find it hard to draft successful proposals for grants, much less manage them effectively.

One sensible rule of thumb when setting out to identify potential funding sources for your project is to look for a close match between the type of initiative a given foundation or agency typically seeks to support and the nature of what it is you want to do. "Most funders," it has been observed, "are astute and demanding. Their goal is not to give away money or to garner a tax deduction. They are using their money to achieve definite goals, their goals."[6] Frequently, "proposal writers focus on their own needs for funds instead of matching their project's goals with a sponsor's priorities."[7]

As Judith Argon advises, a necessary first step is to define your project as clearly as possible and consider what it will take to carry it forward: "Different projects have vastly differing budgetary and programmatic needs; defining the parameters of the project will help direct and identify appropriate funding sources as well as determine the appropriate funding mechanism."[8]

Information on external funding sources is not hard to find. Oftentimes, the best starting point is to visit whatever office in your own institution helps manage grants acquisition and administration. They go by different names: Office of Sponsored Research, Office of Research Support, and so on. Sometimes a facility is associated with Institutional Development and Advancement. In medium-sized and larger schools, it may be conjoined with the university's graduate school.

Staff personnel in these offices generally can assist new faculty in locating likely funding sources. They provide help in fulfilling the specific requirements of current RFPs ("Request for Proposals"), with reviews of the details of grant-writing techniques, and, among other things, useful instruction on how to prepare a detailed budget proposal as a major element of any full-blown application. Most such offices nowadays also make available so-called boiler-plate text describing the institution and its facilities—that is, standardized information about the college or university, its history and development, demographics and current enrollments, and other pertinent data usually called for in a grant proposal.

A second source for information about funding possibilities lies even closer to home—namely, conversations with colleagues who have successful track records in the grantsmanship game. Once again, as Judith Argon suggests, "Rely on the advice of senior colleagues—many will be willing to provide you with the name of their program officer; some will offer to act as an intermediary; and others may suggest preparing a collaborative proposal."[9] Most senior faculty members are more than willing to share their expertise with new colleagues who want to learn the ropes. Beginning faculty should be quick to take advantage of these opportunities and not hesitate to ask for assistance. Above all, ask to see copies of successful proposals that have been funded. If an opportunity opens up, consider becoming part of a grant-writing team—there is really no need to go it alone your first few times.

If your institution lacks a grants officer and few of your colleagues are involved in sponsored research, there are other ways of collecting needed information. Sometimes your best friend is a local reference librarian. Try your campus library. Among the more helpful printed publications and manuals (some of them accessible online as well) are *The Foundation Directory*, *Corporate Foundations Profile*, *Catalog of Federal Domestic Assistance*, *Federal Register*, *Commerce Business Daily*, *The Grants Database*, and several others. Also helpful are notices about funding opportunities sometimes published in professional journals and newsletters in various fields. Your own discipline may be among them.

Internal Funding

Where you apply for funding to support a research initiative ought to depend not only on a match between what you want to do and what a potential sponsor is interested in financing, but also on the level of assistance you are seeking. Not every project requires hundreds of thousands of dollars for its execution. If you are just starting out, it may be prudent to begin with a proposal of very modest proportions. Or develop a preliminary study for which only a small amount of "seed" money is needed. Whereas it is true to observe that funding constraints limit what can be attempted in certain scientific and technological fields, the fact remains that some very good research can still be done in the social sciences and humanities without lavish support. If your proposal is a relatively small one, there may be no need to look beyond your own college or university for support.

The truth of the matter is, in academic institutions where faculty research is prized and rewarded, there is almost always some provision made for awarding small internal grants—that is, for projects requiring, say, no more than a few hundred dollars (usually for basic supplies or to cover manuscript preparation costs, postage, and the like). No particular status or prestige attaches to the receipt of these research incentive funds as such. Small-scale grants are usually awarded noncompetitively in hope that something bigger and more ambitious will ensue later on, or that the faculty recipient will eventually be able to publish something that might not otherwise have seen the light of day. Cliff Davidson and Susan Ambrose emphasize the point that the initiative falls to the new faculty member to obtain seed money or small grants for proposal development from his or her own institution before seeking funding elsewhere. However, they caution, "Don't make the mistake of relying on internal funds for more than a start: academic institutions are not funding agencies."[10] If a few hundred dollars will not suffice to carry out your research program, external funding becomes a must.

External Funding Sources: Grants and Contracts

Oversimplifying only slightly, there are two basic types or categories of funding sources for academic research. The public realm is represented by a mixed array of federal, state, and local governmental agencies. In the private arena are philanthropic foundations and corporations. Public and private sources alike support both grants and contracts, though they tend to operate with different rules, depending partly on the size and character of the projects they prefer to support.

There is a distinction sometimes drawn between grants and contracts, even though the two terms are often used interchangeably. A research *grant* is an award whose terms and conditions almost always are established prior to the issuance of an invitation for applications. Suppose for example, that the Department of Human Services has issued a call for research studies on the habits and lifestyles of people living below the government's official poverty line. Now further suppose that you have had a funding application accepted to study child-care practices among impoverished single mothers. In this example, the grant amounts to funding for a specified piece of research whose focus is congruent with a previously enunciated theme or some predefined sphere of inquiry.

A *contract* may be thought of primarily as an award to perform some type of service or to inaugurate a special program of one type or another. Typically, the various conditions and stipulations are negotiable and tailored to a specific project. For example, a funding agency, whether public or private, is known to support innovative programs for the preservice preparation of elementary or secondary teachers interested in working in inner-city schools. A proposal to accomplish that goal for some targeted school system is submitted by an education department, school, or college. The proposal is funded. In effect, the successful applicant has contracted to furnish a service (in this example, an innovative training program adapted to the needs of urban-school teachers). There may be a research or assessment component added in, depending on how the contract is drawn up, but the delivery of a program or service remains the primary consideration.

Whether it is a research grant or a service contract, the award typically is made to a college or university as such (rarely a subunit thereof). The institution as a whole ultimately bears legal responsibility for managerial oversight of the project and accountability for the administration of funds, no matter what office, individual, or faculty team actually is charged with completing the work. Both grants and contracts usually mandate very specific administrative and reporting requirements throughout the life of the project.[11]

Experienced academics who have applied at one time or another for funding to some federal governmental agency will attest to the complexity of the application and review process. The sheer number of federal programs and agencies, the complicated nature of the federal bureaucracy itself, and the lack of articulation or connection among individual governmental offices all conspire to make the pursuit of funding a daunting prospect for even the most seasoned grant writer.[12] The usual pattern is for a governmental agency to advertise the availability of funding for some specific purpose by issuing a formal request for proposals (RFP). Basically, the agency determines the topic, subject, problem, or range of issues to be treated. Your challenge as an applicant is to design a means of addressing whatever topic or problem has been identified.[13] Proposals are funded on a competitive basis, depending on the perceived relevance of the proposed work to the topic of the RFP and external reviewers' judgments about the quality of each proposal submitted for consideration.[14]

Typically, RFPs from federal sources provide detailed proposal instructions and guidelines for submission. A major advantage in responding to a specific RFP is that the applicant knows ahead of time that funds have already been earmarked to support winning proposals. The trick is to persuade the prospective funding agency that your proposal, one among perhaps dozens or even hundreds received, is deserving of support.

Funding for a given project also can be secured sometimes through an unsolicited proposal, especially if the funding entity is a state rather than a federal agency. The advantage of this approach is that you as applicant are free to select a research topic and approach of your own choosing, assuming there is some rough correspondence between the needs and interests of the agency and the nature of the proposal you submit for consideration. The key disadvantage, of course, is there is no prior guarantee that any funds have been set aside to accommodate the particular request in question, even if the proposal is favorably received.[15]

Some federal governmental agencies have developed special funding opportunities for new faculty. They recognize that neophyte professors are at a real disadvantage when competing for grants against faculty colleagues with established track records. Novice grant writers are well advised to check on the availability and funding priorities of special programs sponsored by the National Science Foundation (NSF), the National Institutes for Health (NIH), the National Endowment for the Humanities (NEH), and the National Endowment for the Arts (NEA), among others.

Private Sector Funding Sources:
Foundations and Corporations

Private foundations and business corporations provide the bulk of private research funding in higher education—in excess of $4 billion annually.[16] Relatively few of them, regardless of their size, stated purpose, or financial genesis, are wholly autonomous entities, independent of control by the individual, family, or business that established them.[17] Foundations come in many different varieties and sizes; and they tend to operate in quite dissimilar ways.

National foundations are large organizations that generally seek to make a tangible difference on a large scale with respect to some specific issue or societal need. They want creative, innovative projects and model programs that promise concrete, measurable results—preferably immediately.[18] Examples of large-scale funding agencies include the Kellogg Foundation, the Carnegie Foundation, the Ford Foundation, and the Rockefeller Foundation. Collectively, these gargantuan foundations account for well over half of all private foundation-giving nationwide.

Community foundations usually originate with an endowment from some public-spirited citizen, the proceeds from which go to help support local or regional undertakings.[19] Research projects or service programs that target a specific community are particularly favored.

Family foundations characteristically represent the special interest of a family or a family member, such as a deceased spouse whose surviving partner as donor wishes to memorialize with a bequest. Many such foundations have defined geographic preferences or a focus on small- and medium-scale undertakings in a specific field or area of endeavor.[20] Foundation executors tend not to issue general requests for proposals, preferring instead simply to receive unsolicited proposals on topics consistent with their interests and priorities.

Many large business corporations have established foundations that fund various academic research projects and service contracts. Corporate foundations vary greatly among themselves in their operations, and are difficult to describe succinctly. Some are purely philanthropic in character. Most, strictly speaking, are not. The latter tend to favor initiatives calculated to benefit their respective corporate sponsors. As Edward Reeve and Davis Ballard emphasize, "Corporations view their grants as purchases. They want something back from the researcher, some kind of direct or indirect benefit for their corporation and their employees."[21]

An example might be a business whose foundation finds it more cost-effective to farm out basic research and development work to academe than to conduct the same activities in-house, or, for the same reasons, uses outsiders to do marketing analysis and other types of field research. Again, a corporation might direct its foundation to sponsor a series of employee-training programs designed and conducted exclusively by human-resource specialists from a college or university instead of by its own staff personnel. Many similar illustrations come to mind.

A hybrid type of funding source for research projects is that represented by a foundation operating under the auspices of a professional trade association. Corporate sponsorship is not through any single business or corporation but, rather, through a consortium or association of like commercial enterprises. In almost all instances, the trade association funds only projects of direct benefit or interest to its sponsoring members within a given industry. A national association of egg producers, for instance, might fund a long-term study of the nutritional benefits and hazards of egg consumption; a consortium of lead manufacturers would be especially interested in research aimed at the development of improved storage batteries for electrically powered automobiles; and so on.

Basic Guidelines

Already mentioned as a commonsense rule when seeking a funding source for your research is the importance of determining whether your proposed project is sufficiently well-aligned with the priorities and interests of the targeted foundation or corporation that it will be accorded serious consideration. Incredible though it may seem, the single most-frequent complaint heard from funding entities is about the inclination of academics to utilize a "shot-gun" approach when looking for funds to support their projects. Absolutely no useful purpose is served by firing off an unsolicited proposal to a funding agency whose institutional interests or priorities are incongruent with what you want to do. Chances of a "lucky hit" are negligible.

Second, the point cannot be overemphasized: Hard-nosed realism is called for when estimating the cost of the research for which support is sought. A "pie-in-the-sky" approach where the total price tag vastly exceeds any reasonable projection of actual likely costs (or benefits) serves only to undermine the credibility of your proposal and practically guarantees its rejection. The opposite extreme is almost equally counterproductive. A "low-ball" cost estimate may result (assuming your proposal is accepted) in funding at a level too meager to allow you to complete your project satisfactorily.

Third, you must consider carefully whether you are able and willing to comply with the funding source's due dates for budgets, progress reports, and so forth, and whether you realistically can expect to complete your research within the time frame designated. A quick way to lose credibility and legitimacy in the eyes of your sponsor is to default on deadlines or fail to complete the work as promised within the time specified.

Fourth, be sure you and your institution meet each and every one of the eligibility requirements stipulated by the funding source.[22] Taking into consideration the amount of work that goes into a proposal and the time needed for it to undergo review, there is nothing so frustrating and disheartening as discovering well into the process that you cannot, or have not, complied with certain eligibility considerations that, if unmet, may preclude further consideration for funding.

Finally, unless you are hoping to be part of a large team of investigators doing "cutting-edge" basic research under the auspices of a major governmental agency or a national foundation, bear in mind when preparing a proposal that most funding sources favor submissions whose focus generates practical applications. As previously mentioned, foundations and corporations prefer to support initiatives capable of leading to early, demonstrable results.[23]

The Grant-Writing Process

The first step preliminary to the actual writing of a grant proposal is to gather in as much information as possible about the funding source to which the request will be submitted. Written materials supplied by the foundation or agency furnish the starting point. Contact with the foundation's grants officer or some other appropriate representative is apt to be helpful as well. Suggestions from others who have had experience working with the targeted foundation can help fill in the gaps.[24] The aim now is not simply to check on the congruity of your project with the basic purpose and goals of the prospective underwriter.[25] It is to confirm how the agency does business, what procedural guidelines it insists on, and what specific features must be incorporated within the submissions it is willing to consider.

As a general rule, public funding agencies require long, detailed proposals ranging from ten to a hundred pages in length, depending partly on the size of the grant contemplated. Private foundations tend to rely on shorter letter proposals of no more than four to six pages in length. Some offices or agencies demand a two-step process: first, a brief "pre-proposal," followed, second, by a lengthier, more extensive document if, after preliminary review, the initial submission looks promising.

Regardless of the nature of the project, it is helpful to remember also that the two most important aspects of a successful proposal are "a powerful new idea or project" and its presentation in a form likely to be found "clear, convincing, and compelling."[26] If you fail to persuade the program officer or reviewers that your idea offers something new or significant, odds are that funding will be denied. By the same token, if your proposal is poorly written or lacks coherence and focus, it will not receive a favorable hearing.

Whether your submission is unsolicited or a response to a request for proposals, it is important to ensure not only that you understand all of the proposal requirements but that you know how proposals will be reviewed. Many stylistic as well as substantive considerations, including how much technical language to include or exclude, will hinge on who will review your submission—outside consultants or internal grant administrators, specialists in your field or generalists lacking intimate familiarity with your particular academic specialty.[27] Naturally, it is also helpful for planning purposes to have in hand some estimate of approximately how much time is required before reviews are completed and funding decisions rendered.

There is no detailed standardized format for a research proposal. In broad terms, the main elements usually include an abstract or executive summary; an introduction; a statement of need or a statement of the problem; a brief explanation of the objectives of the proposal; a summary of the methods to be employed; evaluation procedures; a detailed budget; indications as to how the results of the project will be disseminated; and various appendices, including the vitas of the investigators and letters of support.[28]

- The opening section in most proposals to governmental agencies is a concise summary of the project in its entirety. It is usually the first part to be read and the last written. It should provide a convenient overview of what is proposed and indicate why the project is a worthwhile undertaking.[29]
- The next section is the introduction, consisting of three or four paragraphs of text. The narrative should serve to establish your academic bona fides, underscore the importance of the project, and link the proposal to the funding priorities of the agency to which the submission is made.[30]
- The third section of the proposal, the statement of need, supplies a rationale for conducting the research project. Sometimes a literature review is demanded, which affords you an opportunity to demonstrate your familiarity with relevant work in the field.[31] Here in this section the case must be made that a need exists for the study proposed and that the work for which funding is sought in fact will address that need. Showing how your proposal is distinctive or unique, how it departs in important respects from previous work, may enhance chances

of a successful review.[32] Granting agencies aspire to support projects that are different, that appear to stand out from conventional or traditional approaches to a problem.[33]

- The fourth part of a long-form proposal to a governmental funding agency typically lays out in some detail the objectives of the study you as the investigator hope to conduct. Sometimes it is appropriate to cite a formal hypothesis you intend to test. In other cases, it is sufficient to cite in broad terms the objectives, anticipated outcomes or results, and the expected accomplishments of the study. Judith Argon advises when drafting this section of the proposal to keep in mind that "when sponsors fund your projects, they are literally 'buying' your objectives."[34]

Most experts agree that special care should be taken in specifying the aims of a study. They must be specific. Insofar as possible, they ought to be measurable. Objectives should be practical. They should be made explicit in some systematic way.[35] The specification should be laid out in the order the objectives will be accomplished and should indicate what will be done and when.[36]

- A methods section typically follows the discussion of objectives. As in a research article, you should discuss in some detail how the research will be designed, how it will be conducted, how data will be collected, and what procedures will be employed to analyze the data. A timeline for completion should be included if possible.[37]
- The evaluation section of a proposal is likely to come under close scrutiny by reviewers. Funding agencies are particularly interested in learning how you intend to identify and assess the outcomes of your study or project.[38] They want to know if it will be possible to judge whether the project has had the desired impact—whether, as the colloquialism has it, they are "getting the most bang for their buck."
- Dissemination of the results of funded research matters too. Funding agencies need to know how you intend to share the results of the study within some broader community: through articles, reports, books, manuals, presentations, and so on. Careful thought should go into crafting a response to this question.
- Not counting appendices, the concluding section of a typical proposal is the budget. Many funding agencies mandate the use of budgetary forms of their own devising. Included within your statement of proposed expenditures should be such items as salaries, benefits, travel, secretarial assistance, equipment (if necessary), and so forth. Likewise

to be included are indirect costs, materials, and supplies.[39] Overall, the budget must offer a credible accounting of what it will reasonably require to complete the project you have described.[40]

Practically every novice can expect to need detailed assistance in drawing up a budget.[41] Determining which expenditures should appear where, under what cost categories, can be a major task all by itself. Complicating matters further is that a funding agency may not always be consistent from one RFP to another in specifying what cost items are allowable within a proposal budget and which will be disallowed. Sometimes the guidelines are specific to a special class of awards or funding cycle. Furthermore, each agency (or so it would seem) has a different set of accounting procedures for determining what portion or percentage of a given expense item is eligible for inclusion in a proposed funding package. In most proposals, the budget must be responsive to two types or categories of cost:

- Direct costs are so-called line items in the budget, including wages and salaries, fringe benefits, equipment, materials, supplies, publication expenses, travel, computer charges, and consultant services. All such items represent specific expenses related directly to the execution of the project.
- Indirect costs, sometimes referred to as "overhead" costs, are expenses calculated usually as a percentage of the project's total direct costs.[42] They amount to charges paid in compensation to the institution to defray the cost of utilities, facilities use, administrative expenses, and other items associated with, but not specifically identified with, the project.
- Cost sharing refers to the arrangement whereby some portion of a project's direct or indirect costs are assumed by the proposal author's institution. Often referred to as "shared" costs, they are usually calculated as a flat percentage of the total proposed budget. Commonly included are such items as charges for the use, maintenance, and upkeep of facilities; a prorated portion of the cost of utilities; administrative overhead (variously calculated); and supplies. In essence, cost sharing is intended to underscore the institution's willingness to enter into a "partnership" with the funding agency, supposedly signified by the school's avowed willingness to assume part of the project's expense rather than depending on the funding agency to bear its total cost.

Sometimes indirect costs can be negotiated between a school's grants officer and a funding agency, depending on individual circumstances. Standard operating procedure in many colleges and universities is to work downward from a predetermined or fixed overhead percentage, a strategy intended to enhance the attractiveness of a particular proposal, and thereby increase chances for its favorable consideration—or so it is hoped. Some institutions, however, require a standard overhead percentage and will not deviate from it significantly, if at all. At the risk of over-generalizing, the larger and more prestigious the institution, the higher the indirect cost charged against a grant and the less room left for negotiating adjustments.

Schools differ substantially in other ways besides indirect costs so far as budget building is concerned, just as do funders.[43] Depending on the nature and amount of the grant application, for example, some universities require the applicant to build in salary costs (wholly or in part) and charge them to the external funding agency. Some colleges and universities have user-fee schedules, which must be built into the indirect-cost portion of the proposed budget. For all of these reasons, few faculty members are able to assemble the budgetary portion of their grant applications without help, given its complexities and endless permutations. What holds true for experienced grant applicants applies with special force to novices. Fortunately, most institutions of higher learning are cognizant of the difficulties and have one or more staff persons available to help as needed.

Foundation Grant Proposals

Most private foundations prefer to have a prospective grant applicant initiate contact by letter. The typical "letter proposal" runs between five and six pages in length. It should be drafted more as an informal concept paper than as a detailed proposal of the sort customarily submitted to a state or federal funding agency. If your letter does attract the interest of the foundation's grants officer, you will be asked to follow up with more information, perhaps to submit a more formal, detailed proposal.[44]

Advice givers in the area of private foundations concur that your initial communication should be concise, matter of fact, and straightforward in explaining what you want to do. The narrative should avoid exaggeration or hyperbole and the excessive use of adverbs and adjectives. A certain economy of expression is highly desirable. Your goal, in other words, is to be clear, precise, and credible, without relying on the sorts of rhetorical flourishes that tend to distract rather than support your text.

The usual components of the document you first submit ought to include (not necessarily in a fixed order) the following elements:

- a proposal summary, an introductory overview of the project
- a rationale for the study or project that demonstrates how its subject matter and objectives are consistent with the priorities and interests

of the foundation—in other words, an argument for why the funding agency should find your proposal both pertinent and interesting
- a statement of the problem or need and why it is significant
- a well-reasoned explanation of how the study or project will serve to address the need or problem outlined
- a statement summarizing your capabilities, professional experience, and qualifications to undertake the project for which you are seeking support
- a succinct request for funding, together with a tentative budget summary or other indication of the level of support requested
- a conclusion in which you reiterate the response you are requesting.[45]

All told, your aim, as one writer sums it up, is to demonstrate that you have something to offer—"a new idea, a different approach, a distinctive solution to a significant problem, the time, talent, and energy to get the job done, and the qualifications."[46] As a beginning grant writer, it will be helpful for you to anticipate several weeks or even months of work to plan, research, develop, and submit a viable proposal. Investing the time and energy required is the price to be paid for writing winning grants.

Precisely for this reason, it is critical that you signal your intentions to your department chair, dean, or some other responsible official well before commencing work on an application. In essence, you need to secure authorization to proceed, since if you are eventually successful it may limit your ability to discharge other assignments throughout the period you are working on your project.

Assuming permission has been secured and you have finally sent off your proposal letter, do not expect a speedy response, apart perhaps from a brief acknowledgment that your request has been received. Each foundation makes funding decisions in its own way. Many lack full-time staff members and make extensive use of outside reviewers to evaluate proposals. If your proposal is not immediately rejected out of hand, it will undergo a series of screening steps, the number depending on the foundation's size and style of operation. Should the proposal survive the winnowing process—which may entail months, not to mention requests for successive reworkings of your draft—it must be approved finally by the foundation's governing board.[47]

Avoiding Common Mistakes

As a newcomer entering the arena of competitive grants and contracts, you may find yourself repeating common mistakes that could jeopardize your chances for securing funding.[48] Beginning faculty should be particularly aware of four common myths associated with the grant-application process:

- The longer and more detailed the proposal, the greater the likelihood it will be funded. Actually, there is little or no relationship between the amount of detail included in a proposal and prospects for its getting accepted. The key is to conform strictly to the submission guidelines of the RFP and to make sure you have addressed all of the requirements stipulated. "Padding" the narrative or including superfluous detail serves only to obscure the merits of your proposal.
- The inclusion of currently fashionable jargon, "buzz" words, and technical terminology will enhance changes of getting a proposal funded. To their credit, it may be said of most grant reviewers that they tend to be unimpressed by pretentious verbiage. You are better off writing in as clear and concise a manner as possible.
- A plea of poverty will increase the likelihood of a proposal getting funded. Your rationale for funding should be deployed and supported strictly on the strength of your proposal. The urgency of your financial need is simply not a variable that funding sources are willing to take into consideration. Again, your proposal must stand or fall on its own merits.
- There are funding agencies out there just waiting to hand out money to practically anyone who applies. Most grants are awarded competitively. There are almost always more hands outstretched for funds than there are resources to fill them. Merely submitting an application carries with it no entitlement to whatever funds are available.

A study conducted by Soraya Corley and Cynthia Schienberg of the most common deficiencies in research grant applications offers a top-ten list of weaknesses also worth noting:[49]

- The proposal did not clearly identify and substantiate a significant problem.
- The proposal did not clearly state the nature of the problem or issue.
- The proposal failed to document adequately the existence of the problem.
- The methods specified were not appropriately adapted to the scope of the problem.
- The methods recommended for addressing the problem were inappropriate or inadequate.

- The problem was more complex than could be addressed by the proposal.
- The proposal lacked clarity in terms of indicating how monies were to be expended.
- The proposal lacked a coherent plan for evaluating the research.
- The project's objectives were not measurable.
- The research time line presented in the proposal was unrealistic.

On balance, there may be more reasons to engage in funded research and other projects than there are reasons for not doing so. A great deal depends on your individual circumstances and interests. Your academic field is an important variable affecting a decision, as is the type of institution in which you hold your academic appointment. If the scholarship in which you plan to engage could benefit from external help and be advanced by it, it probably makes sense to seek outside funding for various projects. If—as is true in many fields—the nature of your work does not require support from funding agencies, then there would seem to be little point in investing the time and effort required for successful grant-writing.

Points in Review

- Match your proposal with an appropriate funding agency, one whose interests and priorities are most congruent with what you hope to accomplish.
- Use the Internet, *Federal Register,* and other published sources to identify grant opportunities. Your school's library is a repository of information on federal, state, and private funding sources. Find out if your school has a grants officer.
- Identify faculty colleagues who have been successful obtaining grants or contracts. Pick their brains. Ask to review successful proposals. Offer to collaborate with them on their projects in order to gain experience before striking off on your own.
- Determine if there are internal college funds to support a small project or a pilot study that could be leveraged for a larger grant later on.
- Make sure you have the support of your institution before making commitments to funding agencies.
- Review and avoid the common mistakes that weaken proposals or prevent them from being favorably considered.

CHAPTER 8

FACULTY SERVICE

The Faculty Workload Triad

Virtually every college and university, large or small, private or public, has some type of "Vision Document" or "Mission Statement," an official invocation of the institution's basic purposes and aspirations. Cited in practically all of them is a more or less standard triad of faculty activities: Teaching, Scholarship, and Service. While the first two categories are presumed to be self-explanatory, "Service" becomes the catch-all term designating everything else that cannot be subsumed readily under the first two rubrics. It likewise is represented as an integral dimension or component of the institution's overall mission.[1]

The Role and Mission Statement of one large Midwestern university, as a case in point, stresses the school's "three primary missions of teaching, research, and service," making special mention of its "outreach orientation" as a public land-grant institution. The institution, the document declares, "recognizes its obligation to extend [its] resources . . . beyond the campus and throughout the State . . . to regional, national, and international clientele."[2] A Vision Statement put forth by an historically black school in Georgia highlights as its motto, "Culture for Service."[3] An independent residential college in Missouri, bills itself "as an intellectual and cultural resource for . . . the local community, and the world."[4]

A private research-oriented institution in the Northeast purportedly seeks to maintain high quality in all of the off-campus services it renders to those external constituencies that are the beneficiaries of its undertakings.[5] A large public land-grant institution in Ohio emphasizing outreach and service defines its goal as "the attainment of international distinction in education, scholarship, and public service."[6]

A medium-sized institution in the mid-South describes itself as "the provider of a wide range of public services to people throughout the state and nation" via its "threefold mission of teaching, research, and public service."[7] The service mission of a California technology-oriented institution is to apply "knowledge by participating in the various communities, local, state, national and international, with which it pursues common interests."[8]

Some schools offer specific examples of their outreach and service efforts. One Southeastern state university, for instance, mentions "service to the public through consultation, technical assistance, short-term instruction, training, and other opportunities for continued learning, growth, and development."[9] Another public university in the Southwest cites "continuing education, its museums and libraries, performing arts, public lectures, athletic events, consultative services, and other outreach activities."[10] Many similar examples from across the country could be adduced to illustrate how academic institutions variously describe their service functions.

Ultimately, what the term "service" boils down to for a faculty beginner depends greatly on the nature of his or her disciplinary specialty, on the organizational "home" where his or her appointment is held, and, of course, on the character of the institution as a whole.[11] Unfortunately, no standard nomenclature designates the various types of service in which faculty members are encouraged or expected to engage. Moreover, discussions of institutional responsibilities for social service do tend to refer to overlapping, unbounded spheres of activity.

Once again, the weight assigned to service is apt to differ tremendously in individual situations, depending also on the college or university in question. In large research universities, the school's broader service mission is not likely to affect a faculty newcomer's decisions about career priorities during his or her first few years on appointment. The mandate for individual faculty members, first and foremost, is to conduct research and to publish; and that imperative is made abundantly clear to all concerned.

In regional public institutions and colleges, research is usually assigned a somewhat lower priority. Teaching is emphasized more heavily; service falls somewhere in between. Only in smaller private liberal arts schools and two-year community colleges is faculty service (along with teaching and the mentoring of students) likely to be ranked highest of all in importance. Research and scholarly publishing as an institutional priority is barely mentioned, if at all.

Even in institutions that highlight their service mission, however, it is not always clear from an individual's perspective how much service, of what type, is deemed acceptable and appropriate for a new faculty member. The entire aspect of "service" as a component of a faculty member's work assignment is marked by ambiguity and uncertainty. The service expectation, potentially, generates exactly the sort of confusion a new faculty member wants at all costs to avoid.

Anticipating somewhat, nearly every new faculty member discovers that his or her academic appointment does carry with it certain vague, ill-defined mandates involving service. And service involvements, to put it bluntly, *will* figure to some indeterminate extent in decisions about your reappointment, annual salary increment, promotion, and the achievement of tenure. Seeking to avoid service obligations entirely, therefore, is highly inadvisable.

Paradoxically, however, while service is ostensibly valued by almost all postsecondary institutions, with few exceptions *it is almost never as highly valued as the other two elements in the faculty workload triad.* Nor is service likely to be rewarded proportionately in terms of actual time and effort expended, relative to that required for success in other professorial pursuits.

Herein lies the seeds of a dilemma confronting junior faculty for whom time is a precious commodity: All faculty are expected to do some service, and service contributions typically *do* count to some extent toward raises and even more to tenure and promotion. But by the same token, *insufficient* service activity will rarely figure as the decisive factor in a decision to *deny* someone promotion or tenure, assuming all other performance variables are judged satisfactory.

Institutional Service

One important type of faculty service is "internal"—that is, responsibilities carried out within the sphere of the institution's own campus operations and activities, possibly including the counseling and advising of students, serving as an advisor to a student organization, and participating in institutional governance. As Neil Smelser puts it, the idea of a professional calling—of which individual commitment to the collective enterprise is a part—is still alive in the academic world (even though, arguably, it has weakened in recent decades). One aspect of that calling expresses itself through committee work.[12] Sooner or later, every faculty member is asked to serve as chair, or at least as a member, of one or more committees, at departmental, college, or campus-wide levels.[13] Serving on committees, in short, comes with the job.

Your obligation to accede, Smelser argues, derives from the terms of an implicit bargain struck between the institution and its faculty.[14] A faculty member is accorded a remarkable degree of freedom from oversight or supervision, not to mention the promise of job security symbolized by tenure (or the eventual prospect thereof). In exchange for

WHEN TO ACCEPT A
COMMITTEE ASSIGNMENT:

- ... when the invitation comes directly from the dean or some other high-ranking administrative official.
- ... when the nature of the assignment is congruent with one of your major professional interests.
- ... when it is clear the committee assignment will not be overly burdensome or excessively time- consuming.
- ... when the committee in question will allow you to network with, and become better known by, colleagues with whom you anticipate working in future.
- ... when the committee or task force has a clear charge and a proven track record of effectiveness in dealing with significant issues or problems, thus affording you the prospect of helping to make a significant, positive contribution to the institution.

WHEN TO DECLINE A
COMMITTEE ASSIGNMENT:

- ... when it is obvious nobody else wants the job (there's probably a good reason for the general disinterest!).
- ... when the committee's focus is far removed from your own interests and concerns.
- ... when it is evident that the assignment will call for a significant expenditure of time and effort.
- ... when the assignment will introject you into the middle of some divisive controversy or a highly-charged political dispute that is unlikely to be resolved to everyone's satisfaction anytime soon.

this autonomy—flexibility and independence almost unrivaled among salaried employees in other work settings—every member of the faculty is expected to assist the institution in the pursuit of its collective purposes. This means service on committees (standing or ad hoc), subcommittees, task forces, boards, and other advisory or decision-making bodies. "The effective operation of any [academic] institution," as A. Clay Schoenfeld and Robert Magnan sum it up, "requires a high degree of faculty participation in faculty government, departmental and campus committees, advisory functions, administrative roles, and similar tasks."[15]

In most complex bureaucratic organizations, committees are both ubiquitous and essential. Academic institutions in particular are honeycombed with them; and they serve many important functions. Some are manifest and explicit; others are latent.[16] As faculty cynics are fond of observing, a standard administrative ploy for delaying a difficult decision is to appoint an ad-hoc task force or committee to examine the issues involved and to tender some sort of recommendation. The net effect is that a decision is deferred, hopefully until passions surrounding a particular controversy have subsided ("studying something to death"). The tactic is usually effective.

Another function is to diffuse responsibility for an unpopular or controversial decision. Ascribing a decision to a committee's collective verdict rather than to an individual decision-maker takes one person off the hook by shifting the brunt of criticism to the whole group.

It is important all the same to stress that that the stock-in-trade of most academic committees is rarely direct power or authority as such. It is mainly a matter of influence. Most committees are advisory in nature only—though this in no way prevents them from helping to shape or even control decisions administrative authorities ultimately make in any particular situation.

Committee bodies as elements within an academic institution's governance and operations structure perform many other vital functions as well. Briefly, a college or university committee is a useful tool for conveying, disseminating, pooling, or gathering information on some particular problem or issue ("many heads are better than one"); for entertaining alternatives to the status quo; for acting as imprimatur for a specific policy or course of action under consideration; for serving as a conduit to carry forward the views and concerns of a particular constituency (faculty, staff, students, alumni); as a vehicle for "floating" new ideas and garnering reactions to them; and, as previously noted, for defusing controversy (or at least scaling it down to manageable proportions so it can be dealt with more comfortably).

Standing committees broaden democratic participation in institutional governance. They act as safety valves, so to speak, in providing forums for open debate and catharsis. They find use in hammering out basic policies and procedural guidelines, adjudicating disputes, evaluating personnel, supervising student admissions and dismissals, allocating resources, ensuring fiscal or administrative accountability, identifying goals and establishing priorities, coordinating services, developing or approving curricula, providing administrative oversight of academic units, and a whole array of other functions. In essence, committees are mechanisms for enhancing the functional rationality of the institution's ongoing operations and activities.

TRANSLATING ACADEMIC
COMMITTEESPEAK . . .

"Serving on this committee will be a real professional opportunity for you."
(Translation: "We have to fill a position on this committee—and we've picked you.")

"We appreciate the unique perspective you bring to this assignment."
(Translation: "We needed a minority member on this committee, and we know you speak for everyone who shares your ethnic identity.")

"Do we need to approve the minutes of our last meeting?"
(Translation: "Does anyone remember what we talked about last time?")

"We're going to need to schedule a regular series of meetings."
(Translation: "We haven't accomplished much yet.")

"The challenge is to get everyone on board and to encourage them to assume ownership of this."
(Translation: "We need to diffuse responsibility for this and spread it around.")

"We should break up into subcommittees and let each group address a particular aspect of this problem before we convene again as a committee of the whole."
(Translation: "This big committee isn't getting much done; maybe smaller groups will work better.")

"This is only a preliminary draft report."
(Translation: "If people don't like it, we can always change it.")

"Have all of the major players and stakeholders in this agreed to what we want to do?"
(Translation: "We need to go back and do some consensus-building.")

"Possibly you could rough out some talking points for our next meeting."
(Translation: "We want you to write something for us.")

"Possibly a little background history here would be helpful."
(Translation: "Let me tell you how we got into this mess.")

"Madame Chair, point of order?"
(Translation: "I don't like the way this is going, so I'm going to delay the vote.")

continues

"I hope we can all come together on this and present a united front."
(Translation: "We've got the majority we need for a vote.")

"Given the importance of this issue, perhaps we should appoint a special task force to explore some of the ramifications in greater depth."
(Translation: "We can probably defer a decision on this almost indefinitely.")

"We should run this by the Faculty Senate and give its members some time to review where we are now before proceeding any further."
(Translation: "We don't have to be in a big rush about this.")

Committee Assignments

Committee work tends to be time consuming. The advantage is that it is necessarily a collective undertaking, quite often affording you a welcome contrast from the more solitary pursuits characteristic of professorial life. Participation happens to be an excellent way of meeting people. As a novice faculty member, serving on committees is a means of familiarizing yourself with the institution, of learning how things get done—and, not incidentally, coming to feel you are a decision-maker on the inside of things rather than a passive onlooker.

Accepting a committee assignment is a good way to become better known among your immediate peers as well as by colleagues in other academic units. It is commonly thought to be a way of raising the profile and reputation of your own academic unit within the broader campus community. Finally, there is gratification to be had when a committee successfully accomplishes a particular task and does it well.

Notwithstanding, most experienced faculty members profess to abhor committee service and regard it as an unwelcome intrusion on their daily work routines. Committee work poses a burdensome distraction from more rewarding tasks—which explains why faculty resort to expletives when referring to it.[17] But given prevailing faculty governance patterns in academe, it is exactly because committee work is so indispensable that participation is commonly looked upon as evidence of your collegiality, professionalism, and "good citizenship." By consenting to serve on committees whose meetings may consume endless hours without any guarantee that something important necessarily will be accomplished, you show your willingness to do your fair share and to be seen as a good "team player."

A senior professor who consistently avoids committee work and declines to take on service assignments is liable to provoke the ire and disapproval of colleagues. But the disapprobation of one's peers on this account alone is not necessarily a career-breaker. An untenured junior faculty member who refuses to pull his or her oar, on the other hand, *can* get into serious trouble. If the nonparticipation begins to attract unfavorable attention, the malingerer's prospects for reappointment or tenure sooner or later may be at risk. For all their tolerance of personal idiosyncrasies, it must be observed, academics are not reluctant to show their disapproval of a peer who seems not to be pulling his or her own weight.

Interestingly, unlike the majority of faculty members at any given institution, some few can always be found who actually take great pleasure in working on committees, and, so to speak, have never found an opportunity to serve that they disliked. They represent the real workhorses of the committee system. For some of these hard-working souls, the camaraderie, the give-and-take around a conference table, offers an antidote to the isolation inherent in professorial life.[18] For others, the sense of influence, of being a major player or decision-maker at the heart of things, acts as a powerful intoxicant—such people are derisively if unfairly referred to as "committee junkies" or "service drones." And for some, a ceaseless round of committee meetings offers at least the illusion of busyness and accomplishment, sometimes perhaps the hoped-for counterbalance to lack of achievement in other aspects of faculty life. Finally, of course, there are those whose motives are purely altruistic.

Faculty novices often find it difficult to strike a sensible balance between too much committee involvement and not enough. Reasons vary.[19] For some, heavy service commitments furnish a pretext—conscious or unconscious—to delay conferring attention on something else. (*"I'd like to be a more productive researcher, but I'm getting eaten alive by all this committee work!"*) Expending long hours on committee meetings and reports, in some instances at least, is a classic form of avoidance behavior.

For others, service work offers more genuine satisfaction and psychological reinforcement than does teaching, advising students, or other aspects of their work assignments. (*"Here I feel I can make a positive difference."*) Yet all the while they overdo, most are mindful they are unlikely to be rewarded to a degree commensurate with that accorded instructional excellence or scholarly productivity (*"I know my committee service work will not count for as much as it should, but someone has to do it, and it is important!"*)

By far the most common reason why new faculty members take on too much institutional service is that they are fearful of saying "no." They know full well their academic "citizenship" and "civic spirit" will be judged by others in terms of a demonstrated willingness to help out. Women and faculty of color are often made to feel a special obligation to take on more extensive committee service obligations than their nonminority peers. The theory is that any given committee will benefit from the gendered, racial, or ethnic perspective such individuals presumably bring to the table. Minority faculty members sometimes refer to this expectation as a form of "double taxation."[20]

If committee service cannot or ought not to be avoided, how much is enough? The standard response is to advise faculty novices to strive for minimal involvement at first, and to avoid becoming overcommitted thereafter.[21] One certainly should do whatever is required, it is said, in order to be judged a "good citizen" by one's departmental or college colleagues, but no more than that.[22]

A good start in committee service, observes Gerald Gibson of Roanoke College, "means setting a reasonable limit early on—and sticking to it." He adds, "What is 'reasonable' will vary with the person; some people can handle a little more than others . . . [but] one is well advised . . . to set some limits, to say no when it needs to be said."[23] Again, as Mia Alexander-Snow and Barbara Johnson advise, "Choose wisely which committees you serve on and learn to say no . . . when service obligations will hinder [prospects for securing] promotion and tenure."[24]

The problem with advising junior faculty to "just say no" is the dubious assumption that they are autonomous agents, free to decide as they will. The question is whether they can decline service assignments with impunity, confident there will be no negative repercussions. Given the relations of power within the academy, it has been often noted, it is no small matter for untenured faculty who want to be considered good academic citizens to turn down committee memberships.[25] Nor is it unreasonable to imagine that a junior faculty member might well succumb to pressure to take on a burdensome service assignment for fear of being perceived as uncollegial.

Hesitation could well be justified when, as is sometimes the case, the assignment is "offered" as a splendid "opportunity" by a department head or some other senior person, someone who is positioned to pass judgment on the faculty member later on. Needless to say, deans, department chairs, and program coordinators should be protective of their new faculty hires; and as much as possible ought to try to shield them from excessive service responsibilities during the first two or three years on the job.

Unfortunately, administrators themselves often are the worst offenders when it comes to overloading junior colleagues with service responsibilities. Faced with the problem of finding willing hands to take on some onerous chore nobody else wants to tackle, the temptation runs strong for an administrator to "invite" untenured colleagues to help—those least likely to decline. Moreover, novice faculty members are not necessarily immune from flattery—they may find it gratifying to be asked for help, and so respond in ways harmful to their own long-term career interests.

Some faculty development specialists who have pondered the issue of service overcommitment among junior faculty recommend that a novice limit his or her membership per year to one, at most two, standing committees having regularly scheduled meetings.[26] Robert Boice of the State University of New York at Stony Brook takes an even more conservative approach. He suggests as a rule of thumb that service should be limited to about an hour's work per week for the first four years of one's appointment.[27] Above all, he is typical in urging selectivity: "Some committees . . . are well worth joining, but you'll do well to look out for yourself before committing to them," he advises. "I'm not suggesting you avoid service altogether—just that you moderate your service until you are secure and productive in your start."[28]

"Selectivity" appears often in counsel offered new faculty. The burden of the advice is that it is important to find out how time consuming and demanding a given assignment will be, and whether the body in question has a good track record of accomplishments. Does it have a clear and explicit charge, a mandate to do something? Is it known for its inaction, or does it get things done? Are the committee's recommendations generally heeded or are they ignored by those to whom the body reports? Does the committee have a history of effective leadership? Do former members whose terms of office have expired consider their involvement to have been helpful or ultimately a waste of time? In short, taking on a committee assignment should begin without illusions and with as much background information as needed.

All things being equal, your long-term career interests are better served by a high-profile committee assignment than a less visible one. A service involvement that makes for a palpable difference is obviously better than one that does not. One single committee membership that actually demands effort and commitment is more meaningful—and will be acknowledged as such—than several trivial assignments. (Faculty are perfectly capable of recognizing insignificant "paper" assignments when it comes time to evaluate your overall record of faculty service.) More is *not* necessarily better.

The ideal for you as a new faculty member is to get involved in a service opportunity of genuine personal interest, whether it be an admissions committee, an international programs and studies task force, a curriculum committee, the committee on scholarships and financial aids, a judiciary body, or whatever. It is important, too, for new faculty members to work toward the point where they begin to be assigned a leadership role as chair of one of the committees on which they have served previously as a member.

Finally, it is advisable for you to compile a service record that includes committee work at multiple levels: departmental, school or college, and campus-wide. Inevitably, if you do a conscientious job as a committee member within your own department, you will quickly win appointment or election to decision-making bodies at higher levels. And, ultimately, a record extending over a span of years that documents service rendered both within and beyond your own academic unit is most likely to be considered truly meritorious.

Summing up, the best advice for novice faculty concerning committee service should include the following guidelines and suggestions:

- Find out as much as possible about the nature and charge of a committee before agreeing to serve as a member.
- Choose committee assignments, whenever feasible, on the combined basis of personal interests or concerns as well as institutional need. It is highly inadvisable for you as an untenured faculty member to accept any committee assignment whose operations are likely to prove divisive or to become "politicized."
- Service on a committee reputed to be unproductive or ineffectual should be avoided unless you are prepared to expend exceptional time and effort on the task of trying to improve its effectiveness.
- You should strive to keep service obligations in balance with other assigned workload responsibilities—service responsibilities must be negotiated with the utmost tact, sensitivity, and discretion.
- In matters involving internal institutional service, it is better on balance to do a few things effectively than to take on multiple chores with indifferent results. Probably, taking everything into account, you should not accept election or appointment to more than two standing committees requiring regularly scheduled meetings during the first year or two of an academic appointment.
- Over the span of three or more years, it is advantageous to seek out committee service responsibilities at multiple levels: departmental or divisional, school or college, campus-wide.
- Accepting a position as a committee chair can be a genuine learning opportunity and should not necessarily be declined, time and energy permitting.
- Up to a point of diminishing returns, the satisfaction and psychological rewards of serving on a given committee are roughly proportional

to the effort expended on its business *between* meetings (gathering information, reviewing documents, writing a report, and so on). Effective committee participation demands adequate preparation for every meeting of the committee as a whole.

• With the possible exception of situations involving two-year schools and small four-year colleges, faculty service within the campus community is likely to have a modest but not altogether insignificant influence on decisions involving salary raises, promotion, and tenure. You should be guided accordingly.

Discipline-Based Professional Service

A second arena in which faculty members discharge their citizenship responsibilities is within their respective disciplines and professional associations. External disciplinary service may occur at local, state, regional, national, and even international levels. It assumes the form of participation in, and contributions to, the workings of scholarly societies and professional boards, councils, and associations with which faculty affiliate in some discipline-based specialty. Faculty in all fields—from anthropology to zoology—generally hold membership in at least one, and usually two or three, of these professional and scholarly organizations.

FURTHER THOUGHTS ON FACULTY COMMITTEE SERVICE

No one was ever promoted or granted tenure on the volume of committee work she or he accepted and did well.

—Nellie Y. McKay, "Minority Faculty in [Mainstream White] Academia," in *The Academic's Handbook,* ed. A. Leigh Deneef and Craufurd D. Goodwin, 2nd ed. (Durham, N.C.: Duke University Press, 1995), 56.

A young faculty member who volunteers for, or accepts readily, those extra sections of the freshman course or serves unstintingly on those innumerable committees is likely to encounter gratitude at the moment but a judgment of irresponsibility and unsuitability for a permanent appointment when the tenure decision is at hand.

—Craufurd D. Goodwin, "Some Tips on Getting Tenure," in Deneef and Goodwin, 152.

The first imperative for a new faculty member is to begin attending state and national convocations of one's disciplinary peers. As A. Clay Schoenfeld and Robert Magnan wryly observe of a novice attending a convention, "You've got to start finding your way around. . . . While rendering proper obeisance to the big wheels there, concentrate on acquiring acquaintances with the peers in attendance of your own status. It's often done best, not in a seminar, but at the bar. You'll all agree the old fogies in charge of this menagerie ought to be put out to pasture, and you're just the Young Turks to do it. As indeed you will, in fairly short order."[29]

Merely attending a convention is only a start. The next step is to secure a place on the program, as a discussant, a panelist, a paper presenter, or in some similar capacity. If you become a program participant who consistently shows up year after year and delivers a well-received presentation, you are bound to attract favorable attention from the leadership of all but the very biggest, most impersonal associations.

If the sponsoring group for a national meeting is extremely large, as in the case of the American Psychological Association, the Modern Languages Association, or the American Educational Research Association, and the like, there are almost always more intimate special interest groups worth investigating. Sometimes the newcomer can better network and begin forging collegial alliances with peers from other institutions in a smaller-scale arena. Also, as a general rule, the smaller and more specialized the organization, the easier it is to get noticed and to begin rising up through the ranks to a position of influence within the group, assuming you aspire to do so.

Opportunities to offer disciplinary service abound. Volunteering to serve on (or standing for election to) a board, committee, or task force of a professional group marks a start. One step leads to another. Before long, if you have acquired a reputation as a diligent, conscientious worker you are likely to find yourself being asked to organize or participate in training institutes, seminars, symposia, workshops, continuing education meetings, and special conferences of various types. Elevation to a leadership role comes with invitations to chair one or more of the organization's major standing committees or executive boards.

Discipline-based faculty work assumes many other forms as well. Service on a journal's editorial board, as a referee for manuscripts submitted for publication, authoring a newsletter or some sort of special report, or working as a reviewer for funding agencies—all are appropriate, legitimate expressions of an individual's commitment to the cause of advancing his or her disciplinary specialization.[30]

Colleges and universities have a vested interest in seeing to it that their faculty members become involved in professional organizations. Altruism aside, office-holding is regarded as evidence of your acceptance and endorsement by your scholarly peers. Presumably, the fact that you are active in an organization indicates that you are "current" in your field, possibly even out at the "cutting edge" of inquiry in a discipline.

Service involvement is also considered good for a person's home institution. High-profile activity by a faculty member bearing his or her institutional affiliation on a name tag or in a program guide, so the theory holds, affords the school invaluable "visibility" and attests to its vitality in the competitive arena of scholarly and profession-related activity.

As is usually the case involving internal service within an institution, disciplinary work beyond the campus carries with it the hazard of unwittingly becoming overextended. Professional affiliations should be decided upon with care. Decisions about what tasks to assume and what roles can be carried out to good effect have to take into account your total work profile, including teaching, advising, and other myriad responsibilities within the home unit.

Counterbalancing these legitimate concerns is the need to become known beyond the precincts of your own campus. When the time comes for faculty performance evaluation, letters of recommendation from colleagues at other colleges and universities who are knowledgeable about your scholarship and service contributions to the field may be solicited. The opinions and judgments of these outside peers can figure importantly within the overall review process; and strong expressions of support could make a favorable decision on promotion or tenure more likely.

Community Service and Outreach

Academics simultaneously inhabit several different "worlds" so far as their faculty service responsibilities are concerned. (It is helpful perhaps to think of overlapping or concentric circles of increasing size.) The first, already discussed, is bounded by the campus: the sphere of internal institutional service. A second service arena is that defined by the individual's scholarly discipline and his or her state and national professional affiliations. A third is that of the local community in which one's college or university is located and the larger world beyond.

Postsecondary schools take pride in themselves as "good neighbors." Any self-respecting institution of higher learning wants to highlight its role as a cultural "resource" for its town or city. Hence, it encourages the public to take advantage of its campus facilities and activities: to patronize the

PROFESSIONAL ASSOCIATIONS: ADDITIONAL THOUGHTS

As a new faculty member, you will likely find it essential to belong to at least one scholarly or professional organization—for example, the Modern Language Association, the American Psychological Association, the American Sociological Association, the American Educational Research Association, and so forth, depending on your academic specialty. Membership signifies your link to organizations within your discipline or subdiscipline and connects you to relevant collectivities outside the boundaries of your own local campus.

You also may wish to consider affiliating with and supporting broader-based organizations, such as the American Association of University Professors. Perhaps no other single organization has done more to advance the cause of academic freedom, to safeguard faculty tenure rights, faculty participation in academic governance, and other issues of concern to members of the professorate in general.

Sometimes activities such as organizing panels, delivering papers, or simply attending the meetings of academic societies are described as "service to the profession." This characterization is misleading. "Professional service" is better reserved for those activities that directly support and advance the organization undergirding your discipline: service rendered as a member of a committee, task force, or editorial board, and so on.

Involvement in the life of state, regional, and national associations in your field is important. You become better acquainted with the leading figures in your discipline. You learn more about those who share your research and teaching interests. Meetings afford invaluable opportunities to begin networking and to afford yourself "visibility." Active participation in professional associations helps make possible job forums, membership directories, accreditation standards, legislative initiatives, and other activities of critical importance to your profession.

diverse art exhibitions, museum displays, musical productions, recitals, theatrical performances, and lectures it sponsors, not to mention its athletic extravaganzas. Access afforded the public symbolizes an institution's desire to fulfill its "civic" responsibilities to the local community and to society at large.

Sometimes overlooked is the point that exhibitions, dramatic performances, museum shows, and so on do not just happen. They require work—not just by staff personnel but by faculty specialists who must invest enormous time, effort and energy in bringing them about. Community service, even at the local effort, can be extremely demanding.

More broadly, the "outreach" mission of a college or university means encouraging its faculty to seize the initiative in serving "society" and seeking, both collectively and as individuals, to contribute to the common welfare off-campus. Recent years have witnessed mounting calls for higher education to become more directly responsive to societal needs in this activist sense. University of Vermont President Judith Ramaley's pronouncement is typical: "There is a growing expectation," she claims, "that colleges and universities will be good citizens in their communities and assist with economic and community development, and, in many instances, will become partners in the revitalization of community and neighborhood life."[31]

Zelda Gamson of the University of Massachusetts at Boston, referring to the same mandate, reiterates the call: "Higher education has to become more engaged with societal issues. . . . We cannot count on government alone to deal with the serious social and economic problems plaguing the country. Higher education represents a vast, untapped resource that has yet to be mined," she declares. "We need the expertise and involvement of our faculties if we are to make a difference."[32]

Russell Edgerton, pleading for an enhanced service role for colleges and universities, argues that the issue boils down to one of priorities: "Lots of folks who care about and support higher education," he asserts, "believe that teaching loads in research universities and elite liberal arts colleges have declined to an embarrassing point; that faculty are pressured into doing research that is of no particular value to society; and that there are fewer and fewer faculty to count on to perform tasks of university citizenship." The American public, Edgerton claims, is "calling upon our universities to recapture and redirect faculty energy to agendas of higher social value. . . ."[33]

A. Clay Schoenfeld and Robert Magnan, among countless others, sound much the same theme. "Outreach," they argue, "is fundamentally an institutional state of mind which views the campus not as a place but as an instrument. Translated into an operational philosophy, outreach asks faculty members individually and collectively to make themselves as available as possible to the whole of society, or at least to the constituency from which an institution draws in inspiration and support."[34] As a corollary, "The outreach function brings back to the campus those essential public impulses that enliven teaching and stimulate research." The outreach goal, as they phrase it, is to bring campus and community into "fruitful juxtaposition" so as to enrich the life of both.[35]

Lorilee Sandman, vice-provost at Cleveland State University, professes confidence that college and university faculty do in fact desire to bring about just this sort of juxtaposition. "As their institutions are implored to become more 'engaged,' and 'responsive,' faculty members want to respond appropriately," she alleges. "They want to connect their research and their students with 'real-world' challenges; they want to be co-learners and partners with people outside the academy, to learn more about discipline-related societal problems and to bring their knowledge to parties dealing with such problems."[36]

Lamenting what they see as a mismatch between society's needs and higher education's current priorities, Deborah Hirsch and Ernest Lynton of the University of Massachusetts at Boston claim to hear a "swelling chorus" urging institutions of higher learning "to turn outward . . . to recognize their obligation to use their intellectual resources to help ameliorate the intractable problems of today's society." They declare: "Never before has society had as great a need for the rapid and effective application of knowledge. Never before has it been so important for higher education to play a major role in this effort."[37]

To skeptics who question whether an expanded activist service role for higher education is possible or even desirable, advocates argue that teaching, research, and service are not mutually exclusive aspects of faculty work, as has long been commonly assumed; and that they need not necessarily compete for time in the sense that effort expended in one area necessarily detracts from the energy available for others. Much allegedly depends on how faculty work is viewed. This often-reiterated counterargument builds more than anything else from a position first enunciated in an influential work entitled *Scholarship Reconsidered: Priorities of the Professoriate*, authored by Ernest

ACADEME AND CIVIC ENGAGEMENT

We believe that the challenge of the next millennium is the renewal of our own democratic life and reassertion of social stewardship. In celebrating the birth of our democracy, we can think of no nobler task than committing ourselves to helping catalyze and lead a national movement to reinvigorate the public purposes and civic mission of higher education. We believe that now and through the next century, our institutions must be vital agent and architects of a flourishing democracy. We urge all of higher education to join us.

—*Fourth of July Declaration on the Civic Responsibility of Higher Education* (Campus Compact, 1999), cited in Elizabeth L. Hollander and John Saltmarsh, "The Engaged University," *Academe* 86 (July-August, 2000): 29.

Boyer of the Carnegie Foundation for the Advancement of Teaching, and first published in 1990.

Basically, Boyer's argument is that the traditional notion of faculty "scholarship" as the *discovery* of new knowledge should be thoroughly reconceptualized and significantly broadened.[38] Borrowing from a formulation put forth by Eugene Rice, a former Scholar in Residence at the Carnegie Foundation, Boyer claims that faculty members should be viewed as responsible for carrying out four basic tasks: *advancing* knowledge through original research; *integrating* or *synthesizing* knowledge and reshaping it for multiple audiences; *representing* knowledge, chiefly through teaching and workshops; and *applying* knowledge through professional service in "real-world" settings.[39] Each task is discernibly different, he claims, yet all are legitimate and important manifestations of scholarly endeavor.

Since the time Boyer's thesis was first put forth, proponents of an expanded faculty service role beyond the usual boundaries of academe have relied upon it in various ways to buttress their case. One can easily imagine faculty initiatives, service proponents claim, that so thoroughly combine or mix the tasks first enumerated by Boyer and Rice that they can no longer be usefully differentiated from one another. An ecological biologist who supervises student interns working with governmental policy makers on various environmental legislative initiatives, for example, affords a hypothetical case in point. One might justifiably claim in this instance that the project would simultaneously involve research, teaching, student advising, public outreach, and also the application of knowledge to practical problem solving, all as elements of the whole.[40]

At root, the crux of the argument here and elsewhere is that applied research by faculty should be redefined as a form of public service and be rewarded accordingly in colleges and universities.[41]

Faculty service in the sense of outreach, of course, can and does assume myriad forms, whether or not it is redefined somehow as "scholarship." It might involve teacher-educators working in professional development schools; allied-health professionals seeking to improve clinical practices in health education centers or community clinics; technology transfer projects conducted under the auspices of a joint university-industry partnership; faculty helping to develop venture-capital incubation start-ups, political scientists and economists doing technical policy analysis for agencies in state and local government; or community development experts helping city planners with urban renewal projects.

Other possibilities for service include conducting clinics and workshops, serving on state or local boards, panels, and commissions as experts in their respective fields. Faculty members might serve as program evaluators, or as witnesses in judicial proceedings, or as consultants to government, business, and industry. Professors can be found working with local neighborhood associations, with regional civic agencies, and with state licensing boards in specific professional fields. Demographers, economists, geographers, and sociologists on loan to national and international governmental bodies that benefit from specialized professorial expertise similarly illustrate major expressions of service. Faculty volunteers staffing television or radio programming as a public service suggests still another example of academic outreach at work.

Left unresolved in the midst of all this professorial activism—outreach or service in both its traditional and newer forms—are several enduring issues. One of them has to do with compensation for faculty consulting. The fact of the matter is, faculty in some fields (engineering, law, agriculture, business administration, and applied technical areas especially) have long found ample opportunities to sell their services in the marketplace. So lucrative has the practice become, many universities have found it necessary to place limits on the amount of time their faculty entrepreneurs may allocate to extracurricular pursuits.

The question becomes, can time spent away from campus doing paid consulting qualify somehow as "service" within an assigned workload; and should it "count" as a meritorious activity when decisions are made about salary raises or promotions in academic rank? Or, again, the question arises over who should own the intellectual property rights to products generated as the outcome of some collaborative relationship linking academe and business. If faculty are permitted to line their own pockets as compensation for their off-campus service liaisons, in what sense is it appropriate to think of the work they do as genuine service?

The situation is a bit less ambiguous, perhaps, when it is a matter of external service performed pro bono, that is, without remuneration. Homely examples might include a law school professor who counsels the local school board without benefit of a fee or does volunteer work with the American Civil Liberties Union; a medical school professor who donates his services to a public health clinic; or a biologist who monitors and issues periodic reports on water pollution for a local or state agency.[42] In these or similar instances, it seems easier to make the case for including all such activities as part of a faculty member's regular workload assignment and hence eligible for consideration in terms of faculty incentives and rewards.

A lesser sort of confusion sometimes arises through a failure to distinguish carefully between faculty service that draws upon the individual's scholarly knowledge and disciplinary expertise, on the one hand, and contributions made by a faculty member acting solely in his or her capacity as

a private citizen, on the other. However laudable or commendable the latter might be, few schools nowadays are inclined to assign weight to a faculty member's private charitable or philanthropic efforts. Serving as chair
of the local United Way campaign, for example, while admirable, is unlikely to be counted as a professional advantage when it comes time to
make a decision on promotion or tenure.

Even here, though, there are exceptions. In many small private colleges,
for example, faculty members are actively encouraged to exercise their
civic obligations and to participate as fully as possible in the life of the local
community. Moreover, they *are* rewarded for doing so successfully. Nevertheless, among medium-sized public colleges or larger universities, in the
vast majority of cases such activities are excluded from formal consideration when it comes to professional performance evaluation.

Lofty rhetoric about the importance of academic outreach notwithstanding, there is strong evidence to show that faculty incentive and reward
systems traditionally have not been well aligned with demands for external service.[43] Nor has the situation changed perceptively since the recent
escalation of demands that institutions of higher learning assume a more
active posture in fulfilling their societal obligations.[44] Administrators can
and do exhort faculty members (including newcomers) to render public
service, but they rarely evaluate or reward it to the same extent they do research, grantsmanship, or teaching.[45]

The labor of a teacher in a drama department producing or directing a
play is not likely to be acknowledged or rewarded to the same extent as
would be the teacher's publication of a scholarly monograph about the
theater. An education professor who provides clinical supervision of interns in a school setting may not be rewarded as much as someone who
secures external funding to conduct a research project within a school district. Organizing a public art exhibition may not count as much, in some
institutions, as authorship of a learned treatise on postmodern themes in
the visual or performing arts. All things considered, fulfilling a service role
has at best a modest effect on faculty rewards. For reasons too complex to
review succinctly, service and outreach still remain academic stepchildren
in all but those few colleges and universities where faculty incentives and
rewards have been linked securely to success in service pursuits. The implications that follow for newly hired faculty ought to be fairly obvious:

- Major service commitments to external agencies are hazardous to the
  long-term career prospects of untenured junior faculty, except under
  very special circumstances involving service grants or other short-
  term projects.

- Junior faculty members should strive to minimize or limit their involvement in academic outreach and service activities until they have made a good beginning in registering progress with other assignments, those most likely to be acknowledged and rewarded by the institutions in which they hold their appointments.
- The amount of time and effort expended by an untenured faculty member on outreach should be a conscious, deliberate decision that takes into account internal institutional service responsibilities as well as discipline-related service involvements, the whole representing no more than some appropriately weighted portion of the individual's total workload assignment.
- Scrupulous attention should be paid to documenting your service contributions throughout any given academic year, and should include a broad spectrum of evidence, including a running log of time expended, letters of acknowledgment or testimonials from those with whom you have worked on service projects, and written documents and reports.

Service work can be nothing less than a genuine transformative experience for many faculty members. For some members of the professorate, nothing else quite compares as a source of personal fulfillment and continuing job satisfaction. A professional life spent engaging the

---

PROTECT THYSELF . . .

In academia, as in any walk of life, an individual can be overwhelmed by meaningless activity. This underscores the necessity of making effective choices among alternative activities, given their potential payoffs. The aspiring scholar bent on a successful career must quickly appreciate that no individual has enough time to dispense effort endlessly to all comers without regard to the ultimate consequences. . . .

One should avoid overinvolvement in service activities, but should also take care to do one's fair share—otherwise, one will likely be resented. In this regard, there is typically a price to be paid for saying no. However, there is also always a price in terms of one's time for saying yes.

—Arthur G. Bedeian, "Twelve Suggestions For Optimizing Career Success," *Rhythms of Academic Life,* in Peter J. Frost and M. Susan Taylor, *Personal Accounts of Careers in Academia* (Thousand Oaks, Calif.: Sage Publications, 1996), 6, 7.

world beyond the ivory tower offers rich opportunities for creative self-expression and altruism.

This being said, it is equally important to heed the caveat that faculty service in all of its potential manifestations must be approached with caution and deliberation. As a junior faculty member just beginning to get established in an academic career, the prospect of fulfilling a substantial service role ought to be anticipated perhaps as a pleasure deferred rather than a professional challenge to which you must immediately respond.

Points in Review

- Service is an important but problematic component of the faculty workload triad.
- Faculty service is usually not as highly valued as teaching or scholarship.
- Service contributions figure in decisions regarding tenure and promotion, but oftentimes in complex, indirect ways.
- New faculty should be cautious about accepting committee assignments or appointments for the first year or two.
- Neophytes must learn when to accept or decline internal service involvements.
- Affiliation with, and service in support of, national and regional professional associations is important for advancing your academic career.
- Community outreach is a form of professional service when it is rooted in a faculty member's scholarly expertise.
- Extensive external service commitments may pose a trap for beginning academics.

CHAPTER 9

LEGAL ISSUES AND
THE PROFESSORATE

The Litigious Environment of Academe

A hard truth about contemporary higher education is that colleges and universities (and those who work within them) are increasingly finding themselves embroiled in legal disputes of various types. A 1997 poll conducted by Tillinghast-Towers Perrin, to cite just one example, found that the frequency of legal claims involving academic institutions had more than tripled in the five-year period since 1992. Claims against public postsecondary institutions during that same time span had at least quadrupled.[1] College or university employees accounted for 67 percent of all claims initiated. Meanwhile, it was found that suits brought by students against institutions or their employees had more than doubled and were projected to increase at an even faster pace in future.[2]

Given this rising tempo of judicial disputation, not surprisingly, the authors of a recent guide to legal issues for college teachers warn that the likelihood of a professor being sued is greater today than ever before. "We live in a litigious society," they observe, "and court cases have been filed where college teachers are named as defendants in almost [every] conceivable area of college life."[3] Faculty may find themselves hauled into court on charges of not having taught a course as it was described in a college catalog, for failing to attend class regularly or provide proper supervision and instruction, for allegedly defaming or demeaning students, or for engaging in discriminatory behavior, among other misdeeds. The list of alleged infractions and possible deficiencies that can and do trigger legal action lengthens yearly.[4]

Most legal controversies involving faculty arise in one of two contexts. The first has to do with the legal rights of the individual as an employee, most often those pertaining to promotion and tenure, annual performance evaluations, workload assignments, and academic freedom. In such situations, typically, it is the faculty member who is the plaintiff or aggrieved party seeking redress from the institution or its representative officers.

The second relates to the potential liability a faculty member faces in connection with the performance of his or her job-related duties and responsibilities: teaching, advising, service, and scholarship. In such situations, of course, it is the individual faculty member who is the defendant, with a student, faculty peer, administrator, or the institution at large in the role of grievant. Either way, taking into consideration what may be at stake, anyone just starting out on an academic career is well advised to have a general understanding of his or her legal rights, duties, and responsibilities, and, more broadly, an appreciation for what circumstances are most likely to lead to trouble.

The Costs of Legal Entanglement

The notion of a "mine field" into which the unwary may stumble is invoked all too often by alarmists in describing the legal situation facing members of today's professorate. This overworked metaphor probably claims too much. In fact, the increasing frequency of litigation notwithstanding, a modicum of caution and forethought greatly reduces chances any given individual will ever be named in a lawsuit or grievance proceeding. All the same, any sober-minded assessment of the situation must acknowledge the very real costs, hidden or otherwise, associated with a possible legal dispute. Attorney fees and other expenses involved in preparing for litigation most immediately come to mind, not to mention whatever compensatory damages might be levied against the losing party. But there are other consequences, equally important, as measured by lost time, diminished productivity, lowered workplace morale, psychological stress and strain, the possibility of injury to one's professional reputation or standing in the academic community, and, of course, the prospect of termination or nonrenewal of employment that must be taken into consideration.

The point is an obvious one. Although you as a newcomer to the field of higher education should never work "scared," you do need to be wary of potential pitfalls and adapt your professional behavior accordingly.

Sources of Legal Rights and Responsibilities

There is no single source in law that establishes all of the legal rights and responsibilities of faculty in colleges and universities. The U.S. Constitution and state constitutions jointly establish a common foundation for fundamental guarantees enjoyed by all members of society. These include First Amendment protection of freedom of speech, press, assembly, and religion; the Fourth Amendment's protection against unreasonable search and seizure without a proper warrant; and the Fourteenth Amendment, which ensures due process and equal protection under the law.

Federal and state statutes enacted by Congress and state legislatures provide another important source of law. Federal statutes codified in the United States Code (U.S.C.) provide protection against diverse forms of discrimination, both in the workplace and in the classroom. In addition, federal statutes establish legal rights and responsibilities pertaining to student records and intellectual property. State statutes, on the other hand, often create rules of law specific to academic institutions located within a given state.

Also applicable are administrative rules, regulations and procedures promulgated by certain administrative agencies charged with responsibility for overseeing and enforcing federal and state statutes. Examples include the Equal Employment Opportunity Commission (EEOC) and the National Labor Relations Board (NLRB), both of which impose certain constraints on academic institutions and their employees. The determinations of these agencies are considered binding as statutes and reviewable in courts. Besides rule-making, these agencies also commonly engage as needed in the work of adjudication.[5]

Common law, or case law, is the outcome of judicial precedent—which is to say, a body of law shaped by previous decisions rendered by courts on similar issues.[6] Case law exerts considerable influence in the areas of contracts and torts, which characteristically are not regulated by statutes. Common law also includes courts' interpretations of the meaning of constitutions, statutes, and administrative rules and regulations.

So-called internal sources of law that also directly affect faculty rights and responsibilities draw from the policies, rules, and regulations set forth by individual institutions. Included are policies established by boards of trustees or curators; rules established by campus administrative or faculty governing bodies; and guidelines outlined in faculty, staff, and student handbooks. Individual academic units (schools or colleges, departments, divisions, or program areas) may also stipulate considerations affecting faculty duties and responsibilities. Prominent among institutional regulations are those included in faculty-employment and student-enrollment contracts.

More informal but often decisive in influence are institutional customs and local usages that collectively help define performance expectations and standards.[7] Campus or academic common law in this sense, it is often noted, can be an important guide for decision-making, particularly whenever the school has laid out explicit processes and procedures for conducting student disciplinary hearings or grievances initiated by or against faculty members.[8]

Public and Private Institutions:
A Legal Difference

Often unappreciated is an important legal difference that separates privately controlled colleges and universities from their public counterparts. Whereas public schools are fully subject to the stipulations of federal law, private institutions and their officers are less constrained by them in several major respects. Consequently, the legal rights of faculty and students and the legal responsibilities and duties of institutional employees do vary, depending on institutional setting. Because the Constitution was designed to limit only the exercise of government power, it has been rightly observed, "it does not prohibit private individuals or corporations from impinging on such freedoms as free speech, equal protection, and due process."[9] Sectarian or denominational colleges, for example, legally may impose specific requirements for compliance with doctrinal orthodoxy or require codes of personal comportment from faculty and students that would be wholly unacceptable on the campuses of secular public colleges and universities.

On the other side, while constitutional protections may not exist in private institutions, many other significant sources of law do apply. Most federal statutes prohibiting nondiscrimination against employees and students, for example, pertain to public and private institutions alike. Moreover, common-law remedies such as contract law, agency law, and tort law hold sway in both types of institutions. "At private colleges," it is noted, "most legal rights are based on contractual relations. In the case of students, the contractual relationship is based on a contract of enrollment. In the case of faculty, staff, and administrators, the contractual relationship is based on a contract of employment."[10] In public colleges and universities, contracts are also a major source of law insofar as the legal rights and responsibilities of students and faculty are concerned.

The Faculty Hiring Process: Legal Sticking Points

Most colleges and universities employ a multistep or staged process in recruiting a candidate for a faculty position, relying on a faculty search committee to carry out the project—a phenomenon somewhat unique to higher education. Interestingly, however, most of those (76 percent) who serve as members of a search committee are apt to receive little or no advice concerning the legal issues involved.[11] Yet from first to last—developing selection criteria, publicizing the availability of the position, screening candidates' paper credentials, handling telephone interviews, checking references, conducting on-campus interviews, extending an offer—committee members tend not to be cognizant of certain considerations that by right ought to inform the committee's work from inception to its conclusion.[12]

The single most important legal issue, from the institution's point of view, is avoiding any form of illegal discrimination. The heart of the matter is a focus on job-related considerations and ensuring that all applicants receive equal consideration relative to whatever specific job qualifications have been established.[13] Obviously, the first step is delineating clear and explicit selection standards or criteria. Second is making a good-faith effort to publicize the position in public venues where, theoretically, any and all prospective applicants can apprise themselves of the fact that the position is indeed available. Third is the conscientious effort that must be made to evaluate applications solely in light of whatever selection criteria have been established, without regard for extraneous characteristics or attributes.

Telephone interrogations and face-to-face interviews become problematic when seemingly harmless but inappropriate queries are posed that elicit discriminatory information. Interviewers, for example, must scrupulously avoid probing a candidate's personal life by asking questions about age, marital status, national origin, finances, race or ethnicity, religious beliefs, disabilities and health-related factors, a spouse's future plans, or the candidate's intentions regarding having children. Various federal laws (Title VII of the Civil Rights Act of 1964, the Age Discrimination in Employment Act of 1967, the Americans with Disabilities Act of 1990, and others) make it illegal if the prospective employer uses this type of information in reaching a hiring decision. However artificial it may seem to avoid taking up these matters, extant law constrains institutions from engaging in any such action that might be construed as discriminatory in character.

From a faculty candidate's perspective, the most difficult challenge during an interview is anticipating and handling the sorts of inappropriate questions that often arise naturally during informal "small-talk" or in the course of conversations that transpire outside of the formal interviewing situation. Prudence dictates that insofar as possible the candidate cautiously steer the conversation back to the topic of his or her knowledge, skills, and abilities.

Employment Contracts

As a new faculty member, your legal rights are defined by the specific terms of your employment contract, as supplemented by labor relations law, employment discrimination law, and, in public institutions, constitutional law and public employment statutes and regulations.[14] Many faculty novices fail to recognize what the contract of employment actually includes. It is misleading, for example, to view it simply as a written confirmation of one's initial academic rank, position, salary, and starting date of employment. In fact it is often much more. Once signed, your contract may commit you to the provisions of many *other* documents, including those contained in a faculty handbook or the text of a collective bargaining agreement; not to mention the detailed rules, policies, and regulations of your school's governing board, as specified elsewhere; and even the guidelines of national organizations such as the American Association of University Professors (AAUP). Think of a set of "nested" dolls, in which one figurine contains many others. An essential starting point in understanding your legal rights and responsibilities as a new faculty member is to read your contract carefully (preferably before having signed it) *and all other* relevant documents to which you may be bound by its terms.

Different types of faculty employment contracts confer differing legal rights. Few guarantees or employment rights exist for faculty employed *at-will*. Employment-at-will means literally that the institution may dismiss the professor without notice, for any reason, or for no reason at all. (Correspondingly, the faculty member may terminate employment for any reason whatsoever and without notice.)

Because of the harshness of this rule, courts recognize many exceptions to employment-at-will status. Stipulations preventing an institution from discharging a faculty member without advance notice or cause include situations where the employment contract is for a specified period of time; where the college's policies explicitly state that faculty member may not be discharged except for cause; and where the professor refused to perform an unlawful act or reported the institution for violating state or federal law. In such cases, the teacher's right to employment is protected by a state or federal statute, such as Title VII of the 1964 Civil Rights Act.

MORE THAN MEETS THE EYE: FROM A SINGLE-PAGE FACULTY CONTRACT

The trustees and the Professional are subject to the provisions of the Statutes of the State of Colorado and the *Handbook for Professional Personnel*, which statutes and *Handbook* are incorporated by reference as if fully set forth herein.

A *term* contract indicates that the new professor is employed for a specified period of time, typically an academic term or year. Upon completion of the term specified in the contract, no right or guarantee of successive reappointments is attached. A *continuing* (non-tenure-track) appointment offers near-automatic successive annual reappointments, assuming the holder's performance remains satisfactory, though the contract offers no hard and fast guarantees and does not confer a "right" to future employment. Generally, a faculty member employed under a term contract may not acquire eligibility for consideration for tenure unless—and only in unusual circumstances—the term contract contains a provision for its conversion to a continuing, tenure-track appointment.

A *probationary tenure-track* contract likewise carries with it no guaranteed right of successive reappointments, and may be terminated without cause at the end of any given appointment period. As a rule, nevertheless, termination requires at least some pro forma explanation for cause and substantial advance notice, depending on the contract-holder's length of prior service. Most colleges and universities offer some type of written notice of nonreappointment by a set date and some minimal due-process protection for the person facing dismissal.

Otherwise, assuming satisfactory performance throughout an initial probationary period, the holder of a tenure-track contract may expect to achieve eligibility for tenure consideration once the probationary interval has been successfully concluded (usually after four to seven continuous years of employment). Established usage dictates either that tenure be awarded at this point or that the applicant be placed on notice that his or her service will be terminated by a specified deadline (usually with allowance for an additional

---

FROM THE FACULTY HANDBOOK OF
A PUBLIC, FOUR-YEAR INSTITUTION

Faculty members may receive a term (non-tenure track), [or] term tenure-track . . . appointment. One of these designations shall be on all faculty contracts. A term appointment applies for a specified term of time as defined in the letter of appointment. Full-time, tenure-track faculty members have probationary status of employment and receive term appointments. All faculty appointed to a tenure-track position shall serve a pre-tenure probationary period of six years.

year of employment so that the individual may have time to seek a position elsewhere).

In some places, faculty rights and responsibilities are spelled out in a collective bargaining agreement negotiated between the institution and a faculty union.[15] Where faculty are unionized, terms of employment, including compensation, tend to be laid out more explicitly and in far greater detail than would normally be the case at schools where no such collective agreements exist.

Nondiscrimination in the Workplace

All colleges and universities, public or private, must provide an environment free of illegal discrimination. "Discrimination" in this context simply means treating similarly situated people differently. The major implication is that all employment-related decisions with respect to hiring, annual performance review, promotion, and the awarding of tenure must be based solely on job-specific considerations. Judgments influenced by such "immutable characteristics" as race, national origin, gender, disability, age, or religion are considered discriminatory under both federal and state law.[16] Nowadays, Congress and most states require virtually every employer (including academic institutions) to provide equal employment opportunity for all employees—in other words, giving every individual a chance to succeed according to merit and ability.[17]

Federal antidiscrimination laws serving to protect faculty in postsecondary institutions are both numerous and far-reaching. They include, besides Title VII of the Civil Rights Act of 1964, the Equal Pay Act of 1963,

---

A STATEMENT ON DISCRIMINATION BY THE AMERICAN ASSOCIATION OF UNIVERSITY PROFESSORS

The Association is committed to use its procedures and to take measures, including censure, against colleges and universities practicing illegal or unconstitutional discrimination, or discrimination on a basis not demonstrably related to the job function involved, including but not limited to age, sex, disability, race, religion, national origin, marital status, or sexual orientation.

—American Association of University Professors, *Policy and Documents & Reports* (Washington, D.C.: AAUP, 1995), 147.

the Age Discrimination in Employment Act of 1967, the Pregnancy Discrimination Act of 1978, the Americans with Disabilities Act of 1990, and the Family and Medical Leave Act of 1993. Contained within their lengthy, often-complex provisions are protections against gender-biased salary compensation; prohibition of discrimination against faculty 40 years of age or older; legal protection against the exclusion of pregnancy, childbirth, or associated illness in health or disability insurance programs or sick leave plans; and injunctions against discrimination injurious to individuals with physical impairments. Safe to say, it requires nothing less than the services of a qualified attorney to interpret and explain the specifics of an individual's legal position in any given situation where discriminatory treatment has been alleged.

Academic Freedom

Academic freedom is broadly construed as a "right" or a unique prerogative legitimating the untrammeled self-expression of professors in the conduct of their functions and activities, most particularly in teaching and disseminating scholarship. Historically, the precise meaning of "academic freedom" has proven illusive. Legal scholars William Kaplan and Barbara Lee point out that it draws meaning both from the world of education and the world of law. Educators, they explain, "use the term . . . in reference to the custom and practice, and the ideal, by which faculties may best flourish in their work . . . [whereas] lawyers and judges . . . use 'academic freedom' as a catch-all term to describe the legal rights and responsibilities of the teaching profession. . . ."[18] From a faculty perspective, academic freedom is a necessary dispensation giving professors the autonomy and freedom from hindrance or external interference they must have in order to fulfill effectively their academic duties and responsibilities.[19]

Legally, academic freedom as it is exercised in public postsecondary institutions is usually considered "a variation of rights to freedom of speech or expression" under the protection of the First Amendment.[20] So far as private schools are concerned, academic freedom is respected and protected chiefly through the terms of employment contracts as well as by institutional policies and practices. Most respectable academic institutions, both public and private, also profess to support and abide by the dictates of academic freedom enunciated in a series of policy documents set forth by the American Association of University Professors.

It is important for beginning faculty members to recognize that while they do enjoy academic freedom (or in public institutions, First Amendment rights) in all aspects of their work—freedom of expression through

ACADEMIC FREEDOM: THE AAUP

(a) Teachers are entitled to full academic freedom in research and in the publication of results, subject to the adequate performance of their other academic duties; but research for pecuniary return should be based upon an understanding with authorities of the institution.

(b) Teachers are entitled to freedom in the classroom in discussing their subject, but they should be careful not to introduce into their teaching controversial matter which has no relation to their subject. Limitations of academic freedom because of religious or other aims of the institution should be clearly stated in writing at the time of the appointment.

(c) College and university teachers are citizens, members of a learned profession, and officers of an educational institution. When they speak or write as citizens, they should be free from institutional censorship or discipline. As scholars and educational officers, they should remember that the public may judge their profession and the institution by their utterances. hence they should at all times be accurate, should exercise appropriate restraint, should show respect for the opinions of others, and should make every effort to indicate that they are not speaking for the institution.

—American Association of University Professors, *Policy and Documents & Reports* (Washington, D.C.: AAUP, 1995), 147.

teaching, freedom to publish the fruits of their scholarship, and so on—the rights conferred are by no means unconditional or absolute. Judging from relevant court decisions of recent years, faculty generally may expect to enjoy the greatest amount of freedom in their research and the least amount in the classroom. Moreover, the exercise of academic rights, it is often held, must always be tempered by professional responsibility.[21] "Regardless of the doctrine of academic freedom and First Amendment claims," some argue, "faculty members of state-supported colleges and universities are public employees and . . . a balance must be struck between the interests of the employee . . . commenting on matters of public concern and the state's interest as an employer. . . ."[22] The same caveat may be supported by the courts with respect to the academic freedom of professors employed within the private sector of higher education.

The most practical advice for academic neophytes amounts to this: If you are employed by a private college or university, controversial utterances (inside the classroom or outside of it) should be accompanied by a disclaimer that you are expressing your own views and that they do not necessarily represent some official stance taken by your institution. Moreover, do not expect your remarks to be received kindly (or not to carry an element of risk) if they contravene a position officially and expressly subscribed to by your college or university, or if their utterance plainly violates the terms of your original employment contract. Finally, whether dispensed in or out of the classroom or in print, from a practical standpoint, considerably less protection is afforded views that are *un*related to a faculty member's area of academic expertise than when they reflect the person's own discipline or field of specialization.

If you are employed by a public institution, it is just as important that you issue a disclaimer indicating that your remarks, likely to be found controversial or offensive by some, represent your own views and that in no way are they to be associated with your institution as a corporate entity. In a classroom situation, it should be possible for all possible viewpoints and opinions to be heard, so long as it is understood that a student's grade will not be affected by that individual's assent to, or dissent from, any views and opinions you as the instructor have expressed.

Historically, professors have tended to get into trouble most often when they failed to disassociate their own "extramural" utterances (public speech beyond the campus) from those of the institutions with which they were associated. In a commonsense sort of way, much depends as well on the manner in which unpopular or allegedly subversive views are conveyed. If the mode of expression is thoughtful, rational, and well considered, one's remarks are less likely to arouse popular ire than, say, when they are delivered in an abrasive, confrontational manner. As an old saying has it, it is not what you say (or write), but how you express it that counts.

Faculty Performance Evaluation

Annual performance evaluations of faculty are a well-established feature of academic life. Such reviews serve multiple purposes. One is to inform an individual as to how his or her performance is regarded by his or her peers or by the department chair. In theory at least, the review serves as an indicator of progress and is intended in part to fulfill a developmental function: identifying specific areas where improvement is needed. The most common purpose of the review is to furnish a basis for a decision about contract reappointment or a possible salary increment. Collectively, successive performance evaluations create the "paper trail" needed to justify an eventual decision (pro or con) about tenure or promotion in academic rank.

The point has been stressed elsewhere but deserves reiteration: a new faculty member needs to be clear about how the evaluation process is conducted, about what specific materials or documents must be assembled for inspection, the criteria and standards by which performance will be judged, and about how they may be differentially weighted. Typically, the administrator who superintends the process exercises the initiative in apprising each newcomer as to what is expected and how the process is carried out. If he or she fails to do so, however, it falls to the faculty member undergoing a review to ask questions and otherwise become better informed about what he or she may expect.

From a legal standpoint, courts have been reluctant to engage in second-guessing decisions rendered by peer review committees or academic administrators. The prevailing view is that academic performance evaluation is best carried out by those with the expertise to make informed decisions—namely, academics themselves—and that the legal system is ill-adapted by its very nature to allow effective intervention. While acknowledging that procedural due process is not always afforded and that assessment standards in particular cases may be lacking in objectivity, courts have recognized too that politics and personalities inevitably play a part (though sometimes an indeterminate one) in the faculty evaluation process.[23] In any event, for all of these reasons, academic assessment is an arena into which courts have rarely ventured or intruded.

The practical upshot of that judicial reticence is that a faculty member who is dissatisfied with the outcome of an evaluation has virtually no legal recourse outside the institution. Some colleges and universities make provision—with varying degrees of formality attached—for appeals or grievance procedures through which a rating may be modified. Some of these procedures can be extremely elaborate and complex in nature. Basically, however, all involve successive reviews at ascending levels within the bureaucratic-administrative hierarchy, possibly all the way up to the chief executive officer of the campus or to the school's governing board. Throughout, the burden of proof involving allegations of unfair or discriminatory treatment almost always falls on the grievant. Furthermore, the prospect of achieving a reversal of an unfavorable rating must always be weighed against the political cost of alienating those responsible for the judgment in the first place.

Ownership and Use of Intellectual Property

Technological advances, it is often said, promise within the near future to transform the terms of the traditional interaction between professors and students within academe—that is, a group of learners assembled in the same physical space, listening to and conversing with a live instructor. The most dramatic harbinger of things to come in this respect (or so it is argued by technology celebrants) is the increasing reliance of colleges and universities on so-called distance education. Through the use of Web-based instruction and compressed video, it is fast becoming possible for faculty to teach large numbers of students in remote locations who perhaps rarely if ever set foot on the home campus.

Not yet fully resolved are several legal issues prompted by the growing popularity of "virtual" instruction, primarily questions involving copyrighting "intellectual property." As faculty members become increasingly involved in distance education, they usually are obliged to develop completely new online courses or to make extensive modifications to existing materials for use on the Web. Most such development efforts demand an extraordinary amount of time, effort, and expertise on the faculty member's part. The question is, who owns the course material once it has been developed?

Other questions follow. May others freely make use of material they have not developed themselves? What rights do you have as the creator of your own online material? As the faculty member who did the work, can you copyright the product of your efforts and so preclude others from accessing, modifying, and using what you have worked so hard to produce? And can you take your work product with you if you should elect to secure employment at another institution?

Unfortunately, many institutions venturing into distance education and Web-based instruction have not yet addressed copyright issues in their policies. Traditionally, it should be noted, class notes, outlines, course syllabi, and related instructional resources are presumed to "belong" to—are "owned" by—whoever produced them. However, featured prominently in existing copyright law is a provision referred to as the "work-made-for-hire" rule. In a nutshell, this doctrine holds that in the absence of a signed contract or policy providing otherwise, ownership of materials developed for instructional purposes belongs to the college or university, not to the individual who created them in the first place.

At the risk of some oversimplification, if you produced educational materials as a necessary part of your job assignment, if these were developed during the course of your employment, and if you utilized institutional facilities and resources in their creation and development, then, or so the rule holds, ownership of whatever you produced may belong not to you but to your institutional employer. Yet situations differ. In at least some colleges and universities, ownership customarily is assigned (or tacitly assumed to belong) to the individual faculty member, not to the institution. Anyone extensively engaged in the production of Web-based courses or the teaching of distance-education courses is well advised to ascertain what ownership rights they may enjoy with respect to materials they have generated, whether "work-made-for-hire" or not.

Due Process and Termination of Employment

A complex array of legal considerations governs the conditions under which a faculty member's employment may be terminated. In a landmark 1972 decision (*Board of Regents v. Roth*, 408 U.S. 564) the United States Supreme Court held that "a public college professor dismissed from an [appointment] held under tenure provisions . . . and college professors . . . dismissed during the terms of their contracts . . . have interests in continued employment that are safeguarded by due process."[24] What the Court's decision affirmed, basically, was that a faculty member in a public institution facing dismissal may have a constitutionally protected right to due process under the Fourteenth Amendment, provided he or she can establish the existence of either what is termed a "property" or "liberty" interest.

In the case of public employment, a property interest exists when a professor can demonstrate a claim of legitimate job entitlement (as distinguished simply from a need or desire for continued employment). Tenure status, or an employment contract whose terms have allegedly been violated, offers presumptive evidence of a "legitimate" property interest.

A "liberty" interest, on the other hand, poses a barrier to dismissal when a public college or university levies charges against the faculty member such that they might do irreparable damage to that individual's professional reputation, standing, or association in the community.[25] The stigma presumably attached to the faculty member as a result of the school's action must be of such a character that it would serve to foreclose the possibility of other academic employment opportunities for that individual. A liberty interest, of itself, it is important to note, does not necessarily preclude the interest-holder's dismissal. But it does provide a legal justification for the demand that due process protections be adhered to in whatever review process leads to possible termination of employment.

Constitutional considerations generally do not apply in cases of dismissal from private colleges or universities. Nonetheless, faculty in private institutions, in common with their public counterparts, are entitled to any procedural protections specified in an employment contract or in the official policies of a particular institution. Even in schools where a contract reflects nothing more than at-will status, courts are increasingly inclined to find an expressed or implied promise by the institution not to act arbitrarily in dealing with faculty. In a legal sense, not acting in an arbitrary manner is taken to mean that the school is obliged to offer some limited or rudimentary procedural protection for its academic employees.[26]

The same obligation holds among public institutions in those states having statutes that require "for cause" reasons for terminating a faculty member's employment. At a minimum, the institution is required to spell out the grounds for dismissal and to hold a pre-termination hearing at which the faculty member may challenge or contest the termination decision. Although rarely enumerated specifically by state statute, "for cause" reasons for nonrenewal or termination typically include charges of insubordination, neglect of duty, moral turpitude, incompetence, intellectual dishonesty, abusive conduct, and violation of institutional rules and regulations.

Teaching and Course Management

Most legal actions brought by students against faculty arise in connection with the performance—or, rather, the alleged nonfulfillment—of job responsibilities and obligations. The bulk of them involve allegations of poor teaching performance or, more broadly, about how a course has been developed and presented. Student claims of faculty wrongdoing based on course development and preparation, for example, may range from allegations of fraudulent misrepresentation (the course content did not match up with the published course description), to breach of contract (the teacher did not follow a syllabus), to arbitrary and capricious action in enforcing policies and grading (because they were not spelled out in a course syllabus) or were discriminatory (because they were not applied uniformly).

A university professor, for example, taught a course entitled "Introduction to Educational Media" for students preparing to become teachers. The catalog description indicated that the course was focused on the use of instructional media in the classroom. The professor elected to add several unrelated topics to the course, including issues of bias, censorship, and religion. Students complained to university officials that the teacher was using his class to advance his own particular religious convictions. University administrators ordered the professor to have his course syllabus and textbook orders approved by his department chair.

The professor responded by filing a grievance claiming his academic freedom had been infringed upon. The dispute eventually ended in litigation and required almost eight years to resolve. The U.S. Court of Appeals for the Third Circuit ultimately held that "a public university professor does not have a First Amendment right to decide what will be taught in the classroom." The court went on to observe, "No court has found that teachers'

First Amendment rights extend to choosing their own curriculum or classroom management techniques in contravention of school policy."[27]

In another case challenging the legitimacy of course assignments, a student enrolled in an English composition class was required to read and be tested over the book *Dessa Rose.* The assignment was included on the course syllabus. The student found the book offensive because of its allegedly obscene content. The student demanded an alternate assignment. The professor refused; and the student received a failing grade for not having satisfied the course requirement.

The student brought suit against the professor, claiming course misrepresentation and demanding $850,000 in damages. Four years of litigation followed. They culminated in a dismissal of the case by the Tennessee Court of Appeal on the grounds that the court had no right to review a grade assigned to a student enrolled in a state college.[28]

Lawsuits prompted by claims of arbitrary and capricious behavior on a professor's part are not at all uncommon. A teacher of a computer programming class, for example, announced that if a student missed six or more class sessions, he or she would receive a "0" for attendance (amounting to a third of the student's grade). The instructor was often a half-hour or more late to class himself. Reportedly, he had informed students that he would be delayed sometimes but that they were to await his arrival.

On several occasions when the professor failed to show up for class after a lengthy waiting period, a number of students left. The students always circulated a sign-up sheet at the beginning of class. One student who left class prior to the instructor's eventual arrival, but whose name appeared on the sign-up sheet, received a "0" for attendance. This student was the only one given the failing grade; even though there were others who also had left the classroom. The student alleged that the professor's action was arbitrary and capricious and amounted to a breach of contract. On appeal, the state appellate court agreed that the professor's action in counting the student absent raised an issue as to whether his action was defensible, particularly since the policy was not clearly stated in the course syllabus.[29]

In another case the court considered a claim of inappropriate instructional methods employed by a professor teaching a technical writing class. Throughout, the professor used explicit examples involving sexual intercourse, ostensibly to illustrate the employment of skills needed in technical writing. Several students complained that the teacher had created an uncomfortable and intimidating learning environment. Responding to complaints, the university disciplined the professor. The professor filed suit in federal district court, claiming his First Amendment right to free speech had been violated. The district court sided with the professor by finding pedagogical merit to his teaching methods.[30] Noteworthy in this case, however, was the fact that the court did uphold the professor's claim. Disputes involving claims of inappropriate instruction tend more commonly to be decided in favor of plaintiffs.

Claims of ineffective or poor instruction have prompted an inordinate number of lawsuits in recent years. At one institution, an untenured professor customarily left his class unsupervised during its appointed instruction time. The instructor claimed his absences amounted to a teaching method he used to help his students become more self-reliant and independent in their work. When the teacher received critical student evaluations, the institution elected not to renew his contract. The professor brought suit, alleging a violation of his academic freedom rights under the First Amendment. The court was not impressed. The state's appeals court held that "the record is clear that [the professor] was not denied a contract because of expressing unpopular opinions or otherwise presenting controversial ideas to his students." Rather, the university concluded that he was not an effective teacher and that academic freedom "is not a doctrine to insulate a teacher from evaluation by the institution that employs him."[31]

Breach of promise figures rather often in legal charges brought against faculty. Typical is the case at one university where two students—both self-proclaimed computer novices—enrolled for a course entitled "Fundamental Pascal Programming." The school's catalog advertised the course as a "concentrated orientation" to its subject matter, with no prerequisites required. The text students were required to purchase and use, as it turned out, was actually intended for advanced programming courses. Meanwhile, the instructor reportedly demonstrated lack of preparation in his teaching of the course and was himself unable to solve many of the assigned homework problems. Student complaints mounted. Several of those enrolled eventually brought suit for breach of contract, negligent instruction, and fraud. The state court hearing the case declared that "whether based upon contract or tort . . . the professor . . . owed a duty to teach the course as it was promised and in a competent manner."[32]

Yet another case serves to illustrate how a faculty member can be held accountable for failing to protect students enrolled in a course from foreseeable harm. A student was enrolled in a college-level course intended to instruct prospective teachers how to conduct various play activities in physical education classes. The student in question, along with several of her fellow classmates, was required to participate in a sack race. The professor required each member to hop with both feet in a plastic trash bag (not a burlap sack) on a freshly waxed wooden floor (not outside on the grass). Inevitably, one student slipped and fell, resulting in a serious injury to her foot.

The student sued the professor, alleging negligence. At trial, the court held that the teacher had a duty to use reasonable care in order to prevent student injuries. The faculty member, it was found, had neglected to issue cautionary instructions, had failed to exercise sound judgment, and had been negligent in not providing adequate supervision.[33]

Some Practical Implications

Many similar cases might be adduced to underscore the legal hazards that arise when a college teacher fails to adhere to the provisions of a course syllabus; or does not exercise common sense and courtesy; acts in a high-handed or arbitrary manner toward students; is negligent in conducting instruction; treats students in a discriminatory manner; or otherwise fails to behave acceptably in the course of conducting his or her assigned duties. Based on previous legal challenges brought by students and academic administrators, faculty members—beginners especially—should ponder the following recommendations:

- Supply a syllabus for each course you teach. Make sure the syllabus includes: (1) a clear statement of goals and objectives; (2) an indication of how the purposes of the course will be achieved; (3) an enumeration of course topics; (4) a summary of all course requirements; (5) an explanation of how grading will be conducted; (6) a reference to institutional rules and policies affecting the course; (7) an explanation of the instructor's special rules or policies; and (8) a tentative course calendar or schedule.
- Observe the provisions outlined in the syllabus as closely as possible; and announce any modifications or changes that become necessary.
- Enforce course policies and rules fairly and consistently.
- Avoid behavior or speech (excessive profanity, sexual innuendo, racist remarks, and so on) that could be considered as contributing to an offensive, intimidating or hostile environment.
- Do not accept responsibility for supervising a course in which you lack the requisite subject-matter competency.
- Show up on time for your classes and always come fully prepared.
- Treat students in a nondiscriminatory, respectful, and professional manner.
- Make reasonable and necessary accommodations for students when circumstances warrant special consideration; avoid unreasonable rigidity or inflexibility in dealing with individuals.

• Provide adequate instructions on safety precautions and proper techniques in any classroom situation where there is potential for injury (chemistry labs, classes using special equipment, and so on).

Grading Students

If you are a new instructor, with little or no previous experience in assessing student performance and assigning grades, it is essential that you familiarize yourself with your institution's rules controlling grading, student appeal rights, and protection of student records. It is also helpful to confer with others *before the fact* to learn how your colleagues handle incidents of cheating, plagiarism, and other forms of academic dishonesty if and when they arise—and they do occur as an unfortunate but not uncommon feature of academic life. In all such situations, great caution and tact are called for. Without a doubt, more legal challenges are raised by students concerning grades and assessment of academic performance than anything else.

A student was charged by his professor with cheating on a final exam. Although the teacher did not directly observe the student cheating, two other students reported seeing the alleged offender consulting unauthorized notes during the test. Neither the professor nor school officials informed the student of the evidence against him. The student was found guilty of academic dishonesty. The student then filed suit alleging his due process rights had been violated. The court held that failure to inform the student of evidence used against him did in fact constitute a denial of his due process rights, and ordered a new hearing in which the student would be informed in advance of whatever evidence would be brought forward against him.[34]

In another case involving cheating, a professor grew suspicious that a student had been dishonest on her final exam. The professor observed her holding the exam in the air, looking around the room, and writing her exam on her left thigh, positioning herself in such a way that she was turned toward another classmate seated two places away. At the conclusion of the exam, the professor examined both students' papers—the first seven pages of multiple-choice questions bore identical answers. A statistics instructor informed the professor there was only a 1-in-200,000 probability that the two papers could be identical without collusion. Based on this information, the professor notified the student she had flunked the course. After having exhausted her grievance rights, the student sued the professor for violating her due process rights. The state appellate court held that the teacher's observation of the cheating behavior, coupled with the statistical analysis, constituted sufficient evidence to support the professor's action.[35]

In another case involving grading, a law student was dismissed from school when her grade point average fell below 2.0. The student blamed her dismissal in part on a final grade of "C-" she received in one particular class. The professor explained that she had received no credit on a final-exam question that accounted for 30 percent of her grade. In her answer to a legal query on the test, she had discussed pertinent law from two different states (as she had been advised to do by another law professor). Her course professor only wanted *one* state's law to be considered, although he conceded her answer, as submitted, was factually correct. However, he refused to change her grade.

The student brought suit, alleging that the professor's grading practice was arbitrary and capricious and violated her right to due process. At trial, the professor alleged that "the highly discretionary, professional, and inevitably subjective process of actually grading . . . exams" should be considered beyond judicial review. The state appellate court disagreed. "If a school exercises its discretion to dismiss a student for academic reasons in an arbitrary or irrational fashion," it promised, "the courts will intervene."[36]

In the final analysis, a professor's legal risk in getting sued over a grade dispute cannot be eliminated altogether. Your best bet is to observe a few common sense rules and hope for the best. Practical suggestions include the following: (1) Explain your grading policies to your students in writing and verbally up front. (2) Be clear and explicit about the rules and standards that will govern the assignment of grades in your course. (3) Strive to be objective, fair, and consistent in your grading practices. (4) Treat all students of like circumstances the same. (5) Learn how to prevent or minimize the occurrence of cheating. (6) Protect the confidentiality of student grades. (7) Familiarize yourself with your school's grade appeal process and all policies governing academic dishonesty. (8) Do not assign a failing grade when cheating or plagiarism is suspected without first consulting relevant institutional regulations and abiding by whatever due process rights they preserve for students.

Student Advising and Legal Liability

"When college teachers serve as academic advisors," the authors of a recent legal guide for educators caution, "they should be fully informed as to all requirements for securing a degree." With considerable understatement, they go on to observe, "Inaccurate advising may involve . . . liability [and therefore] it is unwise for faculty to offer casual academic advice."[37]

Unlike teaching, where a single grade awarded in a course may not necessarily have a major impact on a student's overall academic progress, the work of academic advising might be reckoned akin to the service provided by a harbormaster guiding a ship to port. The advisor's task (under some circumstances at least) is to plot out an entire program of study leading to a degree, a program that might very well require years to complete. Advisement, in this situation, resembles an act of directed navigation, a series of instructions on what the advisee must do in order to satisfy all requirements for graduation.

When advisors make mistakes, typically it is the student who must bear the consequences—in extreme cases, the added time and expense needed to finish a degree. To cite only one example of the process gone wrong, a professor of secondary education led a student advisee to believe she could be certified as a high-school English teacher within the span of one year. According to the student, she had a teaching job awaiting her a year hence and wanted to be sure she was qualified to accept the position. On the strength of the advisor's assurances, the student enrolled in the courses to which she was directed. At year's end, however, she belatedly discovered she was eligible to teach Speech but not English. Thwarted in gaining the position for which she had supposedly prepared herself, she sued the professor for fraudulent misrepresentation.

The state court concluded, "In an action for fraud or false representation, a [student] must demonstrate she not only relied upon said representations, but the reliance was justified under the circumstances."[38] Ultimately, the court found in favor of the defendant, but only because the plaintiff was held to have failed on technicalities to justify her reliance on the professor's instructions about what certification to teach English would require of her.

Given the stakes at issue, it goes without saying that accuracy in academic advising can be of critical importance to a student's academic career. It is doubly important for a faculty newcomer whose assigned duties include advising of students to become thoroughly conversant with degree and graduation requirements. Given the complexity of many degree programs, guesswork will not suffice. In other words, take advising seriously. Learn where to get answers if you find yourself lacking reliable information or when questions of authoritative interpretation arise. It is true that the student bears ultimate responsibility for satisfying the requirements of the degree he or she wants to pursue. But that stipulation alone does not preclude the possibility of a faculty member's being sued if he or she has dispensed inaccurate or misleading counsel.

Scholarship and Professional Service:
Legal Ramifications

Happily, very few legal issues pertinent to a new faculty member are likely to arise in connection with scholarship and research. Most of the problems that do surface involve faculty working in research universities where external funding supports scholarly inquiry—for example, disputes over alleged noncompliance with the provisions of grants and contracts, or over intellectual property questions. Intellectual or academic dishonesty issues always remain a possibility for legal action, as does failure to comply with regulations governing research on human subjects. Otherwise, a novice faculty member is unlikely to become embroiled in any sort of legal dispute as a direct result of research and publishing activities.

The same holds true of a faculty member's extramural involvements. Possibly the only major troublesome area under professional service involves external or independent employment and consulting. Before engaging in work for organizations off campus, it is imperative that you determine what your school allows. Many institutions have strict rules governing how much time may be devoted to outside consulting. Some set caps on the amount of compensation one may receive from consulting work. Self-employment in an independent business or consulting firm likewise is likely to be more or less strictly regulated.

Points in Review

- The probability of your becoming involved in a costly legal controversy is not a matter of luck. Rather, it is a question of minimizing risk through the actions you take or avoid.
- Your legal rights and responsibilities as a professor differ, depending on whether you are employed by a private or public institution.
- An applicant for a faculty position is entitled legally to be judged solely on the basis of ability and possession of the required qualifications advertised for the position.
- Your employment contract delineates the conditions and requirements of your work and the nature of the position you hold.
- Virtually all forms of discrimination in the academic workplace are illegal.
- Academic freedom derives from a First Amendment right for those employed in public colleges and universities; and from institutional policies and practices as well as the terms of a faculty member's con-

tract if employed by a private postsecondary institution. Academic freedom is neither unconditional nor absolute.

- Challenges to the outcome of a faculty performance evaluation are handled primarily through grievance and appeal processes internal to the employing institution.
- Faculty members' rights to intellectual property are limited under certain circumstances by the "work-made-for-hire" rule.
- Termination of a faculty member's employment generally requires due process protection for the individual facing dismissal, depending in part on the terms and conditions of his or her employment contract.
- Whereas professors typically initiate lawsuits against the institutions in which they are employed over disputes involving compensation and personnel issues, students are most likely to sue teachers over matters involving harassment, discrimination, poor teaching, or allegedly unfair grading practices.

PART III

CONCLUDING CONSIDERATIONS

CHAPTER 10

FURTHER THOUGHTS

In Retrospect

When major themes from the literature on faculty orientation and development are recast as specific suggestions or guides for behavior, they do end up in the final analysis seeming rather obvious. The opening discussion, for example, stressed the importance of "scoping out" the institutional environment and learning to "read" its organizational culture—understanding the *context* as well as the *content* of one's work. Not much acumen is needed to grasp the advantage of learning how the system works, who are the major decision-makers, and what institutional expectations attach to a person's newly acquired position.

The point, of course, is not to take too much for granted, or to assume that everything somehow will be made plain over time. Most always it falls to you the individual faculty newcomer to exercise the initiative, to determine how your work will be judged, and what standards will apply ("official" policy pronouncements as well as tacit or implicit measures). The idea is worth emphasizing: *One of the most important challenges you confront as a new faculty member is to develop a sense for the performance norms to which your work will be expected to conform and by which it will be judged by others.*

Mention has been made repeatedly of the importance of seeking advice and counsel from others in the first few months and even years on the job. Anyone joining a faculty is well advised to seek out colleagues for tips and suggestions when questions surface. Some of the isolation of academic life is self-imposed; and there is absolutely nothing wrong with seeking to develop relations with those who could prove helpful as mentors, professional counselors, or collaborators on a project. Other benefits aside, whatever sense of personal fulfillment and career satisfaction you derive can only be enhanced through good working relationships with peers. Collegial ties with coworkers is a significant determinant of job morale.

Needless to add, if you are fortunate enough to gain employment at an institution where faculty development is valued and planned for, there will be structured activities and learning experiences designed expressly to meet the needs of new faculty members. Participation in whatever colloquia, in-service seminars and other activities are offered is highly advisable. If nothing else, faculty workshops afford excellent opportunities for networking and becoming better acquainted with colleagues working in other disciplines and departments on campus.

Much has been made of the importance of collegiality and "good citizenship" in academe. Helpful in this connection is the richly textured concept of *simpatia*. Lacking any precise translation into English, the original Spanish term connotes civility and a pleasant demeanor, with overtones of friendliness, warmth, and agreeability. (It in no way suggests or implies sycophancy.) In an academic context, to speak of someone who exhibits *simpatia*—a person who is *simpatico*—is to suggest cooperativeness and collegiality, a congenial member of the academic community. In a setting better known for its irascible curmudgeons and egoists, *simpatia* goes a long way to confirm someone as a desirable and valued peer, the sort of person more senior colleagues will want to retain in years to come.

As has been previously suggested, it is odd that professors as a whole seem to give so little time and attention to matters of classroom pedagogy. Academics prize in-depth scholarship—and properly so. More than a few put in long hours preparing for their classes. But in a quite simplistic way, unfortunately, many professors tend to equate "teaching" with "telling," and suppose that an instructor's thorough mastery of subject matter is at once both the necessary and the sufficient condition for student learning to occur. Research on teaching most emphatically indicates otherwise.

Whereas mastery of subject matter *is* indispensable, command of a body of knowledge is of little avail from an instructional point of view *if* the teacher lacks the ability to impart the information effectively or cannot inspire students to acquire it in some meaningful way. As previously noted, a not uncommon error among new faculty members is to spend hours organizing materials for classroom lectures while giving only cursory attention to planning how that same material will be presented for maximum effect.

There are literally dozens of books devoted to the topic of instructional improvement and innovation currently available for consultation. Taken as a whole, they offer a rich cornucopia of techniques, activities, and approaches worthy of serious consideration by novices and experienced teachers alike. The best among them offer valuable insights into the advantages as well as the limitations inherent in the traditional lecture format, not to mention suggestions for freshening lectures and making them more effective. What almost all of them share in common, moreover, is a conviction that college teaching at its best utilizes a diverse array of strategies to facilitate learning, not just one particular style of instruction. Linear, one-way communication—telling—represents only one such approach, and a somewhat limited one at that.

"Good" teaching—which is to say, instruction that demonstrably accomplishes what it is the professor intends—demands more. And that "more" is likely to involve classroom practices and formats that encourage discussion and, more broadly, active student learning. For faculty novices, the lesson should be clear: Learning to teach well is a complex, demanding undertaking. Dramatic improvements do not happen overnight; failures are always possible. Managing the process of learning requires practice and, to a certain degree, a willingness to experiment, to take risks. In any case, the thoughtful teacher who accepts the challenge and perseveres will discover sooner or later that thinking about instruction ultimately moves away from the question about how to *teach* and more toward questions about what is needed in order for students to *learn*. The two are by no means always one and the same.

Faculties in small, teaching-oriented colleges tend to be relatively free of pressures to publish. In an expanding number of mid-sized and larger institutions, however, the harsh, inescapable reality is one of "publish or perish."[1] For many academics, conducting research and preparing the results for publication or presentation in some public forum comes fairly easily—at least in the sense that they approach writing confident of eventual success. For others, the prospect of having to publish as a precondition for career advancement looms as a seemingly insurmountable obstacle fraught with hazards. For a few, the felt need to get something out and into print is a professorial imperative that inspires nothing but fear and loathing.

Behind all the cant and rhetoric, there are still good reasons why, in certain institutional settings at least, faculty members should indeed strive to be "productive" published scholars. And so far as the actual task of writing is concerned, the best advice reduces to a handful of eminently sensible suggestions: reserving a physical space conducive to uninterrupted work, breaking a large project down sequentially into more manageable parts, establishing goals and a timeline for achieving objectives, adhering to a structured writing schedule (if only loosely and with frequent adjustments as necessary), determining the best times of day to craft or revise text, getting and keeping organized, avoiding unproductive "binge" writing marathons, experimenting with "prewriting," managing source materials efficiently, soliciting editorial suggestions from others, and so on.

Similarly, there is nothing particularly obscure or arcane about the strategies successful authors employ in submitting their work for publication. Clearly, a necessary first step is to match a manuscript with an appropriate publishing outlet, looking to create congruence between the two in terms of topic, documentation, and format. The importance of submitting a "clean" manuscript also cannot be overemphasized—which is to say, a manuscript as free as possible of spelling and grammatical mistakes. Attention to matters of narrative voice and style are of almost equal importance. But in the end, the writing tips and suggestions academic authors need to keep uppermost in mind are no more complicated or extensive than those commonly taught in any elementary-level writing and composition course for college undergraduates.

One of the most troubling finds in recent years of research on how faculty spends their time is a steady decrease in the amount of time devoted to advising and counseling students. Over a span of two decades, from 1972 to 1992, studies indicated that faculty had reportedly reduced the already modest amount of time spent in informal contact with students. There is nothing to suggest things have changed since the early 1990s. Considering the evidence that documents the important role that such contacts have on a wide range of student outcomes, the trend is worrisome.[2]

For new faculty members especially, open-ended time devoted to students represents a mixed blessing. Hours spent getting better acquainted with students outside the classroom or office is a pleasant diversion as well as a highly instructive experience in its own right. Faculty who make themselves accessible to students in a variety of informal settings usually report high morale and an elevated level of personal job satisfaction (admittedly, the causal direction between accessibility and morale presents the usual "chicken-or-egg" conundrum). All the same, prolonged or frequent social interaction easily draws attention away from other pressing responsibilities and obligations that simply cannot be neglected indefinitely.

An afternoon spent in conversation with a handful of undergraduates in some local hangout, for example, is apt to offer a pleasant and entertaining diversion, no matter what the topic of discussion, whether related to a class or not. It is not especially helpful to you in preparing for classes, or for progressing with a writing project, or for addressing any of the other myriad tasks awaiting you back at the office. To put it bluntly, socializing with students is intrinsically rewarding and important. But it is not accorded much weight by most institutions. It garners little recognition and few extrinsic rewards.

Much the same applies to the faculty work category of service. For new faculty members, the hazards of becoming overextended have already been mentioned. For the first few years, it is sufficient to accept membership on a very small number of committees, task forces, boards, or other agencies, unless the particular circumstances of your appointment demand otherwise. Balance is important. Ideally, you should be able to handle a few service commitments within the immediate academic work unit (e.g., the department); one or two assignments at the college, divisional or campus level; and possibly a committee assignment with your professional association.

Otherwise, it becomes important to learn how and when to say "no." It is possible to decline an appointment tactfully without becoming apologetic or unnecessarily defensive about it (for example, *"Sorry, but I have so many other commitments right now, I simply couldn't take on another task and really give it the time and attention it deserves"*). Protecting your time is a learned art. It must be mastered if you are not to find yourself a few years down the road hopelessly burdened with distractions and unproductive responsibilities.[3] The same applies to excessive consulting, too many outreach activities, extensive community service, and, sometimes, commitments to off-campus extension work.

Documenting Work

Not yet adequately considered is the often-overlooked issue of documenting your professional activities and assignments. Almost all faculty members are subject to some type of annual performance audit or review, an assessment that has a direct effect on the amount of your yearly salary increment. On a longer-range basis, faculty occupying tenure-track positions sooner or later are obliged to document their accomplishments over a stipulated period of years and to submit a comprehensive dossier or portfolio for review by the department chair and/or a promotion and tenure committee. The stakes in the impending decision are huge: the prospect of imminent termination of employment and loss of income or the long-term job security conferred by tenure.

The specific time span involved between the date of an initial appointment and the deadline for a decision—four, five, six or more years in some cases—is less important than the fact that responsibility for assembling all of the relevant documents needed in order for colleagues and administrators to render a judgment falls squarely on the shoulders of the person being assessed. The question is how well you have retained and now assembled the requisite information (and supporting documents) so that a favorable decision becomes more likely.

The following composite list serves to illustrate how detailed and extensive is the information typically called for when submitting a file for consideration:

- Employment history: Year of initial academic appointment; number of years of full-time employment; dates of off-campus duty or other assignments or leaves involving activity substantially different from regular duties; brief description, by years, of teaching, research, and service assignments
- Instructional assignments: Courses taught (listed by academic terms) since date of initial appointment or previous promotion in rank, including course numbers, titles, and student enrollments; include information on such additional duties as coordination of multisection courses, participation in unit examination activities such as written or oral examinations for honors or graduate degree candidates
- Teaching evaluations: Submit statements and data on teaching effectiveness, including student and peer evaluations (numerical ratings and representative samples of narrative commentary); include also comparative data for the department or college if available; cite honors, awards for teaching excellence (if any), student accomplishments or performance on national tests (if any); describe activities, if any, intended to contribute to developing greater effectiveness as a teacher
- Advising: Describe advising duties and responsibilities, by year or academic term, for the past five years, including numbers of active advisees by academic terms, level of advisees, procedures and methods employed, and any other details such as advisee evaluations that indicate the range or quality of advising activities; describe activities, if any, intended to contribute to developing greater effectiveness as an adviser
- Professional performance: Submit a comprehensive statement of work assignments or professional duties, including information concerning primary responsibilities, employees supervised, patrons served, or other desired indicators of work accomplished; provide evidence of experience in areas of assigned professional responsibilities and effectiveness in carrying out assigned duties; include evidence of ability and willingness to accept additional responsibility; evidence of leadership; evidence of cooperation in dealing with personnel at all levels and evidence of efforts at self-improvement and development; provide evidence of innovations in program implementation; evidence of the development of special projects, resource tools, and (or) the use of creative techniques in the performance of duties; and evidence of initiative and resourcefulness in solving unit problems; provide evidence of professional effectiveness in the form of evaluations by clientele and peers
- Creative endeavors: List and describe creative endeavors other than those involving publication (if appropriate and relevant), such as in-

dividual concerts, shows, and performances; group performances; and other kinds of professional activity; include information concerning kind of activity, location, audience, number of performances, or period of show, and date; identify juried shows and exhibitions

- Publications: List books (indicate if coauthored or edited, include title, publisher, date of publication, pages); articles in professional and scholarly journals (include complete bibliographic data for each entry); monographs; book chapters; in all cases indicate whether publication was refereed or nonrefereed

- Presentations and reports: List papers presented at national or international meetings or conferences; papers presented at regional, state, or local meetings and conferences (indicate for each entry whether juried/refereed or nonrefereed); written reports prepared for proprietary agencies on research conducted under contract or as a consultant; other papers and reports such as book reviews and publications in proceedings and newsletters

- Support for research and sponsored programs: Supply information on all external grants, contracts, and other kinds of funding for research (title of project, funding agency, period of support, annual and total dollar amounts, role of faculty member); include a statement concerning degree of individual participation: half-time, percent, summer term, and so on; supply information on all research support and grants from the institution: include computing time allowances, research services support, special grants, off-campus duty assignments; provide complete information concerning activities described

- Honors and awards: List and document reviews of published works, shows, performances; letters of commendation or evaluation; honors or awards received; recognition from professional societies and external agencies

- Service: Cite only service activities involving professional competence and related to but not involving teaching, professional performance of assigned duties, or research and creative activities: work with prospective students; work intended to enhance popular understanding of the institution and its contributions to the public; service in professional organizations; service with governmental agencies, commissions, boards, and similar entities; unpaid consulting; contributions to public service agencies; append information concerning the extent and significance of all services rendered, including honors, awards, citations, peer reviews, and patron evaluations

- Previous evaluations: Append copies of all previous yearly evaluations, starting with the first year on appointment, including assessments supplied by colleagues, the department chair, the departmental review board or committee, and other evaluators.

Virtually every college or university has a document outlining the information every faculty member will need for his or her annual performance review. There will also be a statement summarizing what an applicant must supply at the time he or she undergoes review for tenure or promotion in rank.

The first step, needless to say, is for you to obtain a copy of both documents (sometimes they are incorporated within the body of a faculty policy handbook or an institutional policies and procedures manual) and to familiarize yourself in a general way with their contents. The next is to devise a system for collecting and retaining all the pertinent information called for. It remains to observe, only the most shortsighted delude themselves into thinking they can get all the relevant information together and reconstruct their detailed work histories in a brief period of time. The task of assembling your credentials is difficult enough when all the requisite materials are at hand. Without them, it is practically impossible.

The simplest expedient is to reserve space in an empty desk or file drawer as a repository for documents: copies of workload assignments, course syllabi, student course evaluations, letters of commendation, offprints of publications, correspondence with student advisees—anything conceivably relevant to a future performance evaluation. A useful maxim: When in doubt, save it for later, just in case. A correlative: Start saving everything now!

Arguably, the foregoing counsel may qualify as one of the most widely ignored pieces of advice in all of academe.

The critical consideration is to begin the process at the very outset, creating, as it were, a cumulative historical record. To repeat, the task of assembling a portfolio or dossier is infinitely easier when all the documents are readily available, preferably in some semblance of chronological order or organized under work performance categories (teaching, scholarship, advising, service, etc.). But an unorganized pile of papers saved in one place is infinitely better than no file at all!

Another useful expedient is to keep a copy of your curriculum vitae as a computer file and to update it frequently—weekly or monthly, if necessary. A common if ill-founded tendency is to assume that one will remember in future the exact dates of a conference or workshop or some other important event. The vitae should be kept current as a cumulative, running account of your professional activities and accomplishments.

Unrelated to matters of performance evaluation but having to do with organization is another important suggestion: reading and saving copies of even routine administrative memoranda. Junk mail, advertising circulars, conference announcements, and most of the other miscellaneous detritus found littering faculty desks can usually be disposed of safely in short order. In the case of communications from a dean, department chair, or other administrator, however, it is advisable to retain copies of everything received over the course of an academic year.

Buried in the verbiage sometimes are valuable nuggets of information, special announcements, requests, notification of deadlines, or instructions. Disorganized or negligent faculty members who have not complied with some bureaucratic imperative most commonly resort to the timeworn excuse: *"I never got that memo."* Few administrators believe them or even bother to pretend they do. Noncompliance with administrative dictates and requests is forever a needless source of friction within academe; and it is never to a faculty member's advantage to be thought uncooperative or negligent—especially a newcomer. Department chairs and deans greatly appreciate faculty members who are cooperative and who respond to information requests in timely fashion.

Assembling an Academic Portfolio

Determining what materials to preserve in order to document your professional activities and achievements (given the near-certainty you will be called on to do so eventually) is important, but hardly a major challenge for even the most harried, preoccupied faculty member. Keeping documents in some semblance of order over the span of several years is somewhat more difficult. Assembling and organizing materials for inclusion in a formal dossier—in effect, creating a "paper trail"—requires still more care. And the fact of the matter is, nowadays an increasing number of colleges and universities *do* expect a candidate coming up for tenure or promotion to submit a comprehensive portfolio for review. This compilation, reviewed by the faculty promotion and tenure committee, the department chair, the dean, and other decision-makers, furnishes an important part of the basis upon which a judgment about your career will be made. Anticipating well in advance what information should be preserved for inclusion in your portfolio and how to display it is an act of prudence.

Some institutions are rigidly prescriptive about what specific information to include and how materials should be organized. Others, in lieu of a mandated reporting format, offer only general guidelines, leaving it to the candidate to determine what supporting data will be included or omitted.

Essentially, the academic portfolio you develop for submission will furnish an opportunity for you to summarize your professional and academic accomplishments over time and to showcase them to the best possible advantage. In seeking to achieve these two goals, under no circumstances is it advisable to "stuff" every conceivable document possible into a portfolio. The point is *not* to generate an exhaustive, unwieldy compilation of paper documents that serves only to try the patience of colleagues charged with its review. Quite the contrary, your objective should be to offer a judiciously selected assemblage of materials that profiles your work over a given period of time, while also indicating something about the quality of your overall performance.

The *Teaching* section of the portfolio characteristically includes some (though not necessarily all) of the following components:

1. A preliminary narrative (two or three short paragraphs) in which you describe your basic views or philosophy on teaching, the strategies you most often employ, and your instructional goals and objectives.
2. A summary of your teaching responsibilities, including titles, credit-hours, student enrollments, and official catalogue descriptions of each course you have taught, arranged in chronological order by academic term and year. To this summary you might want to append a brief general description of how each course was organized and taught.
3. A representative sample of recent course syllabi that details the content and aims of each course, the teaching methods used, course requirements, evaluation procedures, and assignments.
4. Student course and teaching evaluation data, including both quantitative ratings and narrative commentary from students.
5. Affidavits from faculty peers who have reviewed your syllabi, classroom materials, assignments, testing and grading procedures, and choices of texts and other instructional materials.
6. Commentaries and analyses of your teaching from faculty colleagues who have actually observed your classroom performance or have team-taught with you.
7. Unsolicited letters about your teaching from former students.
8. A record of honors or teaching awards received.
9. A narrative summary of self-initiated efforts at instructional innovation, experimentation, and improvement, including activities involving curriculum development or revision.
10. Records indicating participation in instructional workshops, committees, colloquia, seminars, symposia, or retreats ("teaching camps").

11. Indicators of involvement in research on teaching.
12. Samples of student work.
13. Examples of graded papers that illustrate good, average, and poor work, together with your comments on how and why they were graded as indicated.
14. A videotape of your classroom performance.

The *Student Advising* section of the portfolio can be considerably less voluminous than the *Teaching* part. At a minimum, however, it should incorporate the following:

1. Summary data on the numbers of students with whom you have worked in an advisory capacity, broken down by academic terms or years, and by degree levels (undergraduate or graduate, academic majors or minors, and so on). Some compilers include the individual names of their advisees.
2. A representative sample of records or notes utilized in advisee consultations (with names omitted to preserve confidentiality).
3. Copies of correspondence with advisees.

The *Research and Scholarship* element of a portfolio may be negligible if you are employed at an institution where faculty publishing is neither emphasized nor perhaps even encouraged. Yet when you come up for tenure, even if you are an unpublished faculty member or have never presented papers at academic and professional conferences, presumably you will have made efforts to keep current and to familiarize yourself with the latest scholarship in your field. Those efforts can and should be documented. At the very least, you should present a list of the state, regional, and national conferences you have attended. Also helpful is a listing of the scholarly journals you consult on a regular basis.

Other elements appropriate for inclusion by published scholars in this section of the portfolio include the following:

1. A complete list of publications (furnish full bibliographical citations). Include a one- or two-sentence "blurb" for each journal in which your work appears, indicating whether your article was refereed or nonjuried, or invited. Include something about the standing of the journal itself: approximate circulation, whether supported by a particular professional society or association, and so on. Include citations for monographs, contributed book chapters, editorship of a published anthology, or published books.

2. A list of works submitted and currently under editorial consideration and/or works accepted for publication but not yet in print.

3. A list of papers presented at state, regional, or national meetings (indicate whether each paper was refereed, nonrefereed, invited, precisely when and where it was presented, and under whose auspices).

4. A brief description of works in progress, if any. (Include only projects where significant progress has already been made: Discriminate between works partially completed and those not yet begun, omitting the latter entirely!)

5. A short summary of other activities of a scholarly nature (such as participation as a convention panelist).

6. Offprints of your best articles or published papers.

7. Letters from colleagues at other institutions discussing your scholarship.

Needless to say, the above list may not be appropriate for faculty members in the visual, musical, or performing arts—in which case some modifications in the reporting format are easily effected.

One section of your portfolio should be devoted to *Service*. It is helpful to list various activities under separate categories: internal institutional service (committee memberships and so forth); professional service (involvement with the work of professional and scholarly organizations); and community outreach (unpaid consulting, teaching).

Considering the sheer range and diversity of items that defensibly can and should be included under the catch-all rubric of "service," it is helpful to accompany each item with a brief explanatory narrative. Assume superficial familiarity at best with your work on the part of those colleagues who will review the portfolio. It is extremely important therefore that you explain the meaning and significance of what you have accomplished. For example, if you have invested time and energy serving on a particular task force, board, or committee, indicate how often the body met and in general terms report what was achieved.

Sometimes it is helpful to include work products from a committee, task force, or board, or samples of correspondence involved in a service project.

Overall, the portfolio is an important document. In some instances, the skill with which it is assembled truly can make or break an academic career. It is not a time for excessive modesty or for being self-effacing about one's accomplishments. At the opposite extreme, care should be taken not to succumb to the sin of "puffery." Nothing is so irritating to faculty colleagues as self-serving exaggeration. A candid, matter-of-fact presentation, well balanced and straightforward in its organization and execution, best serves the interests of the individual under review.

Time Management

One of the most frequent laments heard from academics is, *"There never seems to be enough time to get everything done!"* The complaint is just as prevalent in corporate business; and an entire cottage industry has sprung up in recent years to help the chronically disorganized deal with problems stemming from poor time management.[4] That many business people should feel harried and overwhelmed by multiple demands on their time is perhaps understandable. That professors should feel similarly afflicted might seem more surprising. After all, college and university academics control most of their own time. They mostly set their own schedules; and they enjoy broad latitude in determining how they organize their work.

Paradoxically, it may be precisely because professors do have considerable autonomy in the workplace that they feel pulled simultaneously in so many different directions. The diverse pressures and demands on them are real enough, even if many are internally generated. There are always students to see, meetings to attend, classes to prepare for, research to pursue, projects to complete, reports to write, students papers to grade, books and articles that must be consulted in order to keep up in the field, and so on ad infinitum. Keeping everything in balance and within reasonable limits is an ongoing challenge under the best of circumstances.[5]

There are plenty of self-styled efficiency experts and productivity gurus nowadays who charge academic institutions as well as businesses substantial sums of money to instruct their employees how to work in a more time-efficient manner. The key to success, most agree, is effective time *management* since, as it is often observed, one cannot create, buy, sell, rent, borrow, lend, save, or multiply time. One can only spend it. If it is not used, it evaporates. The trick therefore is to manage it productively. Wise use of time requires that a person attend in a deliberate, self-aware way to how it is being expended (or wasted).

Best-selling author Stephen Covey offers an important caveat. Time management, he points out, is actually something of a misnomer. The trick is not really to manage time but, in the final analysis, to manage ourselves.[6] Though hardly a novel idea, his point applies to people in academe as much as in corporate business.

Self-management *is* important, particularly for faculty novices who have not yet established their own personal work routines and habits and who run the risk of failing to use their time effectively. To borrow an often-repeated example, suppose a faculty member "wastes" an hour a day on average—that is, 60 minutes every workday are unintentionally expended in some non-productive or unplanned way. Assuming an eight-hour workday, three weeks of annual vacation and nine or ten holidays, the cost for an individual with a yearly salary of $40,000 amounts to no less than $5,000.

Again, in a society that tends to assign great importance to the monetary value of things, if an individual's annual salary is $40,000, dividing by a factor of "2" reveals an approximate hourly wage of $20. That figure multiplied by the number of hours misspent in any given time period yields an indicator of the hypothetical "cost" of the time lost within that span.

The foregoing examples, obviously, are not intended to imply that a dollar figure or value should necessarily be assigned to every working hour of an academic's day or that all work should be rigidly scheduled. Much depends also on what is considered "unproductive" or "wasted" time. The underlying point, rather, is that there are costs, hidden or otherwise, attached to unproductive faculty time—not the least of which are the frustration and anxiety felt by those who cannot manage themselves effectively and who consequently never seem to get much accomplished.

The simplest, most rudimentary step to better time management is to record and carry around a daily or weekly "to-do" list, crossing off items as they are addressed. A list might not necessarily record tasks in order of their importance or urgency, though at least it indicates what one hopes, intends, or needs to get done. Merely having an enumeration of things to do available as a reminder, for some people, serves as a possible corrective to the tendency to drift through one's workday, heedless of the passage of time.

Another stratagem is to track work time using some type of day planner or appointment book (electronic or otherwise), with specified blocks of time reserved for conferences, writing, working in the lab, and whatever else needs to get done. Some professors claim they could not function without their weekly or daily planners. Others consider them intolerable encumbrances. Either way, no calendar or appointment book can compensate for lack of discipline or the individual's inability or unwillingness to use it for its intended purpose.

A somewhat more elaborate approach to time management urges the individual (1) to sit down once a week and actually write out objectives or goals for the following week; (2) to think through and perhaps record in writing what must be done each day to accomplish those goals; and (3) to assign priorities to the various items identified. Assuming the highest-ranked priority items are addressed first or receive the most attention, presumably at week's end the timekeeper will have registered tangible progress toward—and derived satisfaction from—achieving his or her short-term goals.

There is undoubtedly a great deal of truth to the claim that unforeseen contingencies can and do play havoc with the most carefully constructed schedule. No one, it is said, can plan for the unexpected crisis or problem, the time-consuming diversion or interruption, the task or meeting that ends up taking up far more time than anticipated, and so on. To a greater extent than some time-management experts seem willing to acknowledge, most people as a rule find themselves forced to react to situations rather than being able to control them.

A solution to the problem—if, indeed, there is one—is to build "cushions" into your schedule so as to allow for the unexpected. The basic idea is not to schedule every minute of your time. Nor is it to cling rigidly to a detailed schedule, no matter what. And, of course, some responsibilities can neither be avoided nor postponed to a more convenient moment; they must be dealt with as the occasion demands. The overall aim, however, is to be sure that high-priority items get attended to and that you do not find yourself engulfed constantly by trivial diversions.

Common sense suggests that "time wasters" should be avoided or at least compensated for whenever possible: unscheduled visitors, telephone interruptions, last-minute meetings, crisis situations, and so on. At the risk of seeming too formulaic, there are some strategies worth trying with a view to minimizing wasted time:

- Begin work early when there are fewer people around.
- Maintain generous office hours for scheduled appointments as well as drop-ins; if no visitors show up, the time can be used to handle routine chores.
- Establish priorities and give important tasks the most attention: put first things first.
- Be tactfully assertive with others about time; limit the duration of conferences and meetings whenever possible.
- Make it a habit to complete tasks well before their deadlines.
- When uninterrupted time is essential, keep the office door closed and solicit the secretary's help in screening calls, receiving messages, and barring drop-in visitors.
- Focus on doing one thing at a time.
- Cultivate habits of organization that allow the ready retrieval of documents when they are needed, without having to search through a cluttered, messy workplace.

- Avoid excessive isolation by taking short breaks to converse with colleagues and staff members.
- Reserve some portion of a day or two per week to accomplish work at home that cannot be done in the office.
- When work on a particular task is not going well, master the habit of leaving it alone for a while and work on something else instead.
- Vary work routines so as to avoid premature or excessive fatigue.
- When beginning work on a large or long-term project or task, break it down into parts and work on one part at a time.
- Plan ahead.

Keeping Up

Professors make much of the need to spend time and energy "keeping up" with the latest developments in their respective fields of specialization. Without question, remaining current is an important professional imperative (even though academics as a whole do seem prone to exaggerate what staying abreast of things requires in some cases). Hours must be set aside for reading journals and books in one's field, attending conferences, consulting with colleagues, and much else besides in order—as the saying has it—to stay "in touch" with the latest findings and scholarly developments in one's discipline, or some subdivision thereof. New faculty just entering the academic job market enjoy the advantage over their more experienced senior colleagues in that the former are more likely to be abreast of the latest twists and turns of scholarship than are the latter—at least initially.

In a much broader sense, faculty members have an obligation to stay current with the field of higher education as a whole, not just with the state of scholarship in a particular disciplinary specialty area. Perusing such periodicals as the *Chronicle of Higher Education,* or the magazine *Change,* the *AAUP Bulletin,* and, possibly, the *Review of Higher Education* or *Lingua Franca* comes to mind immediately as a useful way of achieving and maintaining currency in the broader field of postsecondary learning.

As-yet not mentioned are the "tools" of the professorial trade, the skills and knowledge college professors should possess in order to work effectively: research on student demographics, the latest suggestions regarding instructional innovations, new computer software packages, and so on. Whether it is realistic to expect that academics who already find it difficult to find time to sustain their scholarship to keep themselves well informed about the broader field of higher education as well seems problematic. Yet if not professors—then who?

COMPUTER TECHNOLOGY:
WHAT ACADEMICS NEED TO KNOW

New faculty members in business, engineering, the physical sciences, and most of the applied technological fields usually enter the professorate already well versed in computer technology. Others, especially some new faculty in the traditional arts disciplines, tend not to be as familiar with computers and their uses in instruction.

An emerging consensus suggests that, at a minimum all new faculty members need to know:

1. How to set up and operate a multimedia computer system with related peripheral devices, including the installation of software packages.
2. How to employ basic troubleshooting procedures for routine maintenance and correction of computer-related problems.
3. How to use productivity tools for word processing, database management, and spreadsheet applications.
4. How to utilize appropriate productivity tools for creating multimedia presentations.
5. How to use computer-based technologies, including telecommunications and electronic mail, to access information and enhance productivity.
6. How to design and create a website.
7. How to use imaging devices such as scanners, digital cameras, and video cameras with computer systems and software.
8. How to utilize broadcast instruction, audio/video conferencing, and other distant learning applications.

A Professor Comments . . .

"In the late 1970s, I assumed these new-fangled typewriters with television screens attached were a fad destined to fade away in short order."

"In the 1980s, I assumed it made more sense to train secretarial staff in the use of computers than for me to acquire the expertise needed to operate one of them myself."

"In the 1990s I was prepared to concede that my computer offered some advantages over my old typewriter for word-processing."

"I begin my daily work routine nowadays by first checking and responding to my e-mail, posting new updates on my web page, and then preparing computer-generated visuals for my next class. . . ."

SOURCES OF JOB SATISFACTION AND STRESS DURING THE EARLY PHASES OF ONE'S ACADEMIC CAREER

- The first three years are a time of intense adjustment for new faculty members. Retrospectively, they report the early years to be the most difficult period of an academic career, a time of *high* stress and *low* satisfaction.
- Poorly defined work-role boundaries, perpetual time pressures, work overload, and high self-expectations rank among the major sources of faculty stress.
- Junior faculty experience substantial role anxiety and struggle to define their role as faculty members. This struggle takes two primary forms: (1) deciphering institutional expectations for performance and (2) learning to prioritize time and effort appropriately across academic tasks.
- Beginning faculty typically feel a lack of collegiality, both from junior colleagues and from more senior faculty. Newly appointed faculty tend to be preoccupied with defining and meeting institutional expectations, establishing collegial bonds, and negotiating multiple role demands.
- Recent findings appear to show a fairly high, consistent level of satisfaction with the autonomous, intellectually challenging nature of the academic enterprise, and a lower, steadily eroding level of satisfaction relative to issues of compensation and institutional governance.
- Need for recognition and support gives way over time to the more lasting and profession-specific needs for autonomy, challenge, and accomplishment.
- Prioritizing and allocating time and energy appropriately and effectively are key developmental tasks at an early career stage.

Source: Deborah Olsen, "Work Satisfaction and Stress in the First and Third Year of Academic Appointment," *Journal of Higher Education* 64 (July/August 1993): 453–471.

Maintaining the Balance

Although those outside academe might be shocked to hear it, 50- and 60-hour workweeks are not uncommon among members of the professorate. At the outset, the demands made on a newcomer's time can seem both endless and profoundly overwhelming. Most professors as a rule work long hours; and some work to mind-numbing excess.

The hazards and drawbacks of being a workaholic are stressed endlessly in the self-help literature, complete with the usual caveat that good mental health and continued productivity require that a proper balance be maintained between work and play. What applies to people in general applies with special force to those whose work demands a certain amount of creativity—most college and university professors among them. Teaching and writing and most other scholarly endeavors are inherently creative acts. They cannot be done by rote, or without some personal involvement and self-investment. The surest route to "burn-out" and eventual loss of creativity is a work regimen that is arduous, that recognizes no limits or boundaries, and that is sustained without respite for months and even years on end.

The antidote is the living of a balanced life, one whose rhythms include time and space set aside for spouse and family, for relaxation with friends and relatives, for recreational pursuits, and hobbies. Academics who know better but love their work tend to ignore that fundamental need for balance. To a greater extent than anywhere else, they find their chief satisfaction and fulfillment in and through their professional lives. (By now it has become an overworked cliché to observe that no one on his or her deathbed has ever been filled with remorse for not having spent more time at the office.) Ultimately, faculty members must seek to develop a lifestyle that is responsive to their chosen academic calling while still making adequate provision for rest, relaxation, and extracurricular interests.

New faculty members bent on launching their professional careers may find it hard to hear—much less heed—this particular message. Some senior faculty, having spent years in the relentless pursuit of their career interests, never do learn but profess to be none the worse for it. Notwithstanding, in the final reckoning, living an academic life is a rare privilege, one to be greatly treasured. Yet it is important to remember that, as is true of any occupation, although membership in the academy affords great life satisfaction, academic pursuits of and by themselves can never encompass or define the whole of life.

NOTES

Preface

1. Sarah M. Dinham, "Being A Newcomer," in *Faculty in New Jobs,* ed. Robert J. Menges et al. (San Francisco, Calif.: Jossey-Bass, 1999), 1.
2. Dinham, 2.
3. Quoted in Robert Boice, *The New Faculty Member* (San Francisco, Calif.: Jossey-Bass, 1992), 1.
4. Peg Boyle and Bob Boice, "Systematic Mentoring for New Faculty Teachers and Graduate Teaching Assistants," *Innovative Higher Education* 22 (Spring 1998): 157.

Chapter 1

1. Ann Austin, "Faculty Cultures, Faculty Values," *New Directions for Institutional Research* 68 (Winter 1990): 62.
2. George D. Kuh and Elizabeth J. Whitt, "The Invisible Tapestry: Culture in American Colleges and Universities," Report No. 1 (Washington, D.C., ERIC-ASHE Higher Education Reports, 1988), 76–77.
3. Douglas J. Toma, "Alternative Inquiry Paradigms, Faculty Cultures, and the Definition of Academic Lives," *Journal of Higher Education* 68 (November/December 1997): 681.
4. Toma, 683.
5. William G. Tierney, "Organizational Culture in Higher Education: Defining the Essentials," *Journal of Higher Education* 59(1) (January/February 1988): 3.
6. Tierney, 3.
7. Edgar H. Schein, *Organizational Culture and Leadership* (San Francisco: Jossey-Bass, 1988).
8. Stephen P. Robbins and Mary Coulter, *Management,* 6th ed. (Upper Saddle River, Penn.: Prentice Hall, 1999), 86–87. Also see Peter P. Schoderbek, Richard A. Cosier, and John C. Aplin, *Management,* 2nd ed. (Madison, Wis.: Magna Publications, Inc., 1994), 90.

9. A. Clay Schoenfeld and Robert Magnan, *Mentor in a Manual, Climbing the Academic Ladder to Tenure*, 2nd ed. (Madison, Wis.: Magna Publications, Inc., 1994), 4.

10. Robert F. Allen and Saul Pilnick, "Confronting the Shadow Organization: How to Detect and Defeat Negative Norms," *Organizational Dynamics* (Spring 1973): 4.

11. Wendell L. French and Cecil H. Bell, Jr., *Organizational Development: Behavior Science Interviews for Organization Improvement*, 6th ed. (Upper Saddle River, Penn.: Prentice Hall, 1999): 62.

12. John P. Kotter and James L. Heskett, *Corporate Culture and Performance* (New York: The Free Press, 1992), 5.

13. Allen and Pilnick, 1–5.

14. Allen and Pilnick, 10.

15. Allen and Pilnick, 5–10.

16. Peter Seldin, "Personal and Professional," *The Chronicle of Higher Education* (May 8, 1991): A15–17.

17. Schoenfeld and Magnan, 90.

18. Don Hellriegel, John W. Slocum, Jr., and Richard W. Woodman, *Organizational Behavior*, 5th ed. (St. Paul: West Publishing Company, 1989), 311.

19. Schoenfeld and Magnan, 122.

20. Anne Reynolds, "Charting the Changes in Junior Faculty," *Journal of Higher Education* 63 (6) (November/December 1992): 637.

21. William G. Tierney, "Organizational Socialization in Higher Education," *Journal of Higher Education* 68 (January/February 1997): 2.

22. Teryl Ann Rosch and Jill N. Reich, "The Enculturation of New Faculty in Higher Education: A Comparative Investigation of Three Academic Departments," *Research in Higher Education* 37(1) (1966): 117.

23. Jack H. Schuster, "Preparing the Next Generation of Faculty: The Graduate School's Opportunity," in *Preparing Faculty for the New Conception of Scholarship, New Directions for Teaching and Learning* 54, ed. Laurie Richlin (Summer 1993): 27–28.

24. Rosch and Reich, 116.

25. Rosch and Reich, 124.

26. Gerald W. Gibson, *Good Start: A Guidebook for New Faculty in Liberal Arts Colleges* (Bolton, Mass.: Anker Publishing Company, Inc., 1992), 53.

27. Rosch and Reich, 126.

28. Rosch and Reich, 127.

29. Stephen P. Robbins, *Organizational Behavior Concepts, Controversies, and Applications*, 6th ed. (Englewood Cliffs, New Jersey: Prentice Hall, 1993), 613.

30. Rosch and Reich, 128.

31. Rosch and Reich, 129.

32. Lois Calian Trauvetter, "Experiences of Women, Experiences of Men," in *Faculty in New Jobs: A Guide to Settling in, Becoming Established, and Building*

Institutional Support, ed. Robert J. Menges (San Francisco: Jossey-Bass Publishers, 1999), 61–62.

33. Daniel W. Wheeler, "The Role of the Chairperson in Support of Junior Faculty," in Mary Deane Sorcinelli and Ann E. Austin, eds., *Developing New and Junior Faculty, New Directions for Teaching and Learning* 50 (Summer 1992): 88–89.

34. James L. Bess, "Collegiality: Toward a Clarification of Meaning and Function," in *Higher Education: Handbook of Theory and Research* 8, ed. J. C. Smart (New York: Agathon Press), 1.

35. *Webster's Collegiate Dictionary,* 10th ed.

36. Barbara Balsmeyer, Kathleen Haubrich, and Carroll A. Quinn, "Defining Collegiality within the Academic Setting," *Journal of Nursing Education* 35 (September 1966): 264.

37. Rita K. Bode, "Mentoring and Collegiality," in *Faculty in New Jobs: A Guide to Settling in, Becoming Established, and Building Institutional Support,* ed. Robert J. Menges (San Francisco: Jossey-Bass Publishers, 1999), 121.

38. Schoenfeld and Magnan, 138.

39. Carlin Romano, "On Collegiality, College Style," *The Chronicle of Higher Education* (May 26, 1999).

Chapter 2

1. Jean V. Kartje, "O Mentor! My Mentor!" *Peabody Journal of Education* 71 (1996): 116–117.

2. Dorothy Harnish and Lynn A. Wild, "Mentoring: A Strategy for Improving Instruction," *AACC Journal* 64 (August-September 1993): 22.

3. Blake E. Peterson and Steven R. Williams, *Mathematics Teacher* 91 (November 1998): 730.

4. See Terry M. Widman, Susan G. Magliaro, Ruth Anne Niles, and Jerome A. Niles, "Teacher Mentoring: An Analysis of Roles, Activities, and Conditions," *Journal of Teacher Education* 43 (May-June 1992): 212; Rochelle L. Clemson, "Mentoring in Teaching," *Action in Teacher Education* 9 (Fall 1987): 87–90; and Clemson, *The Dynamics of Mentoring in Higher Education: Experiences of Department Chairs,* Ph.D. dissertation, University of Maryland, 1985.

5. See Bruce Joyce and Beverly Showers, "The Coaching of Teaching," *Educational Leadership* 40 (October 1982): 4–10; Barbara Field, "Supervision as Socialisation," in *Teachers as Mentors: A Practical Guide,* ed. Barbara Field and Terry Field (London: Palmer Press, 1994), 46–62; and Laurent A. Daloz, "Mentors: Teachers Who Make a Difference," *Change* 15 (September 1983): 24–27.

6. Eugene M. Anderson and Anne Lucasse Shannon, "Toward a Conceptualization of Mentoring," *Journal of Teacher Education* 39 (January-February 1988): 40.

7. Harnish and Wild, 22.

8. Sarah M. Dinham, "Being A Newcomer," in *Faculty in New Jobs,* ed. Robert J. Menges et al. (San Francisco, Calif.: Jossey-Bass, 1999), 5.

9. Rita K. Bode, "Mentoring and Collegiality," in Menges et al., 118.

10. See Billie J. Enz, "Guidelines for Selecting Mentors," in *Mentoring: Contemporary Principles and Issues,* ed. Teresa M. Bey and C. Thomas Holmes (Reston, Virginia: Association of Teacher Educators, 1992), 67.

11. Gerald R. Crockover, "Reflections on Professorial Mentorships," *Teaching Education* 3 (Spring 1991): 113–114.

12. Frank M. Perna, Bart L. Learner, and Michael T. Yura, "Mentoring and Career Development Among University Faculty," *Journal of Education* 177 (1995): 36. Refer also to Kartje, 124.

13. Ronald D. Simpson and William K. Jackson, "A Multidimensional Approach to Faculty Vitality," in *Enhancing Faculty Careers, Strategies for Development and Renewal,* ed. Jack H. Schuster, Daniel W. Wheeler, et al. (San Francisco, Calif.: Jossey-Bass, 1990), 178. Consult Jonathan David Rohrer, *A Retrospective Study Of How New Faculty Report The Use Of Mentoring Relationships To Make Sense Of Their Multiple Roles (Socialization, Organizational Entry, Culture),* Ph.D. dissertation, Michigan State University, 1998.

14. See Rohrer for details.

15. Gaye Luna and Deborah L. Cullen, "Empowering the Faculty: Mentoring Redirected and Renewed," *ASHE-ERIC Higher Education Reports* 3 (1995): 1–2.

16. Neil R. Wyle, "A Consortial Approach: The Great Lakes Colleges Association," in Schuster and Wheeler et al., 265–266.

17. For an informative account of the New Faculty Program (NFP) developed at Montclair State University in 1994–1995, refer to Gloria Pierce, "Developing New University Faculty Through Mentoring," *Journal of Humanistic Education and Development* 37 (September 1998): 27–38. See also Robert Boice, "Mentoring New Faculty: A Program for Implementation," *Journal of Staff, Program and Organization Development* 8 (Fall 1990): 143–160; and Boice, "Lessons Learned About Mentoring," in Mary Deane Sorcinelli and Ann E. Austin, eds., *Developing New and Junior Faculty, New Directions For Teaching and Learning* 50 (Summer 1992): 51–61.

18. Luna and Cullen, 4.

19. Peg Boyle and Bob Boice, "Systematic Mentoring for New Faculty Teachers and Graduate Teaching Assistants," *Innovative Higher Education* 22 (Spring 1998): 158.

20. Roger G. Baldwin, "Faculty Career Stages and Implications for Professional Development," in Schuster and Wheeler et al., 33.

21. Robert Boice, *The New Faculty Member* (San Francisco, Calif.: Jossey-Bass, 1992), 107.

22. Boyle and Boice, 161.

23. Boyle and Boice, 159.

24. James W. Selby and Lawrence G. Calhoun, "Mentoring Programs for New Faculty: Unintended Consequences?" *Teaching of Psychology* 25 (1998): 210.
25. Selby and Calhoun, 210–211.
26. Selby and Calhoun, 211.
27. Selby and Calhoun, 211.
28. Richard S. Kay, "A Definition for Developing Self-Reliance," in Bey and Holmes, 67.
29. Boyle and Boice, 177.
30. Consult Boyle and Boice, 161, 173, 177; and Boice, "Lessons Learned About Mentoring," in Sorcinelli and Austin, 51–61.
31. Pierce, 30.
32. Pierce, 33.
33. Robert J. Menges, "Dilemmas of Newly Hired Faculty," in *Faculty in New Jobs*, ed. Robert J. Menges et al. (San Francisco, Calif.: Jossey-Bass, 1999), 19.
34. Menges, *Faculty in New Jobs*, 20.
35. Menges, *Faculty in New Jobs*, 20.
36. Menges, *Faculty in New Jobs*, 20.
37. Menges, *Faculty in New Jobs*, 20.
38. Menges, *Faculty in New Jobs*, 26, 30.
39. Dinham, 5.
40. Luna and Cullen, 2ff.

Chapter 3

1. Wilbert J. McKeachie, *Teaching Tips, A Guidebook for the Beginning Teacher*, 8th ed. (Lexington, Mass.: D.C. Heath & Company, 1986), 3.
2. Robert Boice, *Advice for New Faculty Members, Nihil Nimus* (Needham Heights, Mass.: Allyn Bacon, 2000), 12.
3. Robert Boice, *The New Faculty Member, Supporting and Fostering Professional Development* (San Francisco, Calif.: Jossey-Bass, 1992), 52.
4. A. Clay Schoenfeld and Robert Magman, *Mentor in a Manual, Climbing the Academic Ladder to Tenure* (Madison, Wis.: Magna Publications, 1992), 113. See also Boice, "Quick Starters: New Faculty Who Succeed," in Michael Theall and Jennifer Franklin, eds., *Effective Practices for Improving Teaching*, New Directions for Teaching and Learning 45 (Winter 1991): 25.
5. Boice, *New Faculty Member*, 76–79.
6. Alan Wright et al., *Teaching Improvement Practices, Successful Strategies for Higher Education* (Boston, Mass.: Anker Publishing Company, 1995), 59.
7. Wright, 59. Refer also to Robert J. Menges, "The Real World of Teaching Improvement: A Faculty Perspective," in Theall and Franklin, 25.
8. Kenneth A. Eble, *The Craft of Teaching* (San Francisco, Calif.: Jossey-Bass, 1976), 17–18.
9. Maryellen Weimer, "It's a Myth: Nobody Knows What Makes Teaching Good," in *Teaching College, Collected Readings for the New Instructor*, ed.

Weimer and Rose Ann Neff (Madison, Wis.: Magna Publications, 1990), 13.

10. Kay F. Quam, *Ready, Set, Teach: Learn to Teach, Teach to Learn* (Commack, New York: Kroshka Books, 1998), 93–94.

11. Consult Schoenfeld and Magman, 162; and Lynn Sorenson, "Beware the N of One," in *Relative to Teaching*, Teaching and Faculty Support Center, University of Arkansas (April 1996): 1.

12. Neil Browne and Stuart M. Keeley, "Achieving Excellence: Advice to New Teachers," in Weimer and Neff, 39–44.

13. Browne and Keeley, 39.

14. James R. Davis, *Better Teaching, More Learning, Strategies for Success in Postsecondary Settings* (Phoenix, Arizona: American Council on Education, Oryx Press, 1993), 13–14.

15. Louis Raths, et al., *Teaching for Thinking*, 2nd ed. (New York: Teachers College Press, 1986), 185–186.

16. See Quam, 95; and "Effective University Teaching," *Focus on University Teaching and Learning*, Dalhousie University, Halifax, Nova Scotia (March/April 1996):

17. "Effective University Teaching," 1.

18. Davis, 27.

19. Quoted in Thomas Angelo, "Setting Goals—No Problem, Reaching Goals . . . Aah!" *Relative to Teaching*, Teaching and Faculty Support Center, University of Arkansas (April 1994): 1.

20. Angelo, 1; refer also to Quam, 114.

21. Refer to Bill J. Frye, "Goals and Objectives for College Courses," in *Teaching in College, A Resource for College Teachers*, rev. ed., ed. Donald Grieve (Cleveland, Ohio: Info-Tec, 1990), 153–167.

22. Davis, 30.

23. Note the discussion in Davis, 113–114.

24. Rebecca Brent and Richard M. Felder, "It's a Start," *College Teaching* 47 (Winter 1999): 14–17.

25. Karron G. Lewis, "Teaching Large Classes (How to Do It Well and Remain Sane)," in *Handbook of College Teaching, Theory and Applications* ed. Keith W. Prichard and R. McLaren Sawyer (Westport, Conn.: Greenwood Press, 1994), 322.

26. Donald Grieve, "A Planning Model for College Faculty," in Grieve, ed., *Teaching in College*, 153–167.

27. Benjamin S. Bloom, M. D. Englehart, et al., *Taxonomy of Educational Objectives: Handbook I, The Cognitive Domain* (New York: Longmans, Green, 1956).

28. Quam, 130–132.

29. See Linda B. Nilson, *Teaching at Its Best, A Research-Based Resource for College Instructors* (Bolton, Mass.: Anker Publishing Company, 1998), 13.

30. Brent and Felder, 17.

31. Consult Howard B. Altman, "Syllabus Shares 'What the Teacher Wants,'" in Weimer and Neff, 45–46; Brent and Felder, 14–17; Schoenfeld and Magman, 137–139; and Nilson, 20–21.

32. William J. Ekeler, "The Lecture Method," in Prichard and Sawyer, 85.

33. Ekeler, 86.

34. William E. Cashin, "Improving Lectures," in Weimer and Neff, 59. See also Michael D. Sublett, "The Quick Fix: Turning Listeners into Active Learners," *College Teaching* 47 (Winter 1999): 22; Elaine J. Enderson, "Active Learning in the Lecture Hall," *Journal of College Science Teaching* 26 (May 1997): 428; Beth Panitz, "Stuck in the Lecture Rut?" *ASEE Prism* 5 (February 1996): 26; and Barbara Gross Davis, *Tools for Teaching* (San Francisco, Calif.: Jossey-Bass, 1993), 111–130.

35. McKeachie, 69.

36. Nilson, 89.

37. Quoted in Cushin, 59.

38. Davis, 134.

39. Davis, 134; McKeachie, 7.

40. Quoted in part from Schoenfeld and Magman, 118; and in Christopher J. Lucas, *Our Western Educational Heritage* (New York: Macmillan, 1972), 296–297.

41. Joseph Janes and Diane Hauer, *Now What? Readings on Surviving (and Even Enjoying) Your First Experience at College Teaching* (Acton, Mass.: Copley Publishing Group, 1988), 14–15; Raths, 2; Nilson, 76; and Charles C. Bonwell and James A. Eison, *Active Learning: Creating Excitement in the Classroom,* ASHE-ERIC Higher Education Report No. 1 (Washington, D.C.: George Washington University, School of Education and Human Development, 1991), 8.

42. Cushin, 60.

43. Nilson, 75.

44. Nilson, 75.

45. Cited in Bonwell, "Using Active Learning As Assessment in the Postsecondary Classroom," *Clearing House* 71 (December 1997): 73. See also Bonwell and Tracey E. Sutherland, "The Active Learning Continuum: Choosing Activities to Engage Students in the Classroom," *New Directions for Teaching and Learning* 67 (Fall 1996): 3; and Bonwell, "Enhancing the Lecture: Revitalizing a Traditional Format," *New Directions for Teaching and Learning* 67 (Fall 1996): 31.

46. Bonwell and Eison, iv.

47. Janes and Hauer, 5, 14.

48. Davis, 173.

49. McKeachie, 28. See also Mathew Lippman, "Some Thoughts on the Foundations of Reflective Education," in *Teaching Thinking Skills: Theory and Practice,* ed. Joan Baron and Robert Sternberg (New York: W. H. Freedman, 1987), 153.

50. Peter J. Frederick, "Classroom Discussions," in Prichard and Sawyer, 100. Consult Davis, Tools for Teaching, 63–95.

51. Nilson, 87.
52. Janes and Hauer, 35.
53. Maryellen Weimer, "Successful Participation Strategies," in Weimer and Neff, 95–96; Stephen D. Brookfield and Stephen Preskill, *Discussion As A Way Of Teaching, Tools and Techniques for Democratic Classrooms* (San Francisco, Calif.: Jossey-Bass, 1999), 37, 87–90; Andy Farquharson, *Teaching in Practice* (San Francisco, Calif.: Jossey-Bass, 1995), 163; Janes and Hauer, 34–35; Nilson, 87ff.
54. Brookfield and Preskill, 22–23.
55. Brookfield and Preskill, xv.

Chapter 4

1. Arthur W. Chickering and Zelda F. Gamson, *Applying the Seven Principles for Good Practice in Undergraduate Education* (San Francisco, Calif.: Jossey-Bass, 1991), 66. Cited also in Charles A. Lubbers and Diane A. Gorcyca, "Using Active Learning in Public Relations Instruction: Demographic Predictors of Faculty Use," *Public Relations Review* 23 (Spring 1997): 67.
2. Chet Meyers and Thomas B. Jones, *Promoting Active Learning, Strategies for the College Classroom* (San Francisco, Calif.: Jossey-Bass, 1993), xi. Also refer to Raymond F. Orzechowski, "Factors to Consider Before Introducing Active Learning into a Large, Lecture-Based Course," *Journal of College Science Teaching* 24 (March 1995): 347.
3. Bonwell and Eison, iii.
4. Refer to Robert B. Barr and John Tagg, "From Teaching to Learning—A New Paradigm for Undergraduate Education," *Change* 27 (November/December 1995): 12–25; and Michael S. Sublett, "Turning Listeners Into Active Learners," *College Teaching* 47 (Winter 1999): 22.
5. Tom McKinnon, "Five Good Reasons for Avoiding Active Learning," *Relative to Teaching,* Teaching and Faculty Support Center, University of Arkansas (March 1997): 1. Note also Michael P. Ryan and Gretchen G. Martens, *Planning a College Course: A Guidebook for the Graduate Teaching Assistant* (Ann Arbor, Michigan: National Center for Research to Improve Postsecondary Teaching and Learning, 1989), 20. See also Susan A. Stearns, "Steps for Active Learning of Complex Concepts," *College Teaching* 42 (Summer 1994): 107.
6. Meyers and Jones, 59.
7. Ann P. McNeal, "Death of the Talking Heads: Participatory Workshops for Curricular Reform," *College Teaching* 46 (Summer 1998): 90; and McKeachie, *Teaching Tips,* 284.
8. Jo Sprague, "Retrieving the Research Agenda for Communication Education, Asking the Pedagogical Questions That Are Embarrassments to Theory," *Communication Education* 42 (1993): 356.
9. Mel Silberman, *Active Learning, 101 Strategies to Teach Any Subject* (Needham Heights, Mass.: Allyn and Bacon, 1996), 1. See also Barbara Gross Davis, *Tools for Teaching,* chapter V.

10. Nilson, 69, 103.
11. Marilla Svinicki, "Seven Deadly Comments That Block Learning About Teaching," *National Teaching and Learning Forum* 3 (1994): reprinted in *Relative to Teaching*, Teaching and Faculty Support Center, University of Arkansas (November 1994): 1–2.
12. See Barbara J. Millis, "Introducing Faculty to Cooperative Learning," in Wright, 127–139; Richard A. Giboney and Clark D. Webb, *What Every Great Teacher Knows, Practical Principles for Effective Teaching* (Brandon, Vermont: Holistic Education Press, 1998); Roy A. Weaver, Theodore J. Kowalski, and Joan E. Pfaller, "Case-Method Teaching," in Prichard and Sawyer, 171–178; and Paul R. Pintrich, "Student Motivation in the College Classroom," in Prichard and Sawyer, 37–38.
13. Quam, 79.
14. Davis, 57.
15. Meyers and Jones, 36–37.
16. Quam, 79.
17. "How Students Learn, How Teachers Teach, And What Goes Wrong in the Process," *Relative to Teaching*, Teaching and Faculty Support Center, University of Arkansas (September 1994): 1.
18. Thomas G. Carskadon, "Student Personality Factors: Psychological Type and the Myers-Briggs Type Indicator," in Prichard and Sawyer, 69–81. See also Barbara Gross Davis, *Tools for Teaching*, chapter VI.
19. Carskadon, 70.
20. Carskadon, 72–73, 75–76.
21. Victoria L. Clegg, "Tips for Tests and Test Giving," in Prichard and Sawyer, 425. Note the recommendations in Barbara Gross Davis, *Tools for Teaching*, chapter VIII.
22. Nilson, 183.
23. Quoted in J. Hoffman and D. Oseroff-Varnell, "Teaching Effectiveness and Student Ratings: Finding the Missing Link." Paper presented at the 2nd National Conference on the Training and Employment of Teaching Assistants, Seattle, Washington, November 1989, 6; cited in Menges, 21.
24. Joseph Epstein, ed., *Masters, Portraits of Great Teachers* (New York: Basic Books, 1981), xiii; cited in Menges, 21.
25. Menges, 25, 26–27.
26. American Association of University Professors, "Statement on Professional Ethics," *AAUP Policy Documents and Reports* (Washington, D.C.: American Association of University Professors, 1990), 76.
27. American Association of University Professors, "A Statement of the Association's Council: Freedom and Responsibility," *AAUP Policy Documents and Reports*, 77–78.
28. American Association of University Professors, "Joint Statement on Rights and Freedoms of Students," *AAUP Policy Documents and Reports*, 154.
29. McKeachie, "Ethical Standards in Teaching," in Weimer and Neff, 33.

30. Conwell G. Strickland, "Student Rights and the Teacher's Obligations in the Classroom," in Weimer and Neff, 29–31.

Chapter 5

1. Diane W. Strommer, "Advising Special Populations of Students," in Alice G. Reinarz and Eric R. White, eds., *Teaching Through Academic Advising: A Faculty Perspective, New Directions for Teaching and Learning* 62 (San Francisco, Calif.: Jossey-Bass, Summer 1995), 25.

2. Gerald W. Gibson, *Good Start, A Guidebook for New Faculty in Liberal Arts Colleges* (Bolton, Mass.: Anker Publishing Company, 1992), 161.

3. See Wesley R. Habley and Ricardo H. Morales, "Advising Models: Goal Achievement and Program Effectiveness," *NACADA Journal* 18 (Spring1998): 35–41.

4. Wesley R. Habley, "Fire! (Ready, Aim): Is Criticism of Faculty Advising Warranted?" *NACADA Journal* 14 (Fall 1994): 30. See also Kimberly Ann Saving and Maybelle C. Keim, "Student and Advisor Perceptions of Academic Advising in Two Midwestern Colleges of Business," *College Student Journal* 32 (December 1998): 511–521.

5. Quoted by James Kelly, "Faculty Speak to Advising," in Reinarz and White, 15.

6. Quoted in Kelly, 22.

7. Quoted in Kelly, 20.

8. Quoted in Kelly, 19.

9. Gary R. Hanson and Christine Huston, "Academic Advising and Assessment," *New Directions for Teaching and Learning* 62 (San Francisco, Calif.: Jossey-Bass, Summer 1995), 93.

10. A. Clay Schoenfeld and Robert Magnan, *Mentor In A Manual, Climbing the Academic Ladder to Tenure* (Madison: Wis.: Magna Publications, 1992), 164.

11. Habley, *Fulfilling the Promise?* (Iowa City, Iowa: American College Testing, 1993), 1.

12. Ernest T. Pascarella and Patrick T. Terenzini, *How College Affects Students: Findings and Insights from Twenty Years of Research* (San Francisco, Calif.: Jossey-Bass, 1991), 101–102, 394.

13. Margaret C. King, "Academic Advising, Retention, and Transfer," *New Directions for Community Colleges* 82 (San Francisco, Calif.: Jossey-Bass, Summer 1993), 24.

14. Alexander W. Astin, *Four Critical Years* (San Francisco, Calif.: Jossey-Bass, 1977), 223.

15. George H. Douglas, *Education Without Impact, How Our Universities Fail the Young* (New York: Carol Publishing Group, 1992), 176.

16. Robert Solomon and Jon Solomon, *Up the University: Re-Creating Higher Education in America* (Reading, Mass.: Addison-Wesley, 1993), 69.

17. Schoenfeld and Magnan, 165.

18. Marquita L. Byrd, "Academic Advising Ain't What It Used to Be: Strangers in the University," *NACADA Journal* 15 (Spring 1995): 44–47.

19. Elements cited are drawn in part from Norbert W. Dunkel and John H. Schuh, *Advising Student Groups and Organizations* (San Francisco, Calif.: Jossey-Bass, 1998), 132; Gibson, 161–163; Schoenfeld and Magnan, 164–165; and Virginia N. Gordon, *Handbook of Academic Advising* (Westport, Conn.: Greenwood Press, 1992), 19.

20. Matthew Morano, "Challenges Encountered by New Advisers: Honest Answers, Practical Solutions," *The Mentor* (January 1999): 1–3.

21. Morano, 1.

22. Quoted in Morano, 2.

23. Quoted in Morano, 3.

24. Kenneth C. Petress, "The Multiple Roles of An Undergraduate's Academic Advisor," *Education* 117 (Fall 1996): 91.

25. Thomas J. Grites, "Improving Academic Advising," IDEA Paper No. 3, Center for Faculty Evaluation and Development in Higher Education, Kansas State University, August 1980.

26. Carol C. Ryan, "Professional Development and Training for Faculty Advisers," in Reinarz and White, 36.

27. Susan H. Frost, "Developmental Advising: Practices and Attitudes of Faculty Advisors," *NACADA Journal* 13 (Fall 1993): 19.

28. Gibson, 163.

29. Robert M. Berdahl, "Educating the Whole Person," in Reinarz and White, 7.

30. Kenneth Eble, *The Craft of Teaching* (San Francisco, Calif.: Jossey-Bass, 1990), 108.

31. Henry Rosovsky, *The University: An Owner's Manual* (New York: W.W. Norton, 1990), 152–153.

32. Eble, 105, 106.

33. Douglas, xxxiii-xiv.

34. Eble, 107.

35. Page Smith, *Killing the Spirit, Higher Education in America* (New York: Viking Penguin, 1990), 217.

36. Quoted in Smith, 217.

37. Berdahl, 7.

38. Berdahl, 7.

Chapter 6

1. Robert T. Blackburn and Janet H. Lawrence, *Faculty at Work, Motivation, Expectation, Satisfaction* (Baltimore: The Johns Hopkins University Press, 1995), 115.

2. Henry Rosovsky, *The University, An Owner's Manual* (New York: W.W. Norton and Company, 1990), 84–98.

3. Jaroslav Pelikan, *Scholarship and Its Survival: Questions on the Idea of Graduate Education* (Princeton: Carnegie Foundation for the Advancement of Teaching, 1983), 64.
4. Benjamin R. Barber, *An Aristocracy of Everyone: The Politics of Education and the Future of America* (New York: Ballantine, 1992), 196.
5. Robert Solomon and Jon Solomon, *Up the University, Re-Creating Higher Education in America* (Needham Heights, Mass.: Addison-Wesley, 1993), 12–13.
6. William D. Schaefer, *Education Without Compromise, From Chaos to Coherence in Higher Education* (San Francisco, Calif.: Jossey-Bass, 1990), 108–109.
7. See Peter J. Gray, Robert C. Froh, and Robert M. Diamond, *A National Study of Research Universities: On the Balance Between Research and Undergraduate Teaching* (Syracuse, New York: Center for Instructional Development, Syracuse University, March 1992), 6. Consult also Carolyn J. Mooney, "Professors Feel Conflict between Roles in Teaching and Research," *Chronicle of Higher Education* (May 8, 1991): A15.
8. See David S. Webster, "Does Research Productivity Enhance Teaching?" *Educational Record* 66 (Fall 1985): 60–62; and S. D. Neill, "No Significant Relationship Between Research and Teaching, Research Reveals," *University Affairs* 30 (April 1989): 18.
9. The point is adapted from Solomon and Solomon, 13.
10. Solomon and Solomon, 14.
11. Jacques Barzun, *Begin Here: The Forgotten Conditions of Teaching and Learning* (Chicago, Illinois: University of Chicago Press, 1991).
12. See Page Smith, *Killing the Spirit, Higher Education in America* (New York: Viking, 1990), 7, 20, 179, 197–198.
13. George C. Douglas, *Education Without Impact: How Our Universities Fail the Young* (New York: Birch Lane, 1992), 68–70, 100–101.
14. Schaefer, 100.
15. Christopher J. Lucas, *Crisis in the Academy, Rethinking Higher Education in America* (New York: St. Martin's Press, 1996), 187.
16. A. Clay Schoenfeld and Robert Magnan, *Mentor In A Manual, Climbing the Academic Ladder to Tenure* (Madison, Wis.: Magna Publications, 1992), 218.
17. Lucas, 187.
18. Blackburn and Lawrence, 115–116.
19. Joseph M. Moxley, *Publish, Don't Perish, The Scholar's Guide to Academic Writing and Publishing* (Westport, Conn.: Greenwood Press, 1992), xvii, 5, 172.
20. Ralph E. Matkin and T. F. Riggat, *Persist and Publish, Helpful Hints for Academic Writing and Publishing* (Niwot, Colorado: University Press of Colorado, 1991), 26.
21. Matkin and Riggat, 22.
22. Gerald W. Gibson, *Good Start: A Guidebook for New Faculty in Liberal Arts Colleges* (Bolton, Mass.: Anker Publishing Company, 1992), 135.
23. Gibson, 148.

24. Robert Boice, *The New Faculty Member, Supporting and Fostering Professional Development* (San Francisco, Calif.: Jossey-Bass, 1992), 18.

25. Boice, *Advice for New Faculty Members, Nihil Nimus* (Needham Heights, Mass.: Allyn & Bacon, 2000), 22.

26. Boice, *The New Faculty Member,* 102; and Boice, *Advice for New Faculty Members,* 104–105.

27. Kenneth T. Henson, "So You Want to be Published?" *Kappa Delta Pi Record* 35 (Winter 1999): 79.

28. Henson, "Writing for Publication, Some Perennial Mistakes," *Phi Delta Kappan* 78 (June 1997): 781.

29. Matkin and Riggat, 7.

30. Boice, *The New Faculty Member,* 168.

31. Boice, *The New Faculty Member,* 165.

32. Moxley, 29.

33. Moxley, 25, 27.

34. Consult Moxley, 46–47.

35. Donald W. Fiske and Louis Fogg, "But the Reviewers Are Making Different Criticisms of My Paper!" *American Psychologist* 45 (May 1990): 591–598.

36. Tara Grey, "Publish, Don't Perish: Twelve Steps to Help Scholars Flourish," *Journal of Staff, Program, and Organization Development* 16 (Winter 1998–1999): 142.

37. Moxley, 105.

Chapter 7

1. A. Leigh Deneef and Craufurd D. Goodwin, eds., *The Academic Handbook,* 2nd ed. (Durham, North Carolina: Duke University Press, 1995), 217.

2. Cliff I. Davidson and Susan A. Ambrose, "The New Professor's Handbook, A Guide to Teaching and Research in Engineering and Science" (Bolton, Mass.: Anker Publishing Company, Inc., 1994), 113.

3. Lynn E. Miner, Jeremy T. Miner, and Jerry Griffith, "Proposal Planning & Writing," 2nd ed. (Phoenix, Arizona: The Oryx Press, 1998), 4.

4. Miner, Miner, and Griffith, 4.

5. Miner, Miner, and Griffith, 4–5.

6. Kenneth T. Henson, "The Art of Writing Grant Proposals, Part I," *Contemporary Education* 68(1) (Fall 1996): 61.

7. Miner, Miner, and Griffith, 6.

8. Judith K. Argon, "Securing Funding from Federal Sources." in *The Academic Handbook,* 2nd ed., ed. A Leigh Deneef and Craufurd D. Goodwin (Durham, North Carolina: Duke University Press, 1995), 220.

9. Argon, 220.

10. Davidson and Ambrose, 115.

11. Davidson and Ambrose, 117–118.

12. Argon, 220.
13. Edward M. Reeve and Davis V. Ballard, "A Faculty Guide to Writing Grant Proposals," *AACC Journal* (February/March 1993): 30.
14. Davidson and Ambrose, 117.
15. Davidson and Ambrose, 117.
16. Fred E. Crossland, "New Academics and the Quest for Private Funds," in *The Academic Handbook,* 2nd ed., ed. A Leigh Denneff and Craufurd D. Goodwin (Durham, North Carolina: Duke University Press, 1995), 237.
17. Crossland, 237.
18. Reeve and Ballard, 30.
19. Reeve and Ballard, 30.
20. Reeve and Ballard, 30.
21. Reeve and Ballard, 30.
22. Cheryl C. New and James A. Quick, "Steering Your Way to a Winning Grant Proposal," *Technology & Learning* 19(10) (June 1999): 6–12.
23. Crossland, 238.
24. Davidson and Ambrose, 121.
25. Kenneth T. Henson, "The Art of Writing Grant Proposals, Part III," *Contemporary Education* 68(3) (Spring 1997): 197.
26. Argon, 226.
27. Argon, 226–227.
28. See Miner, Miner, and Griffith, 93–138; Reeve and Ballard, 31; Jane C. Belcher and Julia M. Jacobson, *From Idea to Funded Project Grant Proposals That Work,* 4th ed. (Phoenix, Arizona: Oryx Press, 1992), 12–52.
29. Miner, Miner, and Griffith, 136.
30. Miner, Miner, and Griffith, 93.
31. Argon, 228.
32. Miner, Miner, and Griffith, 101.
33. Argon, 228.
34. Miner, Miner, and Griffith, 103.
35. Miner, Miner, and Griffith, 110.
36. Miner, Miner, and Griffith, 107.
37. Miner, Miner, and Griffith, 113.
38. Miner, Miner, and Griffith, 114.
39. Reeve and Ballard, 31.
40. Miner, Miner, and Griffith, 122.
41. Miner, Miner, and Griffith, 122.
42. Miner, Miner, and Griffith, 122–123.
43. Argon, 231.
44. Crossland, 242–243.
45. Miner, Miner, and Griffith, 83–84; Crossland, 243.
46. Crossland, 244.
47. Crossland, 239.
48. Miner, Miner, and Griffith, 5.

49. Sonja M. Carley and Cynthia A. Scheinborg, *Proposal Writing*, 2nd ed., (Thousand Oaks, Calif.: Sage Publications 2000), 36–37.

Chapter 8

1. Bronwyn E. Adam and Alton O. Roberts, "Differences Among the Disciplines," in Robert M. Diamond and Bronwyn E. Adam, eds., *Recognizing Faculty Work: Reward Systems for the Year 2000, New Directions for Higher Education* 81 (Spring 1993): 54.

2. University of Nebraska - Lincoln, "2000 Fact Book," distributed by the Office of Research and Learning, 1; accessed online at http://www.unl.edu/ unifacts/mission.html.

3. Clark Atlantic University, Office of the President, "Vision Statement," 1; accessed online at www.cau.edu/president/index.html.

4. Westminster College, "Mission, Goals and Vision," Graduate Catalogue, 1999–2000, 7.

5. Tufts University, "Vision Statement," 1; accessed online at www.tufts.edu.

6. Ohio State University, "The University Context, Chapter 1: The University Mission;" accessed online at http://www/apo.ohio-state.edu/mp/ mpv1c1.htm.

7. University of Arkansas, 1998–1999 *Catalog of Studies*, 9.

8. Accessed online at http://www.calpoly.edu/%7E-communic/univ/ mission.html.

9. Accessed online at http:///www.lawsch.uga.edu/handbook/uga.html.

10. Accessed online at http://www.edu/smu_mission.html.

11. A. Clay Schoenfeld and Robert Magnan, *Mentor in a Manual, Climbing the Academic Ladder to Tenure* (Madison, Wis.: Magna Publications, 1992), 201.

12. Neil J. Smelser, *Effective Committee Service* (Newbury Park, Calif.: Sage Publications, 1993), 99.

13. Smelser, 208.

14. Smelser, 99.

15. Schoenfeld and Magnan, 202.

16. Smelser, x-xi.

17. Robert T. Blackburn and Janet H. Lawrence, *Faculty at Work, Motivation, Expectation, Satisfaction* (Baltimore: The Johns Hopkins University Press, 1995), 222.

18. Smelser, 41.

19. Robert Boice, *Advice for New Faculty Members, Nihil Nimus* (Boston, Mass.: Allyn and Bacon, 2000), 255.

20. See W. G. Tierney and E. M. Bensimon, *Promotion and Tenure: Community and Socialization in Academe* (Albany, New York: State University of New York Press, 1996), 75; Schoenfeld and Magnan, 203; and Mia Alexander-Snow and Barbara J. Johnson, "Perspectives from Faculty of Color," in *Faculty in New Jobs*, ed. Robert Menges, et al. (San Francisco, Calif.: Jossey-Bass, 1999), 93.

21. Donald K. Jarvis, *Junior Faculty Development* (New York: Modern Language Association, 1991), 73.
22. Schoenfeld and Magnan, 203.
23. Gerald W. Gibson, *Good Start, A Guidebook for New Faculty in Liberal Arts Colleges* (Bolton, Mass.: Anker Publishing Company, 1992), 158–159.
24. Snow and Johnson, 96.
25. Shelly M. Park, "Research, Teaching, and Service, Why Shouldn't Women's Work Count?" *Journal of Higher Education* 67 (January/February 1996): 46–84.
26. Gibson, 158.
27. Boice, 255.
28. Boice, 256.
29. Schoenfeld and Magnan, 211.
30. Adams and Roberts, 55–56, from the Special Committee on Faculty Roles and Rewards in Geography, Toward a Reconsideration of Faculty Roles and Rewards in Geography, American Association of Geographers, 1993.
31. Judith A, Ramaley, "Embracing Civic Responsibility," *AAHE Bulletin* 52 (March 2000): 10.
32. Zelda F. Gamson, "Faculty and Service," *Change* 27 (January/February 1995): 4.
33. Russell Edgerton, "The Re-examination of Faculty Priorities," *Change* 25 (July/August 1993): 14.
34. Schoenfeld and Magnan, 203.
35. Schoenfeld and Magnan, 204.
36. Lorilee R. Sandman et al., "Critical Tensions, How to Strengthen the Scholarship Component of Outreach," *Change* 32 (January/February 2000): 46.
37. Deborah Hirsch and Ernest Lynton, *Bridging Two Worlds: Professional Service and Service Learning* (Boston, Mass.: University of Massachusetts, New England Center for Higher Education, 1995), 3.
38. Ernest L. Boyer, *Scholarship Reconsidered: Priorities of the Professoriate* (Princeton: Carnegie Foundation for the Advancement of Teaching, 1990).
39. Consult Eugene Rice, "The New American Scholar: Scholarship and the Purposes of the University," *Metropolitan Universities Journal* 1 (1991): 7–18. Refer also to Boyer, "The Scholarship of Engagement," Journal of Public Service and Outreach 1 (1996): 11–20; *Making Outreach Visible: A Guide to Documenting Professional Service and Outreach*, A. Driscoll and Ernest Lynton, eds. (Washington, D.C.: American Association for Higher Education, 1999); Lynton, *Making the Case for Professional Service* (Washington, D.C.: American Association for Higher Education, 1995); D. A. Schoën, "Knowing-in-Action: The New Scholarship Requires a New Epistemology," *Change* 27 (November/December 1995): 27–34; Charles E. Hathaway, "Colleges of Education, The New Realities and a Broadened Definition of Scholarship," *Education* 116 (Spring 1996): 340–345; and Gary S. Krahenbuhl, "Faculty Work," *Change* 30 (November/December 1998): 18–25.

40. The example is adapted from Krahenbuhl, 2–5.
41. See Jeffery P. Bieber, "Faculty Work and Public Trust: Restoring the Value of Teaching and Public Service in American Academic Life," *Journal of Higher Education* 68 (March/April 1997): 233–234.
42. Blackburn and Lawrence, 224.
43. See Robert C. Froh et al., "Representing Faculty Work: The Professional Portfolio," in Diamond and Adam, 100; Katherine L. Kasten, "Tenure and Merit Pay as Rewards for Research, Teaching, and Service at a Research University," *Journal of Higher Education* 55 (August 1984): 500–514; Park, 7–8; and Diamond, "Changing Priorities and the Faculty Reward System," in Diamond and Adam, 6.
44. National Center for Postsecondary Improvement, "The Impact of Incentive Systems on Faculty Behavior," *Change* 32 (March/April 2000): 53–56.
45. Boice, 253.

Chapter 9

1. Tillinghast-Towers Perrin, *A Summary of Findings from the 1997 Educators Legal Liability Coverage Survey* (New York: Tillinghast-Towers Perrin, 1998).
2. Tillinghast-Towers Perrin, 1.
3. Patricia A. Hollander, D. Parker Young, and Donald D. Gehring, *A Practical Guide to Legal Issues Affecting College Teachers* (Ashville, North Carolina: College Administration Publications, Inc., 1995), 1–2.
4. Hollander, Young, and Gehring, 1.
5. J. Douglas Toma and Richard L. Palm, "The Academic Administrator and the Law: What Every Dean and Department Chair Needs to Know," *ASHE-ERIC Higher Education Report* 26(5) (Washington, D.C.: The George Washington University, 1999), 8.
6. Toma and Palm, 8.
7. William A. Kaplin and Barbara A. Lee, *The Law of Higher Education*, 3rd ed. (San Francisco, Calif.: Jossey-Bass Publishers, 1995), 17.
8. Kaplin and Lee, 17.
9. Kaplin and Lee, 46.
10. Hollander, Young, and Gehring, 7.
11. See Tillinghast-Towers Perin, "A Summary of Findings from the 1997 Educators Legal Liability Coverage Survey" for survey results concerning legal training of faculty and administrators.
12. See John W. Murry, Jr., "Avoiding Legal Pitfalls in Recruiting and Selecting New Faculty: What Every Academic Administrator Should Know," *Academic Leadership* 7(2) (Summer 2000): 20–22 and Theodore J. Marchese, "The Search Committee Handbook: A Guide to Recruiting Administrators" (Washington, D.C.: American Association for Higher Education, 1988).
13. See generally John M. Higgins and Patricia A. Hollander, *A Guide to Successful Searches for College Personnel: Policies, Procedures, and Legal Issues*

(Asheville, North Carolina: College Administration Publications, Inc., 1987).

14. Kaplin and Lee, 150.
15. Toma and Palm, 29.
16. Toma and Palm, 30.
17. Rita Risser, *Staying out of Court: The Manager's Guide to Preventing Employee Lawsuits* (Paramus, New Jersey: Prentice Hall, 1993), 20.
18. Kaplin and Lee, 299.
19. Steven G. Olswant and Jane I. Fantel, "Tenure and Periodic Performance Review: Compatible Legal and Administrative Principles," *Journal of College and University Law* 7(1): 3.
20. James L. Rapp, *Education Law* 2 (New York: Matthew Bender & Company, 2000), 11.
21. Rapp, 11–14.
22. John D. Copeland and John W. Murry, Jr., "Getting Tossed from the Ivory Tower: The Legal Implications of Evaluating Faculty Performance," *Missouri Law Review* 61(2) (Spring 1996): 282.
23. Copeland and Murry, 246.
24. Kaplin and Lee, 280 (citing the United States Supreme Court in *Board of Regents v Roth*, 408 U.S. 564 (1972))
25. Kaplin and Lee, 283.
26. Rapp, 6–182.76.
27. *Edwards v. California University of Pennsylvania*, 156 F.3d 488 (3rd Circ. 1998).
28. *Lester v. Walker*, 907 S.W.2d 812 (Tenn. App. 1995).
29. *Oschner v. Board of Trustees of Washington Community College District No. 17*, 61 Wash. App. 772, 811 P.2d. 985 (1991).
30. *Silva v. University of New Hampshire*, 888 F. Supp. 293 (D.N.H. 1994).
31. *Carley v. Arizona Board of Regents*, 737 P.2d 1099 (Ariz. App. 1987).
32. *Andre v. Pace University*, 618 N.Y.S.2d 975 (Cty. Ct. 1994).
33. *Yarborough v. The City University of New York*, 520 N.Y.S.2d 518 (N.Y. Cl. Ct. 1987).
34. *Weidemann v. State University of New York at Cortland*, 592 N.Y.S.2d 99 (N.Y.S. Ct. 1992).
35. *Reilly v. Daly*, 666 N.E.2d 439 (Ind. App. 1996).
36. *Susan "M" v. New York Law School*, 544 N.Y.S.2d 829 (S.Ct. 1989).
37. Hollander, Young, and Gehring, 10.
38. Tinninghast-Towers Perrin, 12.

Chapter 10

1. Consult Jeffrey F. Milem et al., "Faculty Time Allocation," *Journal of Higher Education* 71 (July/August 2000): 454–475.

2. Ernest T. Pascarella and Patrick T. Terenzini, *How College Affects Students, Findings and Insights from Twenty Years of Research* (San Francisco, Calif.: Jossey-Bass, 1991).
3. Lorilee R. Sandmann et al., "Managing Critical Tensions," *Change* 32 (January/February 2000): 44–52.
4. A prime example is that supplied in Stephen R. Covey, *The Seven Habits of Highly Effective People* (New York: Fireside/Simon & Schuster, 1989). See also Covey et al., *First Things First* (New York: Simon & Schuster, 1994).
5. Consult Carol L. Colbeck, "Merging In A Seamless Blend: How Faculty Integrate Teaching and Research," *Journal of Higher Education* 69 (November/December 1998): 647–671.
6. Covey, *Seven Habits,* 150.

INDEX

Printed in the United States
36922LVS00002BB/103-639

9 780312 295370